"This book will free Western managers from their own cultural assumptions and let them conduct business more successfully with Chinese entrepreneurs. Ming-Jer Chen has nicely laid out the essence of the Chinese way of doing business."

—STAN SHIH, Chairman and CEO, The Acer Group, Taiwan

"As the 21st century unfolds, no firm that aspires to global competitiveness can afford to ignore the emergence of greater China as a world economic force. Chen's book provides key insights into the values of this huge emerging market and offers advice about how to do business there."

—IAN MACMILLAN, Fred Sullivan Professor of Entrepreneurship, The Wharton School, University of Pennsylvania

"An admirable effort to trace modern Chinese business behavior to its cultural and philosophical roots. Ming-Jer Chen offers managers a clear perspective with abundant real-life examples."

—RONNIE C. CHAN, Chairman, Hang Lung Group, Hong Kong

"In a highly interconnected, global business environment, managers and business leaders can no longer take their values for granted. An important contribution to understanding the intricate influences that underpin Chinese business practices and corporate decisions, *Inside Chinese Business* is essential reading for students and managers in the 21st century."

—LEO I. HIGDON, JR., President, Babson College and former Vice Chairman, Salomon Brothers

INSIDE
CHINESE
BUSINESS

INSIDE CHINESE BUSINESS

A Guide for Managers Worldwide

MING-JER CHEN

HARVARD BUSINESS SCHOOL PRESS
BOSTON, MASSACHUSETTS

978-1-59139-327-6 (ISBN 13)
Library of Congress Cataloging-in-Publication Data
Chen, Ming-Jer
    Inside Chinese business: a guide for managers worldwide /
    Ming-Jer Chen.
        p. cm.
    Includes bibliographical references and index.
    ISBN 1-59139-327-2
    1. China—Economic conditions—1976– 2. Investments, Foreign—China 3.
China—Civilization. 4. China—Social and customs. I. Title.
        HC427.92 .C3544 2001
        306'.0951—dc21

                                                    00-047115

FOR MY MENTOR WILLIAM H. NEWMAN,
AN EXEMPLAR OF EAST-WEST INTEGRATION

Contents

Note to the Reader

TRADITIONAL CHINESE NAMES place the family name first and the given name second—for example, Chen Ming-Jer. Western names work the other way around. Because many Chinese have taken Western first names, I have chosen to arrange Chinese names in the text in the Western style—Ming-Jer Chen. The only exceptions occur in cases where Chinese individuals are widely known by their Chinese-style names—such as **Mao** Tse-Tung, **Chiang** Kai-Shek, or **Li** Ka-Shing. In such cases, I use boldface to indicate the last name.

For the reader's convenience, Appendix 8, "Glossary of Chinese Terms and their Pronunciation," provides a list of the most common terms used in this book with a guide for their pronunciation and translation.

Finally, the Chinese characters used in this book are traditional characters.

Preface:
From the Great Wall to Wall Street

SEVERAL YEARS AGO, the movie *Wall Street* quoted the sayings of the ancient Chinese philosopher Sun Tzu, and after the film was released, the sales of his *The Art of War* increased fivefold. At about this time, I was asked to review a book on the application of Sun Tzu's thought to Western business, and it became clear to me that the Western business community was developing a strong interest in the affinity between its own business practices and Chinese thought.

The relevance of Chinese culture, however, serves an additional purpose today—as a basis for understanding how the Chinese themselves do business. Indeed, as China emerges as the world's most desirable market, and as Chinese entrepreneurs around the world continue to thrive, knowledge of Chinese culture and its impact on modern business conduct is becoming an extremely valuable asset.

This need was made clear to me in 1997, when I led a group of eighty Western executives on a two-week field trip in mainland China and Hong Kong to gain a first-hand experience of Chinese business and society. My aim was to challenge their misconceptions about Chinese culture. It was when I looked for readings that would help me to achieve this goal that I noticed a surprising dearth of books which addressed the *psychology* of Chinese business—that is, books that could "demystify" Chinese business by providing a thorough and practical understanding of its rich cultural and historical underpinnings.

If Westerners have only recently shown an interest in the ideas of ancient Eastern strategists and philosophers, the Chinese have never truly forgotten this rich legacy of thought. Of course, Chinese business practices will vary from country to country, as they adjust to different political systems and sociological climates. Nevertheless, just as the structures of Western corporations stem from the political and military models of Old World Europe, modern-day Chinese business structures have their origins in ancient Chinese culture and philosophy. The works of Sun Tzu, Confucius, Lao Tzu, and other thinkers are more than simply texts to the Chinese; they represent an integrated worldview. To do business with the Chinese, it is therefore essential to acquaint oneself with this worldview. As Sun Tzu wrote, "Know yourself and know the opponent, and you will win 100 battles."

Indeed, the most powerful tool any executive uses is the mind. But minds are powerfully affected by culture, which, in turn, is largely shaped by history and the philosophies of its great thinkers, be they Adam Smith, Plato, Machiavelli, or Confucius. Thus, to truly "get inside the heads" of your business partners and competitors, it is essential to have a thorough understanding of what underlies their thinking.

Many books have dealt with the "hands-on" or "how-to" aspects of doing business with the Chinese, and most investment banks or consulting companies offer excellent up-to-date information and real-time advice. This book takes a different approach. My principal aim is to bring the connections between Chinese culture and business to the surface for the Western businessperson and to outline broad strategic perspectives based on an understanding of cultural foundations. It is an aim that grows out of my personal background: Before leaving Taiwan for business school in the United States in the early 1980s, I had extensive training in classical Chinese history and culture, alongside formal education in business management and contemporary Chinese social sciences. Under the supervision of my master teacher, a cousin of the last emperor of the Qing Dynasty, who studied with the four most famous Chinese philosophers at the turn of the century, I studied extensively the works of the sixteen leading thinkers from the era considered the peak of Chinese civilization (772–222 B.C.).

Even in Chinese, there are few books that offer a comprehensive look into the cultural dimensions of Chinese business. The books that do provide key cultural and strategic insights ignore the question of Chinese business as it relates to global business practices. This gap was brought to my attention during two intensive workshops I conducted in 1997: the first for management professors from all of the fifty-plus M.B.A. programs on the mainland; the second for the sixty leading strategy educators and consultants in Taiwan. On both occasions, a large and diverse group of professionals felt that there was a profound misunderstanding of Chinese business on the part of the West, stemming mainly from a lack of cultural knowledge. Both Chinese professionals and Western executives saw the same need—for someone to take an *outside* look at the *inside* workings of Chinese business.

That is why I hope that the ideas in this book will extend beyond a Chinese-specific context to the formation of a global enterprise model. With the advent of a truly globalized world, it is not only markets but entire cultures that are coming into contact. Current and future business leaders will need to deal with the cultural challenges that arise from doing business on five continents, and I believe Chinese thinking has much to offer them. Chinese culture teaches the kind of self-other integration that makes it possible to develop a truly globally integrative perspective, at both organizational and personal levels.

Inside Chinese Business has several important additional purposes for me—on professional and personal levels. First, over many years of teaching M.B.A.'s and executives, I have found that they always responded well to the "philosophical" component of my classes, and in fact many have told me how it helped them later on in their business careers. I hope this book will similarly offer readers insights into the ways in which philosophical and cultural frameworks can enhance and enrich business and personal performance. Second, as the current chair of the Business Policy and Strategy Division of the Academy of Management, it is my modest professional aim to promote an integrative, rather than a comparative, approach to international business studies. Finally, as a father of two boys who were both born and educated in the United States, I hope that this book will provide a comprehensive but easily accessible guide to Chinese culture and practice for those second- or third-generation Chinese who read primarily in a language other than Chinese. It is my sincere hope that this book may offer these individuals a bridge between their cultural "homeland" and their local homes.

Acknowledgments

THIS BOOK is the result of a truly collective effort. I have benefited tremendously from the advice and perspectives of friends and colleagues around the globe.

In 1997, The Wharton School at the University of Pennsylvania provided me with the opportunity to found the Global Chinese Business Initiative and the freedom to teach slightly less "traditional" academic subjects. This book was written during this period, and drew much from my Chinese business-related activities, and from my Global Chinese Business and East Meets West seminars. The enthusiasm and feedback from business associates and students helped to shape and sharpen my own ideas.

Among the most dedicated contributors to this project were students and graduates from the University of Pennsylvania, including Stuart Paskett, Mark Tang, Guojia Zhang, David Chuang, Donald Huang, Leeanne Su, Max Sung, and Hong Ki Chris Shiu. I owe special thanks to Nelson Ying, who passed up working for his own "Chinese business family" and instead opted to work with me for over a year. Two other fine students, Kathryn Kai-Ling Ho and Cody Walsh, came from Bryn Mawr and Haverford colleges before their graduation to help me with this project.

Three visiting business professors from China provided tremendous assistance with research: Zhiyuan Qiang of the Tianjin University of Finance and Economics, Liqun Wei of the International

University of Business and Economics, and Min Wu of Tongji University. Alberto Hanani, a doctoral candidate at Imperial College of Science, Technology and Medicine, University of London, made tireless efforts to see the book to its completion.

I am fortunate to have worked with several very talented writers and editors. Laura M. Brown helped develop the first draft, assisting greatly in setting the book's structure, and she has helped me to become a better thinker during our collaboration over the last ten years.

Zoë Bower provided major assistance in the writing of this book and did much to steer it toward its final form. Her international background and training gave her the broad scope and the analytical skills necessary to attend to its conceptual tightness. Her extensive reading of background material and Chinese philosophy made her an informed and sophisticated critic. I hope the publication of *Inside Chinese Business* might act as a small wedding gift to her and Dan.

Rob Baedeker was deeply involved in the editing process, and was particularly instrumental in the development and writing of chapters 6 and 9. His background in literary and critical analysis helped make many of the book's cultural concepts more easily accessible. Without his last-minute efforts, the book would not have been completed in a timely fashion. Kris Day, President of the Calico Group, brought a "mandarin" editorial eye to the book and provided essential criticism; her contribution of the "Cultural Dilemma" boxes testifies to her deep understanding of both Chinese and Western cultures. Joe Chapman's editing added a colorful and lively touch, and helped condense and clarify the key messages of the book.

For guidance and criticism, I relied on a truly global group of friends and colleagues: Y. P. Chan of Core Solutions in Hong Kong, whose support and loyalty I cherish; John Michel of the University of Notre Dame, whose "brotherhood" has enriched my life; Shaohua Carolyn Mu of Virginia Polytechnic Institute and State University, who drew on her experiences at the Chinese Academy of Social Sciences to provide keen insights; Rick Niu of AIG in New York, an excellent example of the new generation of globally minded managers; Thomas Reed and Dawn Kelly of the University of Ulster in Northern Ireland, whose support and advice I treasure; Dr. Elena Ai-

Yuan Yang, whose dissertation on Chinese-American entrepreneurs was a great help in my own thinking; Lawrence Landman, President of the American Chamber of Commerce in Denmark; Ji-Ren Lee of National Taiwan University; Paul Jensen, of Young Crown Trading Ltd. in the PRC; Melanie Hayden, instrumental in offering ideas for chapters 7 and 8; and Kuo-Hsien Su of National Chung-Hsing University in Taiwan, whose assistance in the last ten years has been vital. Professor N. T. Wang, Director of China-International Business Project of Columbia University; Kam-Hon Lee, Professor and former Dean of the Chinese University of Hong Kong; my Wharton colleague and friend Ian C. MacMillan; and Stephen Carroll, Jr., my mentor at the University of Maryland, have helped in ways that go far beyond this specific project.

A final group of reviewers, mostly in Asia, provided helpful business perspectives: Edwin King of Morgan Stanley Dean Witter Asia Ltd. and his colleagues; Norman Chen; Alex Hsu; Siu-Chan Kwan; Eva Kwan; and Wenlei Li. Insights were also offered by Jennifer Y. Hsieh; Joni Eu; Dr. Jonathan Brookfield; Bruce Locb. Chris Wei of KG Telecommunications (Taiwan); Conrad T. C. Wong of Yau Lee Holdings (Hong Kong) and his friends and colleagues, including Doreen Tam and Jiao Xin. A thank you also to Chung-Ming Lau, Lu Yuan of the Chinese University of Hong Kong, J. Stuart Freeman, Jonathan Landrath, and Leila Easa.

Over the last twenty years, the following people have strongly influenced my thinking: Professor Jan-Kwei Chiang in Taiwan, who guided me toward the Western management classics; Samuel Kutz, Kenneth G. Smith, Martin Gannon, and Lee E. Preston at the University of Maryland; my former colleagues at Columbia Business School—Donald C. Hambrick, Hugh Patrick, Kathy R. Harrigan, Michael Tushman, Ehud Houminer, John Whitney (whose book *Power Plays* is a model for works aspiring to show the relevance of classics to the modern business world), Dean Meyer Feldberg and his wife Barbara; and finally, Michael Hitt, Paul Hirsch, and Danny Miller.

I am deeply grateful for the confidence and support of Wharton Deans Thomas P. Gerrity and Patrick Harker, and Deputy Deans Janice R. Bellace and David Schmittlein. As this book is published, I will be moving from the home of Benjamin Franklin to that of

Thomas Jefferson. I appreciate the support of the Darden School of the University of Virginia, in particular Deans Edward A. Snyder and James R. Freeland.

I am indebted to the associates and students of the Global Chinese Business Initiative (GCBI), whose dedication to the program allowed me more time to work on *Inside Chinese Business*: the indefatigable Emily Freeman, Lori Wood, Ralf Graves, Paul Tang, Yen-Miao Tung, Adrian Chiu, Cecilia Chan, Edwin Lee, Catherine Gilmore of former AT&T, Len Tischler of the Foundation for Understanding Chinese Business, and Roz Cohen, GCBI's supportive neighbor.

Instrumental in this book's publication were dedicated professionals like Jim Levine, who skillfully handled publishing and promotional arrangements and four editors at Harvard Business School Press: Marjorie Williams, for supporting the project; Amanda Gardner and Sylvia Weedman for coordinating the last stages of publication and promotion; and Nikki Sabin, for tireless efforts in commenting on the manuscript. I had the additional pleasure of getting to know Nikki personally during the editing process, and would like to congratulate her on the new addition to her family.

The calligraphy on the cover of this book was penned by my Master in Taiwan. The four characters mean "Chinese business." To place his words on the cover of this book is but a minuscule reflection of the profound influence his teachings have had on me.

I could fill volumes with gratitude to my mentor William H. Newman. Bill has achieved legendary status in the management world, from his early work with James McKinsey to his founding of the Academy of Management to his lifelong service in business teaching and research. He was among the first four American business educators to teach in China when it first opened to the West in 1979. Bill has led the way toward a truly balanced East-West outlook and toward global integration, and it is for these reasons that I dedicate this book to him.

Finally, I would like to thank my parents, Tsann and Ai-Jen Chen, for the strong values they have instilled in me and for their selflessness and caring. I hope that the eventual publication of the Chinese version of this book will help explain to them my absence over the last twenty years! My two sons, Andy and Abraham, have been a source of support and joy. They are always in my thoughts, and I hope that soon they will be able to read this book and through it understand the love that I have for them.

My wife Moh-Jiun has been the most supportive partner I could ever hope for. Her selfless devotion to the family has allowed me the freedom to pursue my professional goals. Her love has been strongest at those moments I needed it most. I would like to thank my parents-in-law, Tieh-Fu and An-Er Jeng Hu, for giving me their beloved daughter to enrich and complete my life.

I

INTRODUCTION
Who (and Where) Are the Chinese?

In 1996, Asia business expert Hugh Patrick addressed Columbia University's Center on Japanese Economy and Business. In his talk, Patrick surprised his audience by suddenly switching attention from Japan and calling for Japanese and Americans to work together to learn about and better understand Chinese business. In the past his remarks would have been unimaginable. Today they reflect a new reality: The two economic powerhouses of the late twentieth century, the United States and Japan, are now focused on doing business with the Chinese.

IN THE EARLY STAGES of this book's development, a friend of mine suggested a title that would, he said, command more attention than some of the other possibilities I had been considering. His recommendation was to call the book *The Baffling Chinese*. Although I ultimately decided that this title was a little *too* provocative and controversial, I had to admit it made a suggestive statement about the way Chinese business behavior often can appear to Westerners. Indeed, one of the primary questions this book seeks to answer is, How can non-Chinese understand the often puzzling behavior of Chinese businesspeople?

A large part of the answer to that question is that they should pay careful attention to Chinese culture. And much of Chinese culture, in turn, can be understood by looking to prominent Chinese thinkers. The Chinese customs and characteristics that I will focus on in specific chapters—from the reliance on extended family, to saving face, to the use of indirect communication and competition—grow from deep philosophical roots. By unravelling these roots, *Inside Chinese Business* offers Western managers an insider's look at how the Chinese do business at home, and in a global setting.

From this ground, I then propose the possibility of merging some Chinese business practices with Western managerial tradition —an integrative approach that may have special relevance in developing countries across the globe. An understanding of the Chinese and their business behavior will have broad implications for the Western businessperson working not only with the Chinese but also with other "unfamiliar" business cultures worldwide.

This chapter starts the process of understanding where the Chinese are "coming from" quite literally. It begins with a brief overview of the "motherland"—mainland China—and then extends the definition of *China* to include the global community of Chinese emigrants and their descendants—in Hong Kong, in Taiwan, throughout most Southeast Asian countries, and in nearly every other part of the world (see Appendix 1). Most of these people still identify themselves as Chinese (*hua-ren*), even though many are citizens of other countries. Though institutional, linguistic, and socioeconomic differences have a strong impact on Chinese business practices in those countries in which Chinese operate, the Chinese diaspora is still connected by a common cultural and philosophical heritage.

For this reason, I will assume a degree of cultural unity by using the term *Chinese* throughout the book to designate a diverse group of ethnic Chinese (just as, for the sake of argument, I will unavoidably oversimplify by using the terms *West* and *Westerner*). To begin with, however, I will draw an important (if still generalized) distinction between two principal groups of Chinese: the mainland Chinese and the overseas, or nonmainland, Chinese.

Mainland China: A Cultural and Business Geography

Ask a dozen people who have traveled to China for their most vivid impressions of that vast country, and you will probably get a dozen different answers. Some individuals recall a country of cold plains and dreary mountains, where the local economy depends entirely on peasants tilling fields. Others might tell of gigantic cities in a tropical climate, bustling with thousands of small businesses. Still others remember high-tech centers growing in the suburbs of former colonial towns. Finally, some will describe an endless, furnacelike desert inhabited by nomadic tribes. All these people are describing China, one of the most diverse countries in the world. That diversity also extends to the country's ethnicity (fifty-six ethnic groups), its dialects (200 still in use), its eight major cuisines, and a chaotic century of political events that has seen no fewer than four radically different political systems (imperialism, warlordism, republicanism, and communism).

Despite such diversity, there is, in fact, an incredible degree of unity in China. This unity is due in part to the predominance of one ethnic group, the Han, that constitutes 90 percent of the population, and also to the fact that the 200 dialects of Chinese are held together by the same written language.[1] Most importantly, the unity stems from a long tradition of Confucian values that has governed Chinese society unceasingly, to a greater or lesser degree in different periods, throughout China's history. As a cultural structure, Confucianism is unique because it lacks religious dogma or metaphysical theories. Its contrast with traditional Western cultural systems could not be greater. As the late, preeminent sinologist John Fairbank remarked, "Moses received his golden tablets on a mountain top, but Confucius reasoned from daily life without the aid of any deity."[2]

Since Confucian philosophy was preoccupied with the organization of society as an orderly and hierarchical whole, it could easily assimilate the cultures of invading powers, and thus has lasted for over 2,500 years. Confucianism regulates every social relationship, from familial to civic. It pervades Chinese society and in many ways underlies the Chinese business values discussed throughout this book. Understanding how Confucianism governs different aspects of social behavior is thus essential to understanding the Chinese— and to understanding how to do business with them.

China's cultural traditions and history have long served its people as a source of reassurance and pride. In times of adversity, culture was used strategically: when confronted with the possibility

---

Box 1-1:   The Presence of the Past

Any discussion of Chinese philosophical values must include the fact that in present-day China, traditional thinkers—especially Confucius—are increasingly a subject of discussion. President **Jiang** Zemin refers to Confucius regularly and even attended an international conference on Confucianism in Beijing in the late 1980s. The *People's Daily*, or *Renmin Ribao*, the official voice of the Communist Party and the PRC government, carried an article in 1996 calling for a clear understanding of Confucianism, arguing that it provided "many precious business philosophies for the development of a market economy."[a] The article also suggested that Confucianism could help smooth the transition after Hong Kong's repatriation and promote peace with Taiwan.

   Beyond the mainland, Confucianism is alive and well in Asia. During a time of unprecedented social and economic change, many Chinese are reverting to Confucianism for moral and practical considerations. Senior Minister of Singapore, **Lee** Kuan Yew, articulated this turn in an article in *Newsweek* magazine: "[P]owerful forces of new technology . . . [are] sweeping the world . . . [but] there is no reason to abandon our values . . . The basic human relationships, those between husband and wife, children and parents, extended family members and friends, and between a citizen and his government—these do not change."[b]

   This reliance on tradition is a common cultural phenomenon. Chinese people tend to view their lives in the context of Chinese civilization's huge span, thus putting everything into a long-term perspective. As Hari Bedi, author of *Understanding the Asian Manager*, observes of Asian society at large, "Modern life continues to be judged by old values, creating a complexity of behavior in Asians that foreign colleagues often find baffling. Despite Mao and the cultural revolution, an average Chinese still abides by the tenets of Confucianism."[c]

[a] "China: Article Calls for Critical Appraisal of Confucianism," *BBC Monitoring Service: Far East*, 17 August 1996.
[b] Lee Kuan Yew, "Is Confucianism Dead?" *Newsweek* Special Issue 2000, 49.
[c] Hari Bedi, *Understanding the Asian Manager: Working with the Movers of the Pacific Century* (North Sydney, Australia: Allen and Unwin, 1992), 10.

---

of invasion or revolt, the Chinese would "civilize" the agitators. This could be achieved through the sharing of goods and knowledge, for the scope of Chinese culture was not limited to intricate social codes, but also included sophisticated technological advancements. In the eighth century, for example, the Chinese already had a primitive version of the printing press—some seven centuries before Gutenberg! In fact, until the Industrial Revolution, China was technologically well ahead of any other culture in the world, adding to the mystique that surrounded this closed, secret kingdom that fascinated and attracted outsiders as early as the fifteenth century.

Today, it is no longer just "mystique" that draws Western businesses toward China but the country's staggering market potential. With a population of 1.3 billion, mainland China holds one-fifth of the world's people. Starting in 1979, when Beijing opened the country to foreign investment, Western businesses moved in eagerly to claim a share of China's vast markets. Between 1990 and 1996, for example, the number of multinational companies in Shanghai—a city of 17 million people—increased from 300 to 16,000. The People's Republic of China (PRC) continues to attract much more foreign direct investment (FDI) than any other developing country—with an average annual increase of more than 15 percent per year during the 1990s.[3]

Just as they absorbed foreign invasions in the past, the Chinese are assimilating this new economic invasion and are now becoming partners of major Western firms. More than 300 companies from the Fortune 500 now have operations in China. Volkswagen, for instance, with twenty PRC joint ventures, holds 50 percent of the passenger car market on the mainland.[4] General Motors has invested $1 billion to build a manufacturing plant in Shanghai. And Motorola, with six joint ventures, ten cooperative projects, and more than twenty subsidiaries nationwide, generated revenues of U.S. $2.8 billion in the PRC in 1999.[5]

PRC companies have also begun moving beyond the shores of the mainland. Pearl River Piano Group is now the second-largest piano manufacturer in the world next to Yamaha. Haier, the largest home appliance company in the PRC, opened a South Carolina operation in the late 1990s and has seized 20 percent of the U.S. small refrigerator market.

Beyond the Mainland: The Overseas Chinese

While the West has been increasingly attracted to China, many Chinese have long been attracted to the world outside. Since China's western borders were far off and perilous, the sea provided the main route for emigration. Even today, the majority of overseas Chinese families can trace their roots to three regions in mainland China that lie near southern water: Guangdong, Fujian, and Hainan Provinces (see Appendix 2). Among them there are eight primary groups, distinguished by dialect: Cantonese, Fuzhou, Hainanese, Hakka, Henghua, Hokchia, Hokkien, and Teochiu.[6] As members of these groups left China, they tended to settle with people who spoke their own dialect, and so different regions of Southeast Asia are dominated by groups that emigrated from different parts of China. This is important to remember since family home province and native dialect continue to be the major influences in Chinese personal and business relationships.

The history of the overseas Chinese emigration, though full of hardship and survival, has also been one of tremendous economic success. Those Chinese who have made their homes in Hong Kong, Taiwan, and Singapore currently possess combined foreign reserves of $250 billion, an amount equal to the foreign reserves of Germany and Japan combined. The PRC's foreign reserve in 1999 was $154.6 billion. In 1998, the World Economic Forum ranked Hong Kong, Taiwan, and Singapore numbers 1, 2, and 4, respectively, in global competitiveness.[7] And the total assets of the Chinese diaspora worldwide—which includes Vancouver, Sydney, Toronto, New York, and San Francisco, among other Chinese population centers—are estimated at $2 to $3 trillion. In these terms, the overseas Chinese constitute the third-largest economy in the world, trailing only the United States and Japan in total assets.[8] Table 1-1 shows the geographic distribution of the Global Chinese Business 500—the top overseas or nonmainland Chinese companies in terms of market capitalization.

The Chinese Diaspora

In the tenth century, Chinese merchants began to explore the commercial possibilities of the Indian Ocean coast. Chinese communities grew rapidly in such places as the Malay Peninsula and the Strait of Malacca, although the imperial government of the Sung dynasty (960–1279) never looked favorably on sea trade and emigration. Even in 1712 the emperor K'ang-Hsi requested that foreign govern-

Table 1-1: Geographic Distribution of the Overseas Chinese Business 500

Country/Region	1997	1998	1999
Taiwan	183	285	240
Hong Kong	113	105	105
Singapore	49	37	67
Malaysia	91	41	50
Thailand	15	12	13
Philippines	15	11	13
Indonesia	34	9	12

Source: *Yazhou Zhoukan*, 3 November 1997, 2 November 1998, 1 November 1999.
Note: The significant change from 1997 to 1998 in the regional distribution of the top overseas companies is the result of the Asian financial crisis.

ments repatriate Chinese emigrants so that they could be executed. Nonetheless, these expatriate communities, safely distant from imperial authority, prospered more or less unhindered. Wherever they established themselves, these emigrants, the first major wave of overseas Chinese, managed to occupy a merchant gentry status in between the European colonial administrators and the indigenous peoples.[9]

In the late 1800s, with African slave labor outlawed, many Chinese went to Southeast Asia as laborers, and "coolies" became the world's source of cheap labor. The first Chinatowns sprang up around rubber plantations, tin mills, and factories in cities such as Singapore, Jakarta, Manila, and Saigon. Many Chinese came to the United States during the 1800s to mine for gold, build the railroads, and work in logging camps; others worked on sugar plantations on islands across the Pacific. Although some returned home with their savings, many Chinese laborers used their money to begin businesses of their own and never went back to China, instead establishing homes, families, and traditions in their new countries.

Political events have also been a driving force behind emigration. During the civil war that culminated in the 1949 communist revolution and the relocation of the nationalists to Taiwan, thousands of China's elite families fled the country to protect their lives and wealth. Between 1945 and 1951, nearly 500,000 refugees from the

Shanghai area relocated to Hong Kong, bringing with them the equivalent of U.S. $8 billion. Interestingly, the communist government followed imperial precedent and attempted to bring emigrants home. In 1959, **Mao** Tse-Tung (**Mao** Zedong) offered to send ships to pick up any overseas Chinese who wished to repatriate. Of the millions who had left, only 100,000 took him up on his offer.[10]

The period following World War II was a turning point in the development of overseas Chinese business. As the colonial period in Asia drew to a close, the Europeans left their Southeast Asian holdings behind or sold them off for whatever they could get, and the overseas Chinese were able to buy up these former colonial assets. As the historian Sterling Seagrave puts it, "The overseas Chinese were the only ants at the picnic."[11] These businesses—in agriculture, rubber, and sugar—became the basis for growing Chinese empires (Appendix 3 highlights major historical events for Mainland China, Taiwan, and Hong Kong).

Even though they are a small minority in their adopted countries, the Chinese now control a disproportionate share of these countries' national trade. In Indonesia, for example, where the Chinese population is 4 percent of the country's total, it controls 70 percent of the trade. In the Philippines, where the Chinese population is but 3 percent, it also manages to control 70 percent of all business. Thailand's population is 3 percent Chinese, and yet the Chinese control 60 percent of the trade.[12]

The pattern of emigration continued into the second half of the twentieth century, as many Chinese students pursued graduate education in the West and then stayed on as professionals: between 1978 and 1998, 81.2 percent of the students who left the PRC for the United States chose to remain there.[13] Today, 90 percent of all Chinese immigrants are naturalized citizens of their adopted countries.[14] Despite their citizenship, however, they generally conform to Chinese cultural norms and identify themselves as "Chinese." This identification with ancestral roots can continue even after the passage of many generations. Alberto Hanani, a seventh-generation Chinese-Indonesian, speaks no Chinese but carries with him at all times an extensive family tree tracing his roots back to the Fujian Province in mainland China. Alfonso Yuchengo is a highly respected Filipino businessman (chairman of Rizal Commercial Bank) and political leader (ambassadorships to the PRC and Japan) of Chinese origin. Although his family has been in the Philippines for five generations, and in spite of his formal education in the United States and Germany, Yuchengo stays close to his Chinese roots and speaks three Chinese dialects, in addition to English and Spanish.

The emotional attachment of many overseas Chinese to their motherland is indeed powerful, and these people often consider themselves more Chinese, in terms of traditional Confucian values, than their cousins on the mainland. Those who left the country before the 1949 revolution—and those who left because of it—were not exposed to communist attacks on traditional Chinese values such as family loyalty and social hierarchy. So while mainland Chinese were struggling to adopt new social and political values, the émigrés were working equally hard to maintain traditional Chinese values in countries where they found themselves isolated ethnic minorities.

Due in part to their isolation, overseas Chinese communities became extremely close-knit. Clan associations and benevolent societies, often based on common village origin or common dialect, gave rise to tight social networks that served for trade purposes and for protection of their persons and interests. These networks extended to friends and relatives in other regions of the world, creating a globally interconnected social and business community of Chinese— both on and off the mainland.

Financial success for the overseas Chinese has been dependent on these social networks and on long-term planning and saving. Most ethnic Chinese throughout the world have begun life poor, and their memory of poverty continues to drive the wealthiest of them. Yue-Che Wang, the patriarch of Formosa Plastics (valued in excess of $3.9 billion in 1998), refused to fly business class until the early 1990s, when he was in his seventies. As Lee Shau-Kee, head of Hong Kong's Henderson Land, describes it, "The Chinese who left the mother country had to struggle, and that became a culture of its own, passed on . . . through each generation. Because we have no social security, the overseas Chinese habit is not to spend a lot and to make a lot of friends."[15]

Simply put, the overseas Chinese operate with a "minority mentality" in their new homes or adopted countries. Relying on hard

---

Box 1-2: "Life-Raft" Values

In an article in the *Harvard Business Review*, John Kao presented what he called the "life-raft values" of overseas Chinese entrepreneurs.[a] This set of values, which stemmed from the uncertainty of their minority status, points to some of the unique features that have historically characterized overseas Chinese business:

- Thrift ensures survival.

- A high, even irrational, level of savings is desirable, regardless of immediate need.

- Hard work to the point of exhaustion is necessary to ward off the many hazards present in an unpredictable world.

- The only people you can trust are family—and a business enterprise is created as a familial life raft.

- The judgment of an incompetent relative is more reliable than that of a competent stranger.

- Obedience to patriarchal authority is essential to maintaining coherence and direction for the enterprise.

- Investment must be based on kinship or clan affiliations, not abstract principles.

- Tangible goods like real estate, natural resources, and gold bars are preferable to intangibles like illiquid securities or intellectual property.

- Keep your bags packed at all times.

[a] John Kao, "The Worldwide Web of Chinese Business," *Harvard Business Review* 71, no. 2 (March–April 1993): 25.

---

work and adaptability to ensure their survival, they specialize in finding business niches that will help them survive in nearly any setting. A typical Chinese business pattern is to seek out a local need and fill it. People from Fuzhou, mainland China, where my parents are from, like to say that all they need to survive anywhere in the world is one of three knives: a razor, to start a barber shop; a kitchen knife, to start a restaurant; or a pair of scissors, to start a tailor shop! Of course, "local needs" have become increasingly more sophisticated and digitized, and many overseas Chinese are now doing more than trimming, feeding, or clothing their host nation's citizens. Today in the United States, for example, overseas Chinese are prominent in some of the most prestigious laboratories and high-tech companies. In fact, as many as 20 percent of the high-tech start-ups in Silicon Valley are owned by ethnic Chinese.[16] Jerry Yang, cofounder of Yahoo!, is a well-known example.

Investing in the Mother Country

The loyalty of the overseas Chinese to their homeland is reflected in their investments. Even in the wake of the Asian financial crisis, the Chinese of Hong Kong, Singapore, and Taiwan expanded their networks' branches to the extent that they are now the largest "foreign" investors in the PRC, providing roughly 70 percent of China's capital inflow—far more than that of Japan (8.3 percent), the United States (8.2 percent), and Europe (5.2 percent) combined.[17] Surprisingly, in view of more than fifty years of political disagreements and military standoffs with the "motherland," Taiwan ranks second only to Hong Kong in mainland Chinese business investments.[18] The total number of Taiwanese enterprises invested in the PRC is estimated to be 40,000 to 50,000, and their total investment value is estimated at $40 billion.[19]

Ethnic Chinese throughout Southeast Asia are also seizing economic opportunities on the mainland. All in all, the overseas Chinese have set up a large number of businesses in China, including 100,000 joint ventures.[20] Thai-Chinese billionaire Dhanin Chearavanont, leader of the Charoen Pokphand (CP) Group, runs businesses in mainland China ranging from petrochemicals to Kentucky Fried Chicken shops. Malaysian Robert Kuok—whose global enterprises include plantations, sugar refineries, shipping, property, insurance, and hotels, and who has been described by *Forbes* as the shrewdest businessman in the world—was one of the first overseas Chinese investors on the mainland.[21]

Overseas Chinese reinvestment in mainland China also takes the form of charitable contributions. There is a long history of such gifts: Fujian's Xiamen University, for example, was built by Singaporean-Chinese rubber tycoon Kah-Kee Tan in 1921. The university continues to raise large portions of its budget from Chinese alumni families overseas, and one-third of the buildings on campus bear the names of overseas Chinese entrepreneurs. In the 1990s, the Salim Group donated an estimated $100 million to build hospitals, schools, and ports in Fujian Province, the birthplace of its patriarch, **Liem** Sioe Liong, who left China in the 1930s to work on his uncle's peanut farm in Indonesia.[22] The trend continues today. Li Ka-Shing, reputed to be the wealthiest man in Hong Kong, with an estimated personal fortune of $10 billion, single-handedly donated the funds to build Shantou University in his hometown.

Members of the Chinese diaspora worldwide maintain a complex but balanced sense of dual loyalty both to their country of residence and to their ancestral roots. To the Chinese, this balance seems natural. For those who seek to work and do business with them, it is important to recognize both the complexity of the Chinese sense of identity and the continuing influence of traditional Chinese values.

Future Potential: Where East Meets West

Beyond the importance of understanding individual Chinese, there is a larger global trend that cannot be ignored: long regarded as minor players or latecomers in global markets, Chinese businesses worldwide have exhibited increasing influence and attracted greater attention. Over the last decade, business analysts in the West began to recognize the ascendancy of Asian—particularly Chinese—business and started to make predictions about its role in the twenty-first century. For example, as John Naisbitt wrote in *Megatrends Asia*, "The global axis of influence has shifted from West to East. . . . It's no longer just what America and Europe can do. It's what America, Europe and Asia can do to reshape the world."[23] Peter Drucker made a similar argument: One of his six predictions for the twenty-first century was that the "global outfits of the future will be the Chinese clan. . . . The Chinese are likely to make the family into a modern corporation."[24] Maurice "Hank" Greenberg, CEO and Chairman of AIG, sees a similar future. In 1998 he asserted "If you look down the road 25 years, then maybe we will have our corporate head-quarters in Shanghai and an office in New York."[25]

Box 1-3: Weathering the Crisis

With the onset of the Asian financial crisis in 1997, Western exuberance over the promise of Chinese business subsided. However, Asia's steady recovery from the crisis gives new promise to Asian business. While many firms incurred huge losses or failed altogether, Asian business, and Chinese business in particular, reacted quickly and drew on extensive networks to save floundering businesses.

For example, First Pacific, a Hong Hong–based overseas Chinese firm, made a series of rapid strategic moves to seize new opportunities in Asia. To raise money, it sold its crown jewel, Dutch-based Hagemeyer, for $1.6 billion. It radically reduced its involvement in Hong Kong's property market and expanded its commercial leasing business there. It bought back its own Hong Kong stocks. It sold its cellular telephone assets, Pacific Link, to Hong Kong Telecom. Turning to the Philippines, it strengthened its Filipino subsidiary, Metro Pacific, and acquired 53.4 percent of Philippine Long Distance Telephone. It also seized the opportunity to acquire the London-listed Savillas property agency, with the intention of using it as a base for U.S. expansion. Under the leadership of its managing director, Chinese-Filipino Manuel V. Pangilinan, First Pacific generated $1 billion in cash through global restructuring and repositioned itself as a leading pan-Asian player immediately following the Asian financial crisis.

First Pacific is a good example of a firm turning crisis into opportunity, long a strength of Chinese-managed companies. (Chapter 5 will discuss this concept in greater detail.) The story does not end here, though. First Pacific is more than 50 percent owned by the Indonesian-based Salim Group and **Liem** Sioe Liong's close family members and friends. Indonesia, of course, was among the hardest-hit countries during the Asian financial crisis, and many observers assumed that after the crisis the Salim Group was finished. First Pacific not only turned the crisis to its own advantage but also was able to use its newly raised cash to bail out some of its brother and sister companies in the Salim Group.

With a clear understanding of the Chinese and their businesses, Westerners can avoid making mistakes and prevent the tension and misunderstanding that often threaten good business relations between East and West. For example, it is essential that Western businesspeople understand the difference between mainland and overseas Chinese. One of the most shocking experiences of my consulting career came when I met with a top executive of a Fortune 100 company—the global leader in its industry. As we discussed the size and extent of Chinese investments in Southeast Asia, it became clear to me that this very successful executive, who was in charge of his company's entire global operations, actually thought that those investments came from the PRC. In fact, I was obliged to explain the situation three times before he understood that those investments came from the overseas Chinese. For a person in this position to have so little understanding of the region was not just surprising; it also was potentially very dangerous for his company's investments in the region.

Cultural misunderstandings can lead to missed business opportunities and suspicion, as exemplified by hasty and misguided interpretations of the relationship-based (or *guanxi*-based) nature of Chinese business. Because of a series of highly publicized *guanxi*-related scandals, many Western businesspeople now simply equate *guanxi* with corruption or bribery. This view is shocking and offensive to the Chinese, for whom *guanxi* is a cultural form of social networking. (Chapter 3 will discuss *guanxi* in detail.)

Since the 1990s, business gurus have been seeking to learn from the success stories of Chinese companies. John Naisbitt predicted that the unique strengths of the Chinese business network—among them its speed in making decisions, mustering resources, and connecting people—would make the Chinese model the ideal flexible form of social organization for the globally connected world of the future.[26] Whether or not such fundamental social change ever occurs, Naisbitt's speculation underscores the increasing importance of adaptability in all business systems. Just as the strength of Confucian philosophy lay in its ability to absorb and adapt to foreign rule, Chinese thinking has proven itself uniquely suited to conducting business in a wide variety of political environments and economic systems. For Western executives, the very process of learning about such an approach to business can therefore be enriching. As business becomes more genuinely *globalized*—as opposed to simply transnational—the notion of "global business standards" is unlikely to remain exclusively Western. For the future, it may be helpful to adopt a more integrative approach to global business practices, and Chinese business may serve as the basis for this rethinking. In the

Box 1-4: East-West.com

The intersection of Chinese business and the Internet revolution presents both challenges and opportunities for new ways of thinking. On the one hand, Chinese business represents a promising organizational model—especially in the cyberspace era, where speed is important, the emphasis is on network and community, and business can serve as an integrator across national boundaries. Chinese business strategies can provide a framework for operating with limited resources to expand across and around borders.

On the other hand, dot-com entrepreneurs are becoming increasingly aware that traditional Chinese ways of conducting business remain different—even in cyberspace. One obstacle facing Internet business in the Chinese context is the relationship- and trust-based nature of Chinese business transactions. The Chinese, who are used to being able to touch the products they buy and, more important, to establish direct contacts and relationships with the sellers, will need some convincing to spend their money at "virtual" shops.

The direct B2B Internet business formula used in the United States also runs into complications in China. The American model is built around price wars and auctions that have little to do with any real connection with the client. Furthermore, since support businesses in China tend to be limited in scale and scope, business-to-business transactions present formidable supply-chain problems, requiring multiple and diverse sourcing arrangements. In China, the Internet business formula B2B becomes B2B2B2B2B![a]

[a] "China: Let the E-Commerce Games Begin," http://knowledge.wharton.upenn.edu (accessed 1 May 2000).

words of John Stuart Mill: "There is no nation which does not need to borrow from others."

This chapter has provided a brief overview of the some of the cultural and historical influences on Chinese business in East Asia and worldwide. The following chapters will offer a more in-depth look at the structural and organizational concerns of Chinese business, as well as the values and principles underpinning these concerns. The first section of the book, chapters 2 through 4, explains some of the fundamentals of Chinese social structure. Chapter 2 focuses on the structural centerpiece of Chinese enterprise worldwide, the family business; chapter 3 attempts to demystify the Chinese concept of *guanxi*, which is key to doing business in the Chinese relation-based system; and chapter 4 provides a more detailed view of the relation-based nature of Chinese society and explains the importance of social roles in the Chinese context.

The middle section of the book, chapters 5 and 6, examines values and principles that underlie Chinese social roles and business structures. Chapter 5 provides a detailed look at the most important Chinese business values, such as integration and balance, and their application to time and performance; chapter 6 looks into the mind of the Chinese businessperson by tracing the sources of Chinese strategic and competitive thinking.

The last section, chapters 7 through 9, treats the implications of these structures and values in terms of business conduct. Chapter 7 analyzes Chinese communication styles and suggests ways Westerners can "translate" their ideas into language that the Chinese will understand and embrace; chapter 8 explores Chinese negotiation tactics; and chapter 9 is devoted to the special concerns of doing business in the PRC's transitional economy. Finally, in the epilogue, I explore how some of the fundamentals of Chinese business thinking may enrich Western business ideas and practice—both at home and in global markets.

Conclusion: Business without Borders

In the spring of 2000, I was giving a seminar on global Chinese business at a leading business school in the United States. During my presentation, I was interrupted by a distinguished colleague who, without a trace of irony, asked me point-blank, "Are you telling me that we should learn from those economically backward countries?"

I replied immediately: "That's exactly my point." I still hold to this answer. While this book aims, on the most basic level, to provide Western businesspeople with the insight necessary to improve both the quality and the outcome of their business relations with the Chinese, my true hope is to show that an understanding of Chinese culture and business can do more than improve the bottom line and corporate performance.

From an American-led Western perspective, China often is seen as the most foreign of all foreign places. Its culture, institutions, and people appear completely baffling—a matter of absolute difference, not of degree. But China's extreme "otherness" also presents an opportunity for intense *self*-reflection. That is, the "absolute difference" of Chinese society can throw a new analytical light on the West's own cultural and behavioral norms. By studying the cultural roots of Chinese business, Western executives will realize that they seem foreign to the Chinese. Miscomprehension is a two-way phenomenon, and in seeking to resolve it, we cannot take our own cultural presuppositions and standards for granted. The larger goal of this book is to break down culturally constructed self-other dichotomies and point toward the development of a globally integrating perspective. Indeed, when we understand how one culture's way of thinking diverges from our own, we come closer to developing a mind-set that better translates between all cultures, be they Indian, Spanish, Nigerian, Irish, or simply generational. Perhaps this, after all, will be the winning formula for doing business in the twenty-first century.

2

FAMILY BUSINESSES, BUSINESS FAMILIES

One of the most famous sites on the campus of Tianjin University, in the People's Republic of China, is a stone engraved with a copy of the very first diploma conferred on a graduate, when Western-style university education was first introduced into China. Next to the date on the diploma, 1900, the graduate's name is printed, along with the names of his father, grandfather, and great-grandfather. The diploma speaks volumes about the strength of family tradition in Chinese society. Like any individual in Chinese society, the graduate exists primarily in the context of his family. His achievements belong to them all.

FOR THE CHINESE, business has always been connected to family. In fact, in traditional Chinese culture, the family serves as the basis for and prototypical unit of *all* organizations—from social clubs to educational institutions to political parties.

As has been widely noted, the vast majority of Chinese businesses outside mainland China—even the largest conglomerates— are family-owned. From Hong Kong to Taiwan, Singapore to Bangkok, Jakarta to Manila, the family is the foundation for all Chinese business enterprise. Even in mainland China, where fifty years of communist rule sought to replace traditional Chinese regard for family with a patriotic allegiance to the party, the family-based model of business has reappeared. After the open-door policy was introduced in 1979, family business reemerged along with the substantial growth of private enterprise.

Although the conventional phrase is "family business," what the Chinese really have are "business families," the difference being that family, not business, is the focus: family concerns drive business decisions. This paradigm holds in Chinese businesses of all sizes, from small retail stores to massive multinational organizations, in all Chinese overseas communities, and now in the PRC. This "family first, business second" principle establishes priorities different from those generally held in the West. Winston Wang, for example, of Taiwan's Formosa Plastics Group, states: "I have never really thought about creating wealth. I see things more in terms of projects that need to be realized and responsibilities to the family that need to be discharged."[1]

At present, Chinese business families across Asia are in flux. Many businesses failed during the Asian financial crisis, and those that survived have come under tremendous pressure to comply with international business standards and practices. Even those that have thrived must find ways to adapt as they move aggressively into other parts of the world. For most Chinese companies, there is increasing pressure to professionalize management, especially at the very top level, and in general to "Westernize" their businesses.

While strong Chinese cultural values and family traditions continue to exert a counterpressure against these external challenges, the majority of family enterprises are also undergoing transformation from within: A new generation of professionally minded, and often Western-trained, family members are now inheriting business control and leadership. Chinese business families, at least outside mainland China, are at a crossroads, and the form that they assume will be of great importance not only for Asia but also for the global economy.

The family constitutes, and will continue to constitute, the underlying, driving force of activities and decisions in all phases of business affairs. As the anthropologist Margery Wolf says of Chinese kinship networks, "Money has no past, no future, and no obligations. Relatives do."[2] This chapter, therefore, will first review the importance of family in Chinese society and modern-day business, then take a detailed look at the traditional Chinese business family and its modes of operation. It will end with some projections for the future of Chinese business families.

The Family: Cultural and Business Contexts

The business family is the contemporary extension of a historical and cultural tradition that has always promoted the family as the fundamental organizing and working unit of society. Because China was largely an agrarian state, the family unit, through its capacity to amass and share limited resources, provided a measure of protection against the perils of subsistence living.[3]

Following Confucius, the family unit was given a moral dimension. Confucius extended the family beyond its functional role as a natural working unit to serve as the prototype for a broader societal network of morally binding, mutually dependent relationships. Unlike most Western societies, the Confucian state is composed not of "individuals" per se but of their interconnections and interdependencies. Confucian thought prescribes moral social roles to every person and shapes the individual as a link in a social network, cemented and stabilized by the principle of filial piety, among other rules of conduct. Through the assignment of roles, this system internalizes the social code, creating, ideally, a society that is self-regulating.

To this end, family discipline and conventions exert a powerful force that binds generation to generation. In ancient China, all sons had equal rights of inheritance—a practice that extended economic obligations to the whole family. When these social and economic interdependencies began to extend to more distant relatives, the result was the development of the Chinese clan as a social organization. That is why there are entire villages in mainland China where inhabitants share the same last name. The strong social bond among extended families continues to have profound implications for the Chinese today. In 1999, for instance, the Huang clan annual meeting in Bangkok drew more than 40,000 "Huangs" from approximately thirty countries. To exemplify how family respect can be manifested in a business perspective, **Xiang** Bingwei, the president of Weizhi Group in the PRC, instituted a company holiday in honor of filial piety, winning both the loyalty of his employees and the attention of society. He not only named 8 December the Weizhi Festival of Filial Piety but also honored the parents of the ten top employees at the festival. Such family-centered recognitions are echoed in the Chinese saying "When a man gets to the top, all his relatives get there with him; when a man is found guilty, all his relatives go to hell with him."

The contribution of business families to the economy of Greater China is staggering. According to the estimation of one of the top ten Hong Kong fund managers, around 40 percent of Hong Kong's stock market capitalization in 1999 was controlled by fifteen family groups. Excluding government enterprises, sixteen of the top twenty companies in total assets in Taiwan in 1999 were family-owned and family-controlled. This pattern is much the same throughout Greater China and the rest of Southeast Asia. In Indonesia, nine of the top ten businesses are owned by Chinese families; the largest of these, the Salim Group, held an estimated 5 percent of the country's gross domestic product (GDP) in the 1990s. In Thailand, Chinese families own four of the country's largest private banks, including the Bangkok Bank.[4] Table 2-1 provides a few representative examples of these Chinese business families across Southeast Asia, as well as the key businesses that they operate. As a group, these companies represent the most powerful business force in Asia.

The family-based model of business has even made a recent reappearance in mainland China, spurred by the dramatic increase in the importance of the non-state-owned enterprises, which in the late 1990s were estimated to have produced 72 percent of the country's gross value of industrial output with only 54 percent of its resources. Among them, individual-owned enterprises produced 17 percent of the country's gross value of industrial output with 13 percent of its resources. Significantly, almost a third of all these private businesses are run by single families, and their annual growth rate in both gross output and fixed-asset investment averaged 20 percent during this same period.[5] Even such drastic blows to the family as the PRC's one-child policy, introduced in 1979 to curb population growth, have not deterred this renewed interest in the business family.

Because the development of family business in the PRC is still

Table 2-1: Key Chinese Business Families Across Asia

Family	Base	Main Company	Business
Cheng Yu-Tung	Hong Kong	New World Development	Property, telecom, infrastructure
Fung family	Hong Kong	Li & Fung	Trading and retail
Geoffrey (MT) Yeh	Hong Kong	Hsin Chong Construction	Construction
Kwok brothers	Hong Kong	Sun Hung Kai Properties	Property
Lee Shau Kee	Hong Kong	Henderson Land	Property, convention centers
Li Ka-Shing	Hong Kong	Cheung Kong	Property, telecom, sports, energy
Eka Tjipta Widjaja	Indonesia	Sinar Mas	Paper, timber, banking, food, chemicals, property
Liem Sioe Liong	Indonesia	First Pacific	Food, cement, property, consumer goods
Lim Goh Tong	Malaysia	Genting	Casinos, mining, theme parks, hotels
Mochtar Riady	Indonesia	Lippo Group	Bank, real estate, life insurance
Robert Kuok	Malaysia	Kerry Properties	Sugar, property, media, hotels, drinks, food
Quek/Kwek family	Malaysia/ Singapore	Hong Leong	Property, hotels, banking
Lucio Tan	Philippines	Fortune Tobacco	Brewing, tobacco, airlines, hotels, banking
Chang Yung-Fa	Taiwan	Evergreen Group	Shipping, airlines
Koo family	Taiwan	Koos Group	Financial services, banking, insurance, cement
Tsai family	Taiwan	Cathay Life Insurance	Insurance, property
Wang family	Taiwan	Formosa Plastics	Petrochemicals, semiconductors, plastics
Sophonpanich family	Thailand	Bangkok Bank	Banking, insurance, stockbroking
Chearavanont family	Thailand	Charoen Pokphand	Agriculture, food, telecom, aquaculture, property, beer
Lamsam family	Thailand	Thai Farmers Bank	Banking, trading, agribusiness, insurance

Source: *Forbes, Asiaweek, The Economist, Asia-Inc., Euromoney, Asiamoney.*

in its early stages, this chapter will focus on overseas Chinese business families. However, the underlying family concerns are applicable to Chinese business across all regions.

The Four Pillars of Traditional Chinese Business

The world got its first detailed look at the typical Chinese business family from such business researchers as Victor Limlingan, Gordon Redding, and Murray Weidenbaum.[6] Their work focused primarily on the organizational attributes of the Chinese business family, such as small to medium size, family ownership and cross-sharing, centralized and speedy decision making, and high diversification.

The following section departs from the work of these researchers by examining these businesses through a cultural and family lens. This cultural perspective is essential to understanding the driving forces behind the organizational activities, and reveals four main features: (1) family-directed operation, (2) the dominant family head, (3) enduring roles and family obligations, and (4) the family-financed, family-accountable corporation.

Family-Directed Operation

The typical Chinese business family is headed by either a patriarch or a matriarch—usually the individual who founded the business, or his or her direct descendants—and family members hold key positions within the business. This core business may then be linked to a web of subsidiaries and allied companies, typically owned by various members of the immediate and extended family. The family business thus emerges as a complex network of companies, with ownership distributed throughout the extended family, and often cross-held to create intrafamily dependencies. Cross-holdings are often not apparent from the outside, and Chinese families generally prefer to keep this information private, especially in areas where the Chinese constitute a minority population. For the outsider, detecting such cross-holdings and conducting realistic due diligence can be an extremely frustrating process.

The common perception is that Chinese business families are mainly privately owned, but a significant number of them are actually publicly held. This is especially true of the leading corporations in Taiwan, Hong Kong, and Southeast Asian countries. Despite their public ownership, however, most of these corporations remain under close family scrutiny and direction. When going public, the founding family generally ensures that it will continue to control the company's principal operations and businesses. For example, when Yue-Che Wang, the patriarch of Taiwan's Formosa Plastics Group, decided to take four of his family's holdings public, he made sure that his younger brother, his ten children, and his grandchildren kept an average of 33.5 percent of the equity. Wang, whose total assets were estimated at $3.9 billion in 1998,[7] was especially careful with the "crown jewels" of the family conglomerate, ensuring that the Wang family retained ownership and 100 percent control of the seven-biggest Formosa Plastics companies, with combined assets of over $6.7 billion in 1994.[8]

Chinese business family members share the responsibility of business operations and tend to be hands-on. The story of the PRC's instant-noodle company Ting Hsin is a case in point. The founders, four brothers surnamed Wei, had only high school educations and their own business sense to draw on, but they managed to raise $8 million to start a PRC-based noodle company. They divided management responsibilities among themselves: the eldest brother is company chairman and supervises operations; brother number three, Ying-Chung Wei, is executive vice chairman in charge of finance; the second brother, Ying-Chiao Wei, is in charge of business relations; and the youngest, Ying-Hsing Wei, heads up marketing. This family style of management has proven very profitable for the Weis: Ting Hsin is now the biggest company in the PRC's substantial instant-noodle industry, outcompeting both Nissin Food Products, the Japanese company that invented instant noodles, and the global giant Nestlé.[9]

Family-shared business responsibilities often spread across different industries and regions. Robert Kuok, a Malaysian–Hong Kong billionaire who owns the Shangri-La Hotel chain and the *South China Morning Post*, is a case in point. Two of Kuok's sons are in the family business, and his daughter Ruth helps him manage the group's charitable foundations. Kuok's eldest son oversees hotels, real estate, and Coca Cola bottling; the second son supervises Singapore-Malaysia operations and will soon take charge of the edible-oils business. Two nephews and a nephew-in-law also hold important positions.[10]

Another feature of family-directed enterprise is informal decision making, which usually occurs outside the corporate boardroom. Henry Sy, the Filipino-Chinese retail magnate, for example, holds unofficial business meetings with his six Western-educated children—all managers in the family business—by bringing them together and cooking lunch for them every Sunday. During these family gatherings, Sy coordinates the family's social and business activities. Although he has officially ceded control of his business empire to his daughter Teresita, Henry Sy remains in the background, cooking and counseling.[11]

As these examples suggest, family management usually means that a company's organizational chart is not a reliable guide to where the power really lies in the business. In fact, it is useful to think of a Chinese business family as having two organizational charts: the official one for public consumption, and the unofficial one that reflects the real distribution of power in the company. Because family position (the unofficial chart) often takes priority, certain company officers with strong family positions are likely to exercise a power disproportionate to their titular responsibilities.

In fact, job titles may have little relation to a person's actual role in the organization. The title *vice president*, for example, may be assigned to an important decision maker or to a mere figurehead. The challenge facing the outsider, then, is to unravel the real power structure in the Chinese family business. Businesspeople have found that they can significantly increase their chances of understanding the firm's inner workings if they take the time to investigate the family history and attempt to decipher the relationships among key family members.

To begin such research, one very important first step is to gain access to family gatherings and networks. If this option is unavailable, one should use personal contacts to get information on the family's concerns or talk to other companies that have done business with the family in the past. As you learn about the family's diversification, mergers, and other maneuverings, ask yourself, "What's the story behind the story? What's going on in the family?" If a Chinese business family rejects an attractive deal, it may be for family-related reasons rather than financial reasons. Try to discover the family's agenda, which is often different from the organization's public agenda. Paying attention to family interests can lead to new and unexpected business opportunities.

The Dominant Family Head

Western executives looking for the locus of control of a Chinese family business should look to the head of the family. Chances are that he or she is making all the important decisions for the business. This is especially important when the head of the family is not the same person as the business leader, such as **Liem** Sioe Liong of Indonesia's Salim Group and Yu-Tung Cheng of Hong Kong's New World Development Group. Chinese family heads are hands-on executives, and the very best of them are good at both operational details and overall strategy. Since they usually are the entrepreneurs whose hard work and vision initially built the company, family leaders take a deep and personal interest in the business that continues even after their official retirement. They are accustomed to relying on their own judgment in matters ranging from settling minor disputes to allocating millions in investment capital. The family leader has the final say in all major decisions. Even in companies that resemble typical Western corporations—with high global diversity and formal boards of directors—a central figure remains in the background. Without that person's approval, nothing of consequence happens.

These strong family leaders form the core of the business organization. Around them, trusted family members or long-term friends serve as close advisers and supply the family head with much of his or her information. This flat and two-tiered managerial structure distinguishes the Chinese business family from that of the multilayered managerial hierarchy typical of European and North American companies. In the Chinese business family, for example, frontline managers may report directly to the president of the company, depending on their family status, instead of sending information step-by-step through a hierarchy of commands.

This family-centered decision-making system may be expedient and efficient, but it can lead to difficulties.[12] Business responsibilities are sometimes vaguely defined, and conscientious managers can often feel frustrated and left out. Moreover, the lack of transparency can be discouraging to Western businesspeople who do not understand the principles by which the business family system works. Indeed, those Western companies that have proven successful in various Chinese communities tend to be those whose leaders recognize that they are dealing with a different business paradigm. Using this knowledge, they work to establish common bonds with their Chinese counterparts. Examples abound: Coca-Cola and Rupert Murdoch with Robert Kuok; Procter & Gamble and Motorola with Li Ka-Shing; and 7-Eleven, Honda, NEC, Bell Atlantic (now Verizon), and Oscar Mayer with the CP Group. These partnerships are the product of extensive company research and creative strategic thinking. The Western CEOs took the time to understand where the power lay in the Chinese firm, then carefully developed relationships with the business's family members.

Enduring Roles and Family Obligations

The importance of family relationships in the Chinese context is most apparent when a family business is passed from one generation to the next. Heirs feel a profound sense of responsibility and respect for their family and its business tradition. Even today, the family business tends to be more than a source of financial support to its heirs; it is a connection to their past—their parents, their grandparents, and perhaps even generations farther back. As implied in the opening story about the diploma, for the Chinese family pride is as critical as economic success and prosperity.

Succession ensures that both ownership and management remain firmly under the family's control, even when the heirs have not been actively involved in running the business. Shi-Hui Huang, for example, was a St. Louis neurosurgeon who went back to Taiwan to put the family's business affairs in order after his father's death. After spending a year in Taiwan, Dr. Huang decided to remain there to manage his family's conglomerate himself. He gave up his U.S. practice and became chairman of the Ching Fong Corporation, a group of thirty-five global industrial and investment businesses.[13] From the Chinese perspective, Huang's decision to remain was motivated not simply by business opportunities but also, and perhaps more importantly, by family expectations.

The code of succession may extend to non–blood relations if no immediate family is available. Indeed, extended family is almost

Box 2-1: Sibling Success: The Liu Brothers and the Hope Group

The family model of Chinese business lies behind the most successful of private enterprises. The PRC's Hope Group began in 1982 when four brothers generated capital for an agricultural business by selling their own wristwatches and bicycles to raise the equivalent of about U.S. $120. Today, the Hope Group is the largest animal feed producer—as well as the largest private enterprise—in China, with 16,000 employees and 120 enterprises around the country. In addition to its feed business, the Hope Group has expanded into industries such as real estate and construction, and is a major shareholder in Minsheng Bank, the first privately owned bank in China. The company has continued to fend off attacks from formidable MNCs such as Thailand's CP Group, an overseas Chinese business family.

The four brothers jointly own the Hope Group Corporation, Ltd., and each brother is the head of one of the company's four separate (and diverse) divisions. Notably, the "dominant" family head, in the case of the Hope Group, is not the eldest, but the third brother, Liu Yonghao, who formed the New Hope group in 1996 to expand and diversify into areas such as real estate and to increase the international scope of Hope's current business. Liu Yonghao has become a role model for Chinese business entrepreneurs, sitting on several prominent boards and institutions such as the China Enterprise Confederation.[a]

[a] "The Excellent Chicken-feed of Liu Yonghao," *The Economist*, 6 July 1996, 59, and Mariko Hayashibara, "New Hope for China's Entrepreneurs," *Asia Business*, June 1998, 8–11.

always given preference over professional managers. When the daughters of Hong Kong shipping and property magnate Y. K. Pao expressed no interest in running the family business, he divided the family assets and control of the family enterprises among his four sons-in-law: a Chinese doctor, a Japanese architect, a Shanghai banker, and an Austrian lawyer. Despite the fact that none of these men had experience in running a shipping business, Pao did not consider giving the business over to professional managers. In this case, Pao's decision was a prudent one: His business empire is prospering under family management.[14]

But of course nepotism is not usually a guarantee of success—even in Chinese business. Family members may not always be the best qualified for the job, and their privileged position in the company can demoralize professional managers and create resentment among those of senior rank.

Although Westerners have tended to assume that the laws of Chinese business inheritance follow principles of primogeniture—like the Japanese practice of handing down the assets to only one child, usually the eldest or best-qualified son—the Chinese are actually much more flexible. Historically, they have divided everything equally among the sons when passing on the family assets. Although the actual practice of this system has changed over time, the welfare of the whole family is still taken into account when determining succession and planning for the future. The holdings of the Indonesian-Chinese Salim Group, for instance (once over 250 companies spanning fifty to sixty industries), were developed in large part to give appropriate positions to various members of the nuclear and extended family.

It is partly because of this tradition of asset division among offspring that modern Chinese businesses tend to be more widely diversified than their ethnic counterparts elsewhere in the world. Another benefit diversification presents to Chinese companies is that it often prevents sibling rivalries. In any case, this family-driven practice has important commercial consequences: When children do business in different industries, for example, or in distant geographic markets, brothers and sisters not only avoid competing directly with one another but also extend the reach of the family network and assets, thereby diversifying risks.

Family-Financed, Family-Accountable Corporation

Because of their family-centered organization, Chinese businesses do not rely heavily on external institutions such as banks, and they function with a degree of flexibility and independence that is difficult to imagine in a Western business context. The self-reliant, self-contained character of overseas Chinese business families developed partly in response to the historical uncertainties they faced as minorities in other countries. Their resilience makes them less vulnerable to political and economic upheaval; more important, it enables them to adapt and to operate seamlessly across borders.

Box 2-2: Who's Who in the Wu Family

Taiwan's Wu family, based in Tainan City, provides a good example of how Chinese family businesses are organized. Early in the twentieth century, the two oldest Wu brothers started as garment and fabric merchandisers. They later expanded into the textile business, setting up multiple companies. Over time, they became leading players in a wide array of Taiwanese industries—cement, industrial manufacturing, construction and real estate development, and consumer products.

The various Wu family members fit into both the "family tree" and the family business structure as follows: The eldest son, as the head of the family, serves as chairman of about a dozen major companies, including the largest textile and consumer product companies in Taiwan. One of his daughters-in-law serves as the vice chairman of his construction company. The other is president of an industrial college that Wu founded. The second brother is the chairman of several financial service companies owned by the family; his three sons are involved, as either chairman or vice chairman, with several other family businesses. The third brother and a cousin also play a significant role in this family conglomerate, known as the "Tainan Business Gang," in which many other extended family members—and even close friends—are involved.

The flexibility of Chinese business families permeates every aspect of business practice. Organizational reporting, for instance, is much speedier, thanks to the personal nature of relationships among officers. Instead of requiring commitments in writing, agreements may simply be made over a family lunch or at a social gathering. This informal communication process also helps the company keep a low profile. Record keeping also tends to be informal and to remain within the family: "Ledgers are intended for the tax collector; true accounts are kept in the head."[15] But for all their benefits, such communication practices must come at a certain price. Tight family control of vital information can prevent nonfamily professionals from making well-informed decisions.

The typical Chinese business family has its entire organizational structure streamlined to eliminate the need for elaborate and bureaucratic approval processes. The company owner makes all decisions of consequence. Hiring decisions are often based simply on personal recommendations, with background checks consisting merely of

---

Box 2-3: Cultural Dilemma: When Family Is Your Business

The realities of Chinese business families can make dealing with them confusing. The medium-sized Chinese company you have been talking to, for example, may be part of a larger family conglomerate with an agenda that is not apparent to you. The forty-something manager who has been your contact point may not be able to make decisions on his own; he may have to consult the head of the family—who may live in another country. This family head will make his decision based on the interests of the network as a whole. What can you do?

Options and Observations

Dealing with a Chinese business family demands a different frame of mind and set of skills due precisely to the emphasis on family. When approaching a business family, there are a few points that are helpful to keep in mind:

- Do your homework. Find out who your Chinese partner is linked to, learn about the older generation—who makes decisions and what their track record is.

- Do not examine your own deal in isolation, but rather in light of your Chinese partner's dealings with other Western companies.

- If you can, make sure the patriarch or his advisors do not oppose the idea—if they approve, so much the better.

When dealing with a Chinese business family, remember to take both family and business concerns into consideration. Remember that the more attention you pay to the cultural context of the family, the more facility you will have in doing business with them.

---

phone calls placed to close friends or trustworthy contacts. In traditional Chinese businesses, a potential employee's personal reputation is infinitely more valuable than a formal record of achievements or a salary history. Job descriptions also tend to be loose and flexible. On the downside, such informality can lead to confusion about responsibilities and expectations and can create an environment that lacks proper checks and balances.

Under the family-based system, decisions may be arrived at with greater speed and lower costs, and the emphasis on personal trust dramatically cuts both paperwork and the need for external institutions, such as lawyers and banks. It is not unusual to find enterprises such as Indonesia's Salim Group making—in one dramatic instance—a major acquisition in only seventeen days. Furthermore, the political and social circumstances conditioning the development of overseas Chinese business families have lent them an independence and adaptability that are highly favorable to global enterprise. Given the quickening pace of communications and information accessibility in the global economy, speed and flexibility provide the Chinese companies with a significant competitive advantage.

As Chinese companies adapt to compete in a new Western-led global reality and expand beyond the family's reach, the business family's basic structure will be subject to growing tensions. Some of these tensions are indicated in Table 2-2, which highlights the major differences between traditional Chinese and Western business practices. The strict Confucian hierarchy of roles and relationships that has characterized the overseas Chinese business family must now absorb the more innovative spirit required by modern high-tech industries. Indeed, many of Taiwan's high-tech companies have moved away from the family business model. The following section examines how Chinese business families must—and almost certainly will—reconfigure themselves in the new economy to reduce the tension between traditional approaches and globalization pressures.

The Chinese Business Family in Transition

The traditional Chinese business family is in transition around the globe, as more and more Chinese companies expand beyond their home markets and beyond Asia into other parts of the world. The PRC's Hope Group, for example, has expanded into a number of Southeast Asian markets. Taiwan's biggest food company and 7-Eleven's local partner, President Enterprise Corp., acquired Girl Scout Cookies in 1990 as a basis for building its global consumer product empire. And Hong Kong's Cheung Kong Infrastructure, owned by the Li family, obtained the port management rights for the Panama Canal. However, to thrive in foreign markets, Chinese

---

Box 2-4: Dealing with the Chinese Business Family: Some Tips

- "Family" means something different in every culture, and paying attention to cultural idiosyncracies will prove invaluable.

- If you happen to meet an unassuming, modestly dressed old Chinese gentleman on the golf course in Palm Beach, Florida, pay careful attention and be respectful. Despite appearances, you may be talking to an extremely powerful person.

- Suppose you are interested in working with Chinese Family A. Unfortunately, you have no contacts within the family. You do, however, have a strong relationship with Chinese Family B. Does Family B know Family A? Find out. If the answer is "yes," you can begin to approach Family A through this connection. Use the network.

- When you approach a Chinese company, the pitch may take a while, but the execution will be speedy and the benefit long-term.

- Look beyond the figures in the annual report. Most Chinese companies are not valued in the same way as Western ones, and their intangible assets are hard to pin down.

---

business families are gradually adopting global business standards and practices. The Asian financial crisis and the resulting regulations introduced by the International Monetary Fund are already increasing information transparency and standardizing organizational practices.

Indonesia's Sinar Mas Group exemplifies some of the more dramatic changes being implemented by overseas business families. It has restructured itself into four separate holding companies and listed them on the Jakarta Stock Exchange. Much of the organization is now managed by trained professionals, many of whom are not ethnic Chinese. The company's founder, who is now much less active in management, meets with the family only once a week to discuss business. Sinar Mas has also experimented with new ways of raising funds and has adopted new financial practices—for instance, managing exchange rate and interest rate risk. But perhaps the most telling sign of change is the company's activity in corporate commu-

Table 2-2: Traditional Chinese versus Western Business Practices

Chinese	Western
Dominant purpose of company: serving family interests	Dominant purpose of company: maximizing stockholder wealth
Protection of financial data about company and family	Required audits of financial reports and other company data
Financing of company by family and other friendly families	Financing of company by public sale of stocks and bonds; use of investment bankers, listing on stock exchanges
Not for sale due to obligations to extended family	Mergers; unfriendly acquisitions via control of blocks of stock
Unadvertised sale of company products, often based on family network	Brand promotion via advertising and customer service; stress on competitive market position
Senior managers recruited from within family, often by the family patriarch	Professional managers, based on merit; attracted by money and stock options
Stress on very long-term view of family prestige	Stress on short-run, bottom-line profits and current changes in market value of stock

nications and public relations—an area usually all but ignored by Chinese businesses.[16]

According to Richard Li, chairman and CEO of Hong Kong's Pacific Century and the son of Li Ka-Shing, business operations now require managers familiar both with Western culture and with an increasingly standard set of global business practices. Echoing the thoughts of many second- or third-generation heirs to Chinese business empires, Richard Li believes that to become internationally competitive, business families must push for more specialized and professional management: "Before, the qualities we valued in people were persistence, hard work, loyalty, street smarts. Those are still important, but now a good manager has to have something in addition: he has to have specific knowledge of his industry or technology, and he has to be a creative and a strong team player."[17]

Succeeding the Generation Gap, Chinese Style

The strongest impetus for change in traditional industries, such as manufacturing, real estate, and banking, comes from a major feature of the Chinese family business tradition itself: succession. Handing businesses down from one generation to the next was once the principal means of maintaining a family heritage and tradition. Today it creates the opportunity for reorganizing a business as it is passed on to the next generation.

Succession is now forcing businesses to adopt new, and often foreign, practices. The new generation of heirs frequently receives a Western education or attends professional business schools in Asia. Eighteen out of thirty-three heirs apparent to the largest Chinese conglomerates have a Western education and/or work experience (see Table 2-3). Professional education not only brings knowledge and experience back to the family business, but working and studying abroad offer a chance to the younger generation to break away from the tight family network and traditionalist conservatism of the family business and to launch new, independent ventures of their own.

Succession—and, consequently, new management—may also provide the means by which Chinese business families move smoothly into the new economy. Indeed, the (mostly professionally trained) children of many Chinese patriarchs are already playing an important role in keeping their parents' businesses competitive. A case in point is that of V-Nee Yeh, who, after school in the West and jobs with the investment firm Lazard Freres in New York and London, returned to Hong Kong in 1990 to help his father's struggling construction company. With his Wall Street expertise he helped reorganize the company, Hsin Chong, and made it profitable. After taking the company public and incorporating it offshore, he advised his father to take it private again in a leveraged buyout; it is clear that without his help his family's company might have failed.[18]

Transformation Paths

There is no single path followed by every Chinese family in transition (see Figure 2-1). Any business family has three options in the field of corporate ownership (widely held, familial, and individual) and another three in management control (traditional familial,

Table 2-3: Succession in Major Overseas Chinese Business Families

Li Ka-Shing Family (Hong Kong)

First generation
Li Ka-Shing (born 1928)

Main company: Hutchison Whampoa

Business lines: Telecom, cable TV, and international hotel chain

Second generation
Victor Li Tzar-Kuoi (born 1963)—son of Li Ka-Shing

Education: Bachelor's degree in civil engineering and master's degree in structural engineering from Stanford University

Main company: Cheung Kong

Business lines: Hong Kong's utilities, port facilities, retailing, and real estate

Richard Li Tzar-Kai (born 1966)—son of Li Ka-Shing

Education: Computer engineering and economics from Stanford University

Working experience outside the family business: Investment banker with Gordon Investment Corporation (three years and eventually becoming executive director and partner)

Main company: Pacific Century CyberWorks (PCCW)

Business lines: Satellite broadband service, invest in dot-coms, develop Hong Kong's cyberport, telecom

Li & Fung Family (Hong Kong)

First generation
Fung Yiu-Hing
Li To-Ming

Second generation
Fung Hong Chu—son of Fung Yiu-Hing

Third generation
Victor Fung—son of Fung Hong Chu

Education: Bachelor's degree in electrical engineering from MIT and Ph.D. in business economics from Harvard University

Working experience outside the family business: Victor Fung—former professor at the Harvard Business School

William Fung—son of Fung Hong Chu

Education: Bachelor's degree Engineering and business economics from Princeton University
M.B.A. from Harvard Business School

Main company: Li & Fung

Business lines: Trading and retailing

Geoffrey Yeh Family (Hong Kong)

First generation
K.N. Godfrey Yeh

Second generation
Geoffrey (M.T.) Yeh (born 1931)

Education: Civil engineering degree from Harvard University

Main company: Hsin Chong Construction Group

Business line: Construction

Third generation
V-Nee Yeh—son of Geoffrey Yeh

Education: School of Law at Columbia University

Working experience outside the family business: Lazard Houses (in New York, Hong Kong, and London) working in the field of corporate finance, capital market and risk arbitrage (1984-1990)

Professional credentials: Member of the California Bar Association (1984)

Main company: Value Partners Ltd., HK

Business line: Investment fund management

Table 2-3: Succession in Major Overseas Chinese Business Families (continued)

Robert Kuok Family (Malaysia/Hong Kong)

First generation
Robert Kuok Hock Nien (born 1923)

Main company: Kuok Brothers Sendirian Berhad

Business lines: Food industries, commodity trading, hotels, shipping, plantations and mining, property, entertainment, and retailing

Second generation
Kuok Khoon Chen/Beau (born 1955)—eldest son of Robert Kuok

Education: Bachelor's degree in economics from Monash University (Australia)

Main company: Shangri-La Hotels

Kuok Khoon Ean (born 1951)—son of Robert Kuok

Education: Unknown

Main company: South China Morning Post, Kuok Group in Malaysia and Singapore

Kuok Khoon Loong (born 1953)—nephew of Robert Kuok

Education: Master's degree in economics from University of Wales

Main company: Kerry Properties

Hong Leong Family (Singapore/Malaysia)

First generation
Kwek Hong Png
Kwek Hong Lye (Malaysia)
Kwek Hong Khai
Kwek Hong Leong

Main companies: Hong Leong Corporation Ltd. Group
City Development Ltd. Group
Hong Leong Co. (Malaysia) Berhad

Second generation
Kwek Leng Beng (Singapore)
Kwek Leng Chye (Singapore)
Kwek Leng Chan (Malaysia)
Kwek Leng Seng (Malaysia)
Kwek Leng Hai (Hong Kong)

Main companies: Hong Leong Investment Holdings
Hong Leong Finance
City Developments
Hong Leong Industries Bhd (Malaysia)
Hume Industries (Malaysia)
Hong Leong Overseas (Hong Kong)

Professional credential: Kwek Leng Chan—qualified solicitor in London

Salim Family (Indonesia/Hong Kong)

First generation
Liem Soei Liong/Soedono Salim (born 1916)

Main companies: Indofood
First Pacific

Business lines: Property, food industry, finance, telecom, infrastructure

Second generation
Andree Halim—eldest son
Anthony Salim—youngest son

Education: Singapore High School
Undergraduate degree, UK

Manuel Pangilinan—professional friend of Anthony Salim

Education: M.B.A. from Wharton School, University of Pennsylvania

Working experience outside Salim Group: Manuel Pangilinan—PHINMA Group, Bancom International, and American Express Bank

Table 2-3: Succession in Major Overseas Chinese Business Families (continued)

Riady Family (Indonesia/Hong Kong)

First generation
Lie Wen Chen/Mochtar Riady (born 1929)

Main company: Lippo Group

Business lines: Banking, life insurance, real estate

Second generation
James Riady (born 1957)—son of Mochtar Riady

Education: Accounting and economics degree from University of Melbourne (Australia)

Working experience outside the family business: James Riady—Director of Worthen Bank in Little Rock, Arkansas, U.S.

Main company: Lippo Group in Indonesia

Stephen Riady (born 1960)—son of Mochtar Riady

Education: University of Southern California

Main company: Lippo Bank in Hong Kong

Charoen Pokphand Family (Thailand)

First generation
Chia Ek Chaw
Chia Seow Whooy

Second generation
Dhanin Chearavanont (born 1940)

Professional recognition: Dhanin Chearavanont—honorary doctorate, Thammasat University (commerce and accountancy), adviser to prime minister (1990), Hong Kong affairs adviser to the People's Republic of China

Main company: Charoen Pokphand

Business lines: Agriculture, aquaculture, international trading, automotive and industrial products, real estate, petroleum, and petrochemical

Third generation
Supachai Chearavanont (born 1968)

Education: Boston University graduate

Main company: Telecom Asia

Business lines: Telecom

Lamsam Family (Thailand)

First generation
Choti Lamsam

Second generation
Bancha Lamsam (Ngow Pang Jien)—died 1992
Banyong Lamsam (Chairman)—brother of Bancha Lamsam

Third generation
Banthoon Lamsam (president)—son of Bancha Lamsam

Education: Engineering graduate from Princeton University

Main company: Thai Farmers Bank

Business lines: Banking, trading, finance, insurance

Table 2-3:   Succession in Major Overseas Chinese Business Families (continued)

Wang Family (Taiwan)

First generation
Wang Yue-Che

Main company: Formosa Plastics

Business lines: Petrochemicals, plastics, PVC

Second generation
Winston Wang—son of Wang Yue-Che

Education: Doctor in chemistry from Imperial College of Science, Technology and Medicine (UK)

Main company: Nan Ya Plastics

Charlene Wang—daughter of Wang Yue-Che (and her husband Chieng Ming)

Main company: First International Computer Co.

Business line: Computers
Cher Wang (daughter)

Main company: Everex Systems (U.S.)

Business line: Computers
William Wang—nephew of Wang Yue-Che

Main company: Formosa Chemicals

Business lines: Fibers, nylons

Chang Family (Taiwan)

First generation
Chang Yung-Fa

Second generation
Chang Kuo-Hua—eldest son
Chang Kuo-Ming—second son
Chang Kuo-Cheng—third son

Main company: Evergreen Group

Business lines: Shipping, airlines, hotels

Koo Family (Taiwan)

First generation
Koo Chen-Fu

Main company: Taiwan Cement Co.

Professional recognition: One of the founding fathers of Taiwan Stock Exchange (in 1962)

Second generation
Dr. (Hon) Jeffrey Leng-Song (L.S.) Koo—nephew of Koo Chen-Fu (born 1933)

Education: M.B.A. from NYU School of Business (1962), Hon. Ph.D. from De La Salle University (1989)

Main company: Chairman and CEO, Chinatrust Commercial Bank

Chester Chi-Yun Koo—son of Koo Chen-Fu (born 1952)

Education: M.B.A. from Wharton School, University of Pennsylvania (1979)

Main company: President and CEO, China Life Insurance

Third generation
Jeffrey John Leon (J.L.) Koo Jr.—son of Dr. Jeffrey L.S. Koo (born 1964)

Education: M.B.A. from Wharton School, University of Pennsylvania (1991)

Main company: President of Chinatrust Commercial Bank

Source: Adapted from Nelson Ying Jr. and Yen-Miao Tung, "Succession Patterns in Overseas Chinese Business" (seminar term report, The Wharton School, 1998).

Figure 2-1:   Chinese Business Family Transformation Paths

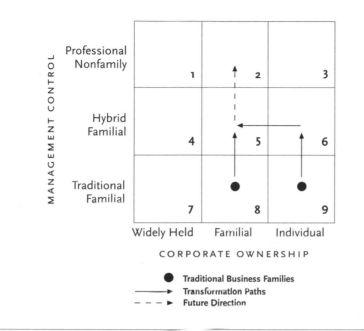

hybrid familial, and professional nonfamilial). The traditional Chinese business family stands in cells 8 and 9, either family-owned or individually owned, but both with traditional familial management. Although still representative of a significant portion of Chinese enterprises—particularly in the PRC—this once-dominant form of Chinese business family has become much less prominent. Because of succession, globalization, and professionalization pressures, many companies have been moving to cell 5 (directly from cell 8; often passing through cell 6 from cell 9). A few companies have even moved all the way to cell 2, as illustrated by the Salim Group's First Pacific.

Cells 1, 4, and 7—where the family relinquishes its ownership position to become mere investors, like many Western family businesses—are unlikely paths. In spite of the pressure to access global capital markets and technology development, and despite losses incurred during the Asian financial crisis, Chinese business families have proven extremely reluctant to sell off their assets. The family running the Bangkok Bank, for example, has remained in control of both its corporate boardroom and its management despite having drastically reduced its equity position after the crisis. This was not a matter of mere stubbornness: In the Chinese cultural context, business success or failure reflects the glory or disgrace of the family.

In view of these considerations, the majority of companies will most likely end up in cell 5—hybrid familial management, familial ownership—but in various forms. Sinar Mas, for example, has reduced its equity ownership and hired professional management, but it nevertheless retains majority ownership and family control. A growing number of companies leave the family head in charge of traditional industries while letting the younger generation advance business in high-tech or emerging industries, such as Internet and telecommunications, or expand into foreign markets. Hong Kong's Li and Cheng families, Taiwan's Koo and Miao families, Thailand's Lamsam and Chearavanont families, and Malaysia–Hong Kong's Kuok family all fall into this category.[19]

According to Alex Liu, of AT Kearney, "The top family companies are trying to create a kind of hybrid organization that combines the best managerial aspects of the East with those of the West." As Liu sees it, the goal of this integration is to keep the best of Asian business practices—the emphasis on entrepreneurship and a sense of family—while adapting the most useful of Western practices: formal strategic planning, clear and consistent accounting, and a focus on innovation, customer service, and quality.[20]

In the PRC, the future of family enterprise must take additional factors into account. There the one-child policy has reduced the family to its minimal nuclear unit. With no siblings, aunts, or uncles, the individual building a family business must reach out to family friends and extended family. In this respect, PRC businesses will diverge from the overseas Chinese business family model and will map out their own development and transformation paths. Nonetheless, there are signs that the family tradition is still strong in the PRC: In the spring of 2000, the heads of its four leading township enterprises all announced their plans to pass on their businesses to their sons!

Conclusion: Will the Family Stay in Business?

The Chinese business family will undergo organizational transformation and strategic redirection over the next twenty years, as internal and external pressures challenge the traditional Confucian principles that have informed Chinese families and businesses throughout their history. Nevertheless, for now there is no sign that the "family first, business second" priority is being abandoned. Dr. Samuel Yin, chairman of the Ruentex Group, Taiwan's sixth-largest conglomerate and Liz Claiborne's longtime partner, exemplifies the perseverance of the traditional model. After his father's death, Dr. Yin founded a hospital to memorialize him. Spending every Thursday evening with his mother—for years before her death—Dr. Yin exemplified the traditional dedication to family values. Such cases of filial piety are rare in the busy corporate schedules of the West, but in the Chinese context, business responsibilities are not seen as being in conflict with family duties.

Will there still be a place for "Chinese values" in the newly adapted businesses? As the Bank of East Asia's CEO David Li puts it, "As any good Chinese entrepreneur knows, crisis and opportunity go together."[21] If one of the key features of the Chinese business is its adaptability, there is little reason to suspect that the pressures exerted by a global marketplace, and by recent crises, will result in its collapse.

Such a balanced adaptation is best represented by Hong Kong's Li & Fung Ltd. which, over the last thirty years, has been setting a precedent for the successful transformation of Chinese business families. The two sons, Victor and William Fung, both returned from Harvard to professionalize their family's company. In 1973, they advised their father to take the company public. They initiated a management buyout in 1988 and made the trading division of their company public again in 1995. In all these changes, one detects the interplay between business and family concerns.

Most important, Li & Fung's transformation demonstrates the successful continuation of Chinese family heritage in resolving the tension between Chinese tradition and Westernization. In the words of Victor Fung: "As we have transformed a family business into a modern one, we have tried to preserve the best of what my father and grandfather created. There is a family feeling in the company that's difficult to describe. We don't care much about [corporate] title and hierarchy. Family life and the company's business spill over into each other."[22]

Indeed, the sense of family heritage and loyalty is so strong that it often overcomes economic logic. A good example is the fifth-generation Thai Chinese Wanglee family, which in the year following the Asian financial crisis still hung on to every parcel of land its great-grandfather had bought 130 years earlier. In Thailand, the family name Wanglee is every bit as recognizable as Rockefeller or Carnegie in the United States, and the family members are struggling against enormous odds to keep the name from being sold off. "What belonged to our family 100 years ago still belongs to us," said Vuttichai Wanglee, a managing director of the family's banking concern. "It is our culture not to risk what great-grandfather built."[23] A family tradition that has endured for more than 100 years and survived many crises is not likely to disappear anytime soon.

3

NETWORKING AND *GUANXI*

Ren zhe ren ye (人者仁也): "The meaning of person is *ren.*" Embedded in this phrase is a universe of meaning that reveals how the Chinese regard themselves and their relationships with others. The third character, transcribed as *ren,* means humanity, as well as core, or the seed of a fruit. The character *ren* (仁) is composed of the characters for "two" (二) and "person" (人 or 亻). This etymology ("two people") suggests that in the Chinese context, no person exists except in relationship to another, and that this relationship is the birth of all possibility.

IN CONTRAST to the West's transaction-based business culture, Chinese business society is relationship-based. In the Chinese business context, relationships are a form of social capital, owned by businesspeople and associated with the companies they run. Whereas in the West a successful businessperson is spoken of as "wealthy," in the Chinese context he or she is described as "well connected." This phenomenon led the *Economist* to describe *guanxi* as "the chief asset" of most Chinese companies.[1]

This chapter will explore the concept of *guanxi,* how Western businesspeople can begin to develop their own *guanxi* networks, and how those networks can be nurtured over the long term. Because establishing *guanxi* is fundamental to the world of Chinese business, this chapter takes a pragmatic and hands-on approach to the subject.

What Is *Guanxi* (關係)?

Guanxi has received a great deal of media attention in the West. There is no direct English translation for the word *guanxi*, a fact that has created much confusion over its precise meaning. The conventional translation as "connections" touches on only one aspect of its meaning. *Guanxi* does consist of connections, but more specifically of connections that are defined by reciprocity and mutual obligation. Ideally, these connections are also supported by a sense of goodwill and personal affection.

Of course, all business cultures depend on informal networking to some degree. Japanese *wa*, Korean *inhwa*, the English old school tie, the American country club—all provide the members of their group with a measure of confidence and trust necessary to underpin business transactions. *Guanxi* differs from these both in its pervasiveness and in its heavy emphasis on family ties and shared experiences.[2]

Guanxi is too often misunderstood as a form of cronyism and influence peddling and is associated with bribery and corruption. *Guanxi*, which has been perceived as emanating from an innate Chinese fear and distrust of others, has been blamed for everything from China's struggles with modernization and economic expansion to the Asian financial crisis. While many *guanxi* relationships have indeed been abused and misused, simply viewing *guanxi* as a form of corruption is highly misleading. Western businesspeople in the Chinese commercial world must take a more comprehensive view.

Guanxi is grounded in trust, mutual obligations, and shared experiences. The concept itself traces its roots back to ancient Chinese social customs wherein reciprocity and other modes of social exchange were used to build and maintain interpersonal relationships throughout society. Not surprisingly, the strongest *guanxi* occurs with both immediate and extended family members, but *guanxi* relationships may also form among individuals who have shared a deep and meaningful experience—old friends, former classmates, colleagues from military service, former coworkers, and so on. Since the Chinese in general prefer to do business with people they know, or with friends of friends, they devote a substantial amount of time and energy to establishing relationships with people they find respectable. It is this commitment of time to building relationships with others that truly defines *guanxi*.

With its focus on relationships and shared history, *guanxi* is a manifestation of the Confucian respect for the past, a value that many—but not all—Chinese cherish. Although the Communist Party, notably during the Cultural Revolution, attempted to erase all traces of this Chinese heritage, *guanxi* remained an important social mechanism, albeit with a slight twist: It was used as a way to work around the country's lumbering state bureaucracy.[3] In fact, it formed the basis of a secondary, unofficial economy in the PRC and provided an alternative means for finding jobs, housing, health care, and various goods. This situation continues today. In the PRC, for example, reliable information may not be available through official channels, and *guanxi* networks are often used to provide it. Similar issues exist throughout the Asian-Pacific region, where having a good source of information on a timely basis can mean the difference between success and failure to a company.

An equally important benefit of *guanxi* networking for business is the protection it offers from threats and uncertainty. In some instances, while legal protections may exist, uniform enforcement of the law does not. Singapore's Senior Minister **Lee** Kuan Yew states that "overseas Chinese use *guanxi* in China to make up for the lack of the rule of law and transparency in rules and regulations. In that hazy business environment, speaking the same language and sharing cultural bonds is a vital lubricant for any serious transaction."[4] In these cases, strong *guanxi* can shield companies from unexpected challenges, or it can minimize costs. For the overseas Chinese, *guanxi* has provided a safety net in their host societies where, although citizens, they are treated as outsiders and often regarded with suspicion.

Types of Guanxi

Guanxi exists in various forms based on the closeness of the relationship between the parties involved. For simplicity's sake, it could be said that the Chinese see relationships as existing on one of three levels, each describing the degree of social proximity.[5]

The first type, *jiaren*, denotes the closest possible relationships in the Chinese context—relationships with extended family members. While blood relations certainly constitute the strongest bonds of obligation, the Chinese will consider highly trusted non–blood relatives as family members. If any person, Chinese or non-Chinese, is accepted as part of an extended family, he or she is considered *jiaren* and accorded the status of a true insider.

The second type of *guanxi* relationship occurs among *shuren*— non–family members with whom one shares a significant connection. Connections considered significant in the Chinese context include people from the same town or village, former classmates, members of the same clubs or societies, or friends of friends.

The third category involves strangers, or *shengren*. From a Chinese perspective, nothing is known about first-time visitors, hence there is little basis for trusting them. This is not to say that the Chinese will immediately assume the worst about strangers, but they are more likely to regard them with suspicion. A wait-and-see attitude is common when dealing with *shengren* and often is a source of impatience and frustration for outsiders who fall into this category.

Despite the Chinese emphasis on *guanxi*-relationships in business, it is nevertheless possible for outsiders who have not firmly established *guanxi* to conduct business with the Chinese. However, since they lack a broader personal or emotional context, the focus in relationships between Chinese and *shengren* tends toward short-term benefit. As a general rule, unless these business relationships transform into a social *guanxi*-relationship—*shuren*—they will not endure in the long term.

Guanxi can be exclusive, but it is not impenetrable. The three concentric circles in Figure 3-1 illustrate the various levels of *guanxi*, starting from the core of most intimate family ties and extending out to nonfamilial affiliates. The interlocking circles represent the various interpenetrating *guanxi* networks. Even if you are a *shengren* standing on the outside, the interlocking circles show that your connections can link you to the inner circle. Indeed, it is even possible to be a *shengren* in one network and a *shuren* or *jiaren* in another. In fact, everyone—Chinese or not—occupies some level of *guanxi*,

Figure 3-1: Interlocking *Guanxi* Networks

depending on how they relate to the network involved. But wherever you stand, you are connectable with all the other parts.

Renqing (人情)

Renqing is a crucial concept for both understanding and cultivating Chinese *guanxi* relationships. The term *renqing* is used to express the unpaid "debts" or favors that accrue through *guanxi* relationships, but it can be literally translated as "human empathy" or "human relationship" and has come to mean "favor" or "gift-giving." As this range of meanings suggests, *renqing* obligations weave networks of relationships through reciprocal offerings of gifts and favors, creating mutual indebtedness that continues indefinitely and becomes a basis for *guanxi*.

Renqing obligations must always be repaid, but there is no specified time frame for the return of favors, and indebtedness may continue over a number of years, even from generation to generation.[6] As one Chinese businessperson says, "Owing someone a favor is like giving that person a blank check without an expiration date." But it is precisely the nonspecific nature of the time frame that makes *renqing* obligations so binding, and *guanxi* networks so enduring and pervasive. The Chinese tend to have long memories, and they will return favors to the family of their benefactors years, even generations, later. This is particularly true when kindnesses were rendered during times of adversity.

The exchange of favors does not have to be equitable. In fact, it is preferable if favors do not balance each other out. Where imbalance exists—and favors are still owed—relationships and interactions continue. Indeed, it is part of *shuren guanxi* to maintain an ongoing exchange and interaction. As the Chinese like to say, "You honor me with a foot; I honor you with a yard. Receive a droplet of generosity; repay like a gushing spring."

Cultivating *Guanxi*

Westerners entering Chinese business encounter a world where personal relationships determine much of what goes on, where every individual has his or her own web of acquaintances and connections, and where each individual's web is one among thousands of intertwining nets of relationships of varying degrees of intensity, many of which are invisible to the outside observer. Confronted with such an opaque business environment, newcomers may feel at a loss—until they begin to cultivate their own network of relationships.

As Figure 3-2 illustrates, you can view *guanxi* from two perspectives. From one point of view, you stand outside the interlocking rings and must establish several connections to reach the center. From another vantage point, however, you already occupy the center of your own *guanxi* network, and the interlocking rings surround you: You can view those connections you already have as possible *guanxi* relationships. Indeed, by shifting perspectives, it is possible to move from being the frustrated "outsider" to being an active "insider." *Guanxi* is not about *gaining access to* a network but about cultivating, expanding, and nourishing your own network.

*Overseas and Western-Trained Chinese:
A Bridge to Greater China That Starts at Home*

Both Western-educated Chinese and Chinese immigrants can be a valuable networking asset to a company seeking to do business in

Figure 3-2: Steps in Managing Extending Networks

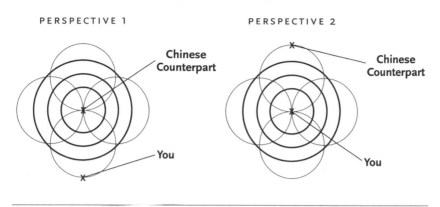

PERSPECTIVE 1   PERSPECTIVE 2

Chinese Counterpart

You

Chinese Counterpart

You

Greater China, especially if they have kept up their cultural and social connections in Asia. Their familiarity with both cultures and business settings can provide an important bridge between East and West. In fact, many companies have already entered the PRC market through bicultural third parties—usually Asian-American employees or consulting companies.

Western businesses should nevertheless be aware of the risks of going through a nonofficial third party whose familiarity with Chinese cultural, business, and social practices might be difficult to assess. Also, Western-trained or Western-born Chinese sometimes encounter resentment from Chinese nationals, who may envy those who have had the opportunity for higher education or employment in the West and may be suspicious of their commitment to the homeland. Chinese ethnicity may facilitate entry and communication, but it does not *necessarily* guarantee an individual's Chinese expertise and status.

Once you begin establishing relationships with third-party Chinese, you may be given the name of a contact person to look up while you are in Asia. The relationship you are expected to have with the Chinese contact is generally indicated by the type of introduction your associate extends. If, for example, you are asked to "give regards" to the friend, the subtext could be that the person is a reliable contact and trustworthy to deal with. Generally, the more elaborate and personal the message, the more attentively the contact is expected to treat you. Letters, in particular, are usually a very serious form of introduction, one intended to establish a strong relationship between you and the contact.

Meeting People

When you first meet a Chinese associate, the types of questions he or she asks will reveal an interest in establishing common ground. Where a Westerner may ask about one's profession, the Chinese will ask, "Where are you from?" and "Do you happen to know so-and-so there?" These questions are intended to place you in a social context and establish whether there is a preexisting connection for potential collaboration. Despite their apparent reticence in dealing with strangers, the Chinese are actually very eager to establish connections with the people they meet. For example, when one American businesswoman meeting her Chinese counterpart in Los Angeles mentioned that her father had been born and raised in Shanghai, the revelation drew a delighted response of *tong xiang!* (fellow villager!) from her new acquaintance, himself a Shanghai native. Such simple connections tend to elicit tremendous goodwill and can form the foundation for ongoing and fruitful relationships.

The discovery of a common ancestry or birthplace carries more weight in the Chinese context than it does in the West. While a Westerner may delight at discovering that a new acquaintance went to the same primary school, or has parents living in the same town, the Chinese view such discoveries in the framework of *lao xiang* ("compatriot" or "old family"), immediately situating a new acquaintance in the innermost circle of relationships.

The Chinese esteem for *lao xiang* can actually lead them to perceive that Westerners, and in particular Americans, do not respect family values and are therefore less trustworthy. This misconception is often compounded by the notion that American businesspeople are interested only in quick profit and short-term business benefits. You must be aware of this stereotype and avoid being trapped by it. Some Westerners have deepened this impression among Chinese by building *guanxi* through giving gifts and hosting lavish banquets, then dropping the relationship once a particular deal has been concluded. It is extremely important that Western business managers

---

Box 3-1: Beware of "Meat and Wine Friends"

One American executive wanted to expand his company into the PRC. Understanding that a good relationship with local government officials was vital to the success of his enterprise, he hosted dinners for various government officials. In fact, he devoted most of his first six months in China to hosting a series of expensive banquets. Inevitably, his business hit a bureaucratic snag one day, and he turned to his former dinner guests for help. To his surprise, none of these officials lifted a finger to help him. He knew that they were able to resolve the problem, but they put him off with vague excuses. The American was left feeling baffled and angry because he had spent time and money building what he thought was *guanxi* with these officials. Why didn't they hold up their end of the bargain?

The mistake this executive made was in thinking that *guanxi* can be established simply by hosting banquets, a common misperception in the West. In the eyes of his Chinese guests, he was a "meat and wine friend," a person who makes a great show of friendship but whose commitment to his friends is in fact superficial. The Chinese, of course, are famous for their enjoyment of food, and they take dining together very seriously. But even more important to them is the sincerity of your friendship. Anyone can pick up the tab at dinner, but only a true friend can be trusted to weather the ups and downs of life and business dealings—and the Chinese are looking for friends and business partners who will be with them over the long term.

Should you host dinners for your Chinese associates? By all means. But be sure to follow these dinners with gestures that express your sincere interest in them and demonstrate your commitment to an ongoing and deepening relationship.

---

not underestimate the personal—and sometimes the emotional—connection involved in Chinese relationships.

During the early stages of a relationship, showing interest in a new acquaintance's background can facilitate the development of *guanxi*. If a new Chinese acquaintance mentions, for example, that she studied at an American university, ask about her experiences there and try to establish a common ground. Such small gestures can be important signs of interest and attentiveness, and a first step toward expanding a *guanxi* network.

Nevertheless, it is important not to indulge in insincere praise or to push a relationship too quickly. In the words of a Hong Kong manager, "You can't expect to parachute guys in and get instant *guanxi*."[7] Indeed, it can take several years to build up a relationship with the Chinese, starting with paying visits to their office, receiving them at yours, finding out slowly about their background, which topics of conversation they favor, and even what type of food they most enjoy.[8] Generally speaking, if your Chinese associates feel that you are trying to take shortcuts to building *guanxi*, either by rushing things or by being less than sincere with them, it will be very difficult for you to succeed in business.

Networking with Individuals, Not Organizations

Guanxi is nurtured and maintained through relationships among individuals, not organizations, and the consequences of this fact are far-reaching. A Western expatriate manager, for example, who comes to Greater China to replace a colleague will inherit that colleague's desk, responsibilities, and address book, but *not* his *guanxi* network. The new manager may not have to start from square one, but he will have to work to establish his own relationships and build his own network. This has serious implications for Western companies considering staffing changes.

But there are ways around this problem. Some companies bring the new employee in early to be introduced to his or her predecessor's network. Once the transition has occurred, inviting the original employee back for important corporate events can help maintain stability. Another means of maintaining *guanxi* over time is to remain in contact with former employees, particularly those who initially helped develop the company's business and establish *guanxi* connections in Asia.

It is equally important to ensure that one's own *guanxi* network extends beyond a single employee in a company. If this employee leaves the company, your account will certainly be transferred to another representative, but your standing with the firm will be radically changed. Also, remember to treat lower-level employees with respect: they, too, have powerful networks that may leave with them

---

Box 3-2: How Many Kevin Wu's Does It Take to Run a Company?

Chinese businesses value consistency and stability in their *guanxi* networks and relationships. This preference for continuity influences a wide range of business decisions, from job changes to the staffing of negotiation teams. As the following story illustrates, they will sometimes go to great lengths to preserve continuity—or at least the appearance of it!

> When the Dutch manager of the technical support department learned that his contact person in the Taiwan headquarters had been replaced because of job rotation he complained because it had taken him some time to establish this relationship which he referred to as his window to Acer in Taiwan. The Taiwanese managers understood his worries and promised to find a solution. After some time, however, they came up with the following suggestion: "To keep Kevin Wu we have to allow him to gain additional experience, but to keep your window to Taiwan we will call his successor also Kevin Wu."[a]

[a] Kai Fuan, "Acer In Europe", Case 592-038-1 (Fontainebleau, France: INSEAD-EAC, 1992), 12.

---

if they feel slighted, or that might be used to take revenge for a slight—even at a much later date.

Cultivating a Diverse Network

To avoid competing loyalties and to keep all of your bases covered, focus on cultivating a diverse network of *guanxi* connections, because a wide network gives you greater maneuverability. Indeed, the opportunities afforded by a good *guanxi* network are practically endless—it can connect you with almost anyone in and beyond Asia. Taiwan's prominent **Koo** Chen-Fu, for example, once held no fewer than ninety-eight titles in different businesses and organizations, with each title representing a *guanxi* network.

Since a *guanxi* network is a delicate chain of one-to-one personal relationships, and the chain itself is only as strong as its weakest link, it is important to know and trust the people with whom you are establishing *guanxi*. Given the strong influence of individual connections on the network as a whole, be sure to check someone's credentials—whenever possible use multiple independent sources —before entering into a *guanxi* relationship. Bear in mind that most individuals who have *guanxi* do not generally advertise it. Chuck Leng Joo, a well-known Hong Kong businessman, said: "Who I know in China is exclusive information. I hardly make it known even to friends."[9]

If, as is frequently the case, you need to rely on your instinct about a person, remember the Chinese saying: "If you are going to depend on someone, test them with a small task first." If you find that you have entered into a relationship with an individual with a poor reputation, for instance, you must immediately but subtly begin to distance yourself from that person before the acquaintance alienates you from other *guanxi*.

Finally, when cultivating your *guanxi* network, do not place too much emphasis on politicians—a common mistake among Westerners. While the goodwill of government representatives is central to business success in the PRC, and helpful in other countries, diversity of *guanxi* is important. Not all connections in China are useful business affiliations. You must examine the background of any connections offered by third parties to make sure that your *guanxi* will advance your firm's entrance into the Chinese market, not hold it back.

It Is *the Thought That Counts*

In the Chinese context, the giving of gifts is vital in both building and maintaining *guanxi*. Gift-giving promotes *guanxi* by providing a way for people to express their interest in one another and by establishing a basis for continued interaction. For the Western businessperson (Americans, in particular), however, such a pretext for continued interaction can cross the ethical line into a conflict of interest that borders on bribery. Compounding this concern is the fact that most U.S. companies enforce gift-giving policies, and under U.S. law (Foreign Corrupt Practices Act of 1977) giving a gift to a government official could be illegal.

While examples of corruption have been well documented, gift-giving need not be unethical.[10] In the first place, gifts do not have to

---

Box 3-3: Cultural Dilemma: Quid Pro Quo and *Guanxi*

My company has specific criteria stating that suppliers are to be selected based on such factors as cost and quality. A manager in my factory in China is discouraging me from shifting to a less expensive supplier, stressing the importance of the long-term relationship with our current supplier, who apparently has been able to assist us in other, unrelated matters. What should I do?

Options and Observations

Recognize that in China's relationship-based society, such long-term arrangements may in some instances make business sense and are not necessarily considered improper. Before making a final decision, consider the bigger picture. Talk with the manager further and try to determine the following:

- What is the basis for his recommendation? How does this supplier fit into your company's *guanxi* networks?

- In what ways was the supplier able to assist in the past?

- In return for your paying a higher price, is some kind of quid pro quo expected?

If there is a quid pro quo, is it acceptable? If not, carefully consider how to communicate the rationale for your position to your colleague and guide him or her in ways to change the relationship with the supplier in a face-saving way.

---

be expensive. For the Chinese, the exchange of gifts presents an opportunity to cultivate and advance *guanxi* through social interaction. For them, gift-giving is not just a material exchange but also, and more important, an exchange of growing bonds of friendship. Giving a gift with symbolic value is a way of respecting Chinese tradition while remaining under your company's financial cap.

Appropriate presents for your Chinese associates or friends demonstrate that you have noticed what is important to them. Common business gifts in the West, such as company promotional items, are generally too impersonal for the Chinese. When choosing a gift for a Chinese associate, make an effort to select a gift the recipient needs or would be particularly pleased to have. At the 1999 Fortune

> **Box 3-4: Gifts to Avoid**
>
> As a general rule, do not give flowers—Chinese view them as superficial. Beware especially of white flowers, which are a sign of death in the Chinese culture. Also, note the many superstitions about gift-giving: Never give a clock or a fan for a birthday present, for example, and avoid the number 4, all of which are associated with death. And do not give scissors or knives, which can "cut" your relationship. Most important, avoid the "potlatch" syndrome—the giving of extravagant gifts that are more likely to embarrass your Chinese friends than please them. Expensive or elaborate gifts are difficult to reciprocate.

Global Forum in Shanghai, Gerald M. Levin, chairman of (then) Time Warner, gave a special gift to the president of the PRC, **Jiang** Zemin. Aware that Jiang liked to amuse Western visitors by reciting the entire Gettysburg Address, Levin presented his Chinese host with a bust of Abraham Lincoln. According to an executive who was present, Jiang beamed with pleasure.[11] A more typical example is the executive who, on a visit to a Chinese friend's office, noticed that he was having trouble with his phone. On his next visit, the executive appeared with a new phone—a useful and modest gift that demonstrated his sensitivity to his associate's needs.

Another appropriate gift is an item that is meaningful to *you*. This could be something for which your hometown is famous, or it could be even more personal. At a very special moment in my career at Columbia University, my colleague Hugh Patrick presented me with his favorite tie as a sign of friendship and support. He has worked closely with Asians over the last forty years and understands which gestures are valued and meaningful in the Chinese context. Even if your Chinese friends do not like the present you choose for them, they will remember your willingness to share with them something you care for!

How to Maintain *Guanxi*

The durability of *guanxi* depends on a number of factors, including the intensity of the relationship and the way in which it is maintained. In some cases, *guanxi* may last for life with little or no maintenance, as is the case with *jiaren*. People who have been through a powerful experience together, often early in life, may establish an enduring relationship. Providing help for someone at an important stage—assisting them, for example, when they are young and inexperienced—will likewise establish a lifelong *guanxi* relationship, even with very little contact later on.

For the Western businessperson, the key to maintaining *guanxi* lies in continued interaction with your Chinese associates. In this respect, it is important to remember that a relationship once established should never be taken for granted, and that there are a few gestures that must always be made, whether you are building a network or maintaining one. For example, stay in touch with your friends— even occasional notes or phone calls will keep things going. Inquire about their families and keep the reciprocity alive. Maintain a steady and appropriate exchange of thoughtful gifts and favors. You are not expected to reciprocate immediately—in fact, it is a sign of trust on your part to remain indebted for some period of time. Although any favor should be repaid with a slightly larger one, proceed conservatively at first. If you suddenly overwhelm your friend with a dramatic gesture, the reciprocity will not have evolved naturally and both parties will be embarrassed. Your friend may find it impossible to reciprocate, and it is the continuous building of reciprocity in the relationship that develops *guanxi*.

Bad Times Make Good Friends

When the PRC opened its doors to Western business in the late 1970s, AIG was the first foreign insurance company given permission to reenter the Chinese market. The Chinese remembered the company with feelings of solidarity because several of AIG's senior executives in Shanghai had been imprisoned by the Japanese occupation army during World War II. The fact that AIG had shared China's suffering was remembered when the company applied to reenter the PRC market.

The Chinese believe that adversity is the best test of a relationship. For this reason, they generally do not despair when business deals fall apart or fail to live up to expectations, instead preferring to see crisis as opportunity. A failed business deal represents an opportunity for partners to reconfirm their commitment to one another and strengthen their relationship. The Chinese put a high value on *huan nan zhi jiao*, which translates roughly as "the relationship has survived a difficult time."

Respect for Family

Family life is central to Chinese society. Many Chinese businesses are family businesses, and family-like behavior comes naturally to the Chinese in most of their business relationships. Because the Chinese do not draw a line between their business and social lives, it is considered appropriate—and desirable—for business associates to take an interest in one another's families. One of the best ways to demonstrate sincerity and maintain *guanxi* is to make the effort to get to know the families of Chinese associates.

Although it may conflict with Western notions of the privacy of family life, it is a valued gesture, once you have an established relationship, to include a Chinese colleague's spouse in dinner invitations. Making a point to ask about the children and paying attention to the answer are also appreciated. Small gestures, such as buying a little souvenir for a child, help demonstrate a personal interest. Dr. David Ho, director of a leading HIV/AIDS research institute, actually makes it an obligation to know all the birthdays of all the children of the people who work for him. All kinds of favors to family are appreciated: providing information, making introductions, helping to solve problems large and small. Once you are on a friendly basis with a Chinese, it is not going too far to ask about the family each time you meet; in fact, once you have met the family members in question, it would be remiss not to do so. As you establish ties with families, you build *guanxi*.

Traditionally, parents are an especially important family relation to recognize. Asking about parents, sending gifts to them, and doing favors for them are all powerful ways to demonstrate one's commitment to a relationship. When you meet the parents of a Chinese associate, paying a compliment to them on the excellence of their child brings your associate back to his social and family context. You not only show your cultural sensitivity but also ensure that everyone is complimented and pleased.

Box 3-5: Cultural Dilemma: When and How to Blow the Whistle

How can I encourage employees in China to come forward if they have problems or if they witness misconduct?

Options and Observations

Since family-like relationships among Chinese employees are not uncommon, it can be very difficult to encourage individuals to come forward to report on a coworker. However, you can take some steps to make it easier for an employee to do so:

- Reinforce the rationale behind the importance of whistle-blowing— for example, the consequences to the company, reputation, or economic losses that may result from not reporting misconduct.

- Set up anonymous and confidential reporting channels for employees. These channels should be equipped to communicate with employees in Chinese. Even better, designate a local contact person. Carefully investigate who would be most appropriate in this role— sometimes a Chinese-speaking foreign manager may be considered more trustworthy than a Chinese by local employees. It is critical that the person have credibility and a reputation for integrity among the other employees.

- Periodically remind employees of the importance of raising concerns. Emphasize that this action is viewed as "raising concerns" rather than "reporting." The raising of concerns should always be done in a private session rather than in a large public forum.

Whistle-Blowing

It is crucial to recognize that in the Chinese context the social network as a whole is as important as any of its component parts. The Chinese term for "individual," *ge-ren*, literally means "unit (*ge*) of mankind (*ren*)." The Chinese consider any important event or transaction in light of its potential effects on the network, because maintaining one's relationships is almost always more important than the details of any individual deal. Sometimes, striking a balance between immediate concerns and long-term networking can be extremely challenging, if not actually dangerous to business success.

The following example illustrates the ambiguity that surrounds "misconduct." An American executive was running a business in mainland China with a Chinese partner when, early in their relationship, he began to see that other businesspeople were overcharging them. The American brought the situation to the attention of his Chinese partner and suggested they confront the parties at fault. His partner refused and recommended that they ignore it. Baffled by what seemed to be his partner's tolerance for being cheated, the American nevertheless accepted his suggestion and waited to see how things developed. As time passed, he began to see a larger pattern emerging: either they made a large profit on a subsequent business deal, or the associates he thought were overcharging them introduced them later to new business opportunities.

Entering the Chinese marketplace can be a daunting prospect in the best of circumstances, and the advice to be acquiescent in the face of loss is difficult to understand. How long should you put up with the situation? When will it turn around? What if you are doing something fundamentally wrong? How do you know? Unfortunately, there are no easy answers to these questions. The best defense in ambiguous situations is strong *guanxi* with your business partners: Networks act to protect their members, and no one loses in the long run.

Guanxi as Strategy

Since the focus of Chinese business is on social dynamics, relationship-building is the fundamental aspect of strategy in Chinese business.[12] Forging relationships in order to accomplish company goals is key to the operation of Chinese businesses worldwide and historically has been a key to its success. Members of a business group or network contribute more than mere capital. They bring a constant flow of people, information, and other assets to the company. Given the Chinese habit of integrating different areas of life, individual assets can easily become organizational assets.

One Chinese-born Indonesian tycoon, Mochtar Riady, leader of Indonesia's Lippo Group, illustrates how "personal" Chinese relationship building can be.[13] In 1990, when Indonesia normalized relations with Beijing, Riady went on an eight-month automobile tour of China, speaking to everyone from academics and economists to waiters and villagers. Chinese officials throughout the country honored him, and his ancestral home in Fujian Province, due to be razed for redevelopment, was preserved until his visit. By 1992, a Lippo executive in Hong Kong could confidently claim that "all the major CEOs in China are friends of Dr. Riady."[14]

In Chinese business, relationships are considered one of the most important company assets. Hong Kong's giant trading firm Li & Fung has built a powerful business by maintaining strong relationships throughout generations. Victor Fung likes to relate a story about his company's creation of a database of its suppliers. One of his colleagues worried that if a competitor got into the system, it could steal "one of the company's greatest assets." Fung, however, was not worried: "Someone might steal our database, but when they call up a supplier, they don't have the relationship with the supplier that Li & Fung has. It makes a difference to suppliers when they know that you've been honoring your commitments for 90 years."[15]

Eric W. K. Tsang has suggested that Western companies operating in China should conduct "*guanxi* audits" in order to assess the strengths and weaknesses of their various relationships, and to cultivate or nurture important links with "outside stakeholders such as customers, suppliers, and government bodies."[16] Some Western companies, he notes, have successfully used *guanxi* as a preemptive strategy against competitors, moving in early and establishing representative offices to fortify relationships and networks in advance of the "real" operations. Indeed, establishing *guanxi* confers undeniable benefits—a fact attested to in the West by a recent surge of interest in network- and relationship-building. Articles such as Rosabeth Moss Kanter's 1996 "Using Networking for Competitive Advantage" attest to this trend.[17]

In the PRC, non-Chinese companies such as Nokia, Boeing, Motorola, Corning, and AIG have built and maintained strong *guanxi* over extensive periods of time, largely due to the personal efforts of their leaders to form trusting and continuing relationships with partners and associates in China and elsewhere (Morris Greenberg of AIG, Jamie and Amroy Houghton of Corning, and Jorma Ollila of Nokia are some prominent examples). Boeing, to take one example, has solidified its position in the PRC by contributing to

---

Table 3-1:   Chinese-Western Networking Differences

Chinese	Western
Personal relationships have organizational implications, and vice versa	Clear distinction between individual and organizational relationships
Personal and trust-based	Contract-oriented
Symbiotic relationship between networked organizations	High independence of networked organizations
Motivated by economic and social concerns	Motivated primarily by economic concerns
Flexibility and informality	Formality and clearly defined roles

---

the development of a modern air-traffic control network, donating flight simulators to local colleges, and training mainland mechanics and pilots in the U.S.

It is critical for Western firms to recognize that relationships are in many ways the "real" operations in Chinese business dealings. In other words, companies that seek to operate successfully in a relationship-based system must be able to treat relationships not as incidental accessories to their strategy, but rather as the strategic *starting point* for doing business in the Chinese context.

Conclusion: Another Look at *Guanxi*

Reporting on conditions in Asia following the financial crisis, McKinsey & Company stressed the significance of the relationships that inform *guanxi* networks: "Doing business in Asia is still . . . driven by relationships . . . that . . . are often the product of networks developed over decades and give companies that enjoy them an undeniable lead over foreigners in these markets."[18]

Although it is true that the Chinese business world is still largely driven by relationships, in different markets the actual influence of *guanxi* can vary greatly. High-tech industries, for example, rely little on the power of human connections, while in more traditional businesses, such as real estate, it remains an important factor. As more and more Chinese companies enter nontraditional markets, the pull of *guanxi* will most likely be felt less and less. Nevertheless, business between Chinese and Western companies could be vastly improved were Westerners to take a more considered, informed, and proactive approach to *guanxi*.

The introduction of relationship concerns into Western business practices does not necessarily entail a conflict of interest or disturbances to a company's ethical guidelines, government policies, and cultural principles. Even if in its worst forms *guanxi* may be used to change or break the rules of business, it is generally only a way to facilitate business processes within the legal boundaries. *Guanxi* is extra insurance for the deal, but not the deal itself. It is equally important to remember that *guanxi* is primarily a personal relationship between two individuals, one that comes and goes with those individuals. To this end, *guanxi* operates in and around the role-relationships prescribed by Chinese culture, but it never replaces role obligations.

But the relevance of *guanxi* to business interests has broader implications. Relationship management has become increasingly imperative in the context of global alliances and partnerships. Managing relationships is fundamentally different from management based solely on the bottom line and requires a mind-set open to the complexities of human interactions. Understanding *guanxi*—what it is, and how to cultivate and manage it—not only can be a valuable tool in doing business with the Chinese but also can provide a foundation for managing business networks, both personal and organizational, throughout the world.

.

4

ROLES AND RULES OF THE SOCIAL FABRIC

For the Chinese, relationships, reciprocity, and respect span time and place as well as social and business spheres.[1] When my first son was born in the United States, my wife and I decided to give him both an English and a Chinese name. We chose the English name Andy, but, in a traditional sign of respect for the parental role, we gave the choice of the Chinese name to my mother. My mother, in turn, paid respect to another traditional role relation and asked her high school teacher from fifty years before in China to pick a Chinese name for her first grandson.

This type of role-relation behavior is not unusual—there is even a special compound word in Chinese, *shigong* (teacher-grandfather), that I always use to address my mother's teacher. The intricate process of naming my son exemplifies the extent to which respect paid to roles and relationships brings together the various elements of the Chinese social and organizational context. Such an intermingling of spheres—which in many parts of the West are generally considered separate—has broad implications for business practices. Family, social ties, and organizational networks are inseparable—within and beyond the realm of Chinese business!

MOST OF US IDENTIFY with our given names: They were chosen by our parents (or grandparents and other close relations), they often carry an evocative meaning, and they may be the word in the language that we feel most "belongs" to us. But this is a Western perspective. For traditional Chinese, the family name comes first. This prioritization points not simply to the privileging of family over individual identity but to a completely different conception of identity itself.

In the West, personal identity is based on the notion of the self. In Chinese society, however, this idea of the self is replaced by that of the role. Family relations, and by extension societal relations, are structured by a hierarchy of roles that define all individuals. To put it in extreme terms, the individual acts and thinks as a cog in a larger mechanism. Condon's witty comment, "had Descartes been Japanese, he would have written, 'We think therefore we are,'" applies equally to the Chinese.[2] This is not to say, however, that in the Chinese system individuals all think alike, but rather that they think according to their place, or their role, in the whole.

This chapter will first describe the cultural significance of roles in the Chinese social and organizational context and then highlight the importance of *mianzi* (face) and reciprocity as two cultural attributes that sustain the role relationships that make up Chinese society. Finally, we will inquire into the ways in which social roles impact relationships formed both inside and between organizations.

Social and Business Roles in Chinese Life

Social roles in Chinese society have historical roots that trace back to the "five relationships" of Confucian thought: ruler/subject, father/ son, husband/wife, elder brother/younger brother, and friend/ friend. These five relationships (*lun*), believed to form the core of human society, provide individuals with morally based, predetermined social roles intended to order and stabilize society from top to bottom.[3] Since they are defined interdependently (one cannot be a son without a father, or a ruler without subjects), these relationships weave individuals into a harmonious, mutually binding social fabric.

In the Chinese context, social roles begin in the family—the locus of three of the five Confucian relationships—and extend to society at large. Within the typical Chinese family, individuals are usually addressed by their family role rather than their personal name. Parents, for example, are addressed as "father" and "mother,"

Box 4-1: Chinese Role Relationships

The Chinese language has a variety of special terms to describe role relationships—terms that even allude to the obligations and expectations that these relationships carry. Here are a few examples:

- *Shi jiao* (generational relationship): Ties between two families whose grandparents are friends.

- *Huan nan fu qi*: Husband and wife who have been through difficulties together.

- *Sheng si zhi jiao*: Relationship with someone for whom one would die.

- *Qing tong fu zi*: Like father and son.

- *Jie bai xiong di*: Sworn to be brothers.

- *Tong chuang*: Classmates. (Literally "study against the same window.")

---

siblings as "elder sister," "younger brother," and so on. Relatives, too, are addressed relationally, as "first aunt," "fourth uncle," "big cousin," "youngest maternal uncle," and so on. By designating the position occupied within the family hierarchy, this form of address functions as a sign of respect and makes explicit the status of the person in relation to other family members. To name a person by his or her family title is to call up a host of attendant social expectations.

Family roles commonly extend outside the nuclear family to include close friends and associates. For example, children often call their parents' close friends *ayi* (auntie) or *shu shu* (uncle). Family titles may also be used within the broader social context. In the neighborhood, for instance, the elderly may be respectfully addressed as "grandfather" or "grandmother." In business, too, an understanding of the broad application of Chinese family relations is highly relevant. One of the many things that McDonald's did right when it entered the PRC market was choosing a Chinese family name for Ronald McDonald; he is known to millions of Chinese children as "Good Uncle"!

As a consequence of their emphasis on role relationships, the Chinese have a vastly different view of personal achievement than do Westerners. Social psychologist Edwin C. Nevis has found that the

Chinese tend to focus on group actualization rather than individual achievement.[4] To the extent that the Chinese conceive of personal fulfillment, they usually view it as the realization of personal potential in relation to the needs and well-being of the immediate family or business group. This means that a manager's pride may not result as much from what he or she views as a personal accomplishment as from the contribution made to the growth of the company and the pride this has brought to the family. The owner of the Empire Szechuan restaurant chain in New York opened a second restaurant for the sole reason that she had too many chefs in her first restaurant. Because she considered her personal attainments in relation to the well-being of the social group as a whole, firing a few chefs was not a viable option.

In a well-known and widely applied cross-cultural study titled "The Confucius Connection: From Cultural Roots to Economic Growth," Hofstede and Bond compare Chinese and American society along several dimensions, including "power distance," or "the extent to which the less powerful members of organizations and institutions (like the family) accept and expect that power is distributed unequally." The authors surmise that the Chinese are high in power distance and low in individualism.[5]

But to conclude that the Chinese belong to a collectivist society that values high "power distance" is not as culturally sensitive as saying that the Chinese social order is conceived through the distribution of—and differentiation among—role relations. This is particularly important in business transactions. Powerful Western businesspeople who express their status by positioning themselves specifically in a traditional role relation will be more successful in doing business with the Chinese. More important, the concept of roles explains how the Chinese can be collectivist and entrepreneurial at the same time.

Chinese people view their lives holistically, and they strive to meet the expectations and obligations of all their roles. A Chinese man will simply consider himself a "good person," rather than distinguishing between roles and viewing himself as either a "good father" or a "good businessman." Traditionally, a wealthy and successful businessman will never forget that he is also a dutiful son who owes obedience to his parents, no matter how comfortable he may be with his role as leader of a large business enterprise. Because roles are viewed with regard to the whole, they do not assume the connotations of superficiality or deception that role-*playing* carries in the West. Instead, they are considered to be a socially responsible act.

The Chinese carry over this holistic view of life to their encounters with others: In meeting Western businesspeople, they will want to become acquainted with the individual and not simply the businessperson. In fact, the notion of knowing a business associate only through the business relationship can seem incomplete and unsatisfactory to the Chinese. From their perspective, a functional role such as a job title, a position in the corporate hierarchy, or a departmental affiliation is merely one of many relevant pieces of information about a person.

Chinese businesspeople also have social roles that often outweigh their functional or titular roles in the company. When a group of students from the Wharton School visited China Trust, for example, they were hosted by its owners, the Koos—a prominent Taiwanese business family and generous patrons of Wharton. The Wharton alumni were welcomed by Jeff Koo Sr., functionally speaking the highest-ranking person in the organization and also the person with the highest social rank. When Jeff Koo Sr. had to leave, the role of host was taken over not by the next-highest executive in the business but by Jeffrey Koo Jr., who was socially—not functionally—the next in command.[6]

In mainland China, this issue of roles is further complicated by the Communist Party, which is not just a political body but also a social organization with tremendous influence over most aspects of life, and a group with members who have deep ties of loyalty and friendship to each other. After all, the word *comrade*, though sometimes joked about in the West, was intentionally chosen to represent and reinforce the notion of comradeship, of deep friendship and personal loyalty, among the older generation of party members.

The equal consideration given to social and functional roles in Chinese companies can present a challenge: It is not always clear, even for the Chinese, which role should dominate in any given context, and this ambiguity can lead to miscommunication and inadvertent signs of disrespect. While trying to remember one's correct

Table 4-1: Chinese-Western Role-Relation Comparison

Chinese	Western
Roles culturally defined	Roles negotiable
Reliance on obligations, based on roles and unstated rules	Reliance on expectations and open communication for clarification
Defined through relationships	Defined through performance
Self = part of network	Self = individual
Joint consideration of functional and social roles in business setting	Functional roles dominate in business setting
More focus on interpersonal relations and group dynamic	More focus on institutional rules

Source: Elena Yang Ai-Yuan, "The Role of Culture in Business Networking: A Field Study Comparing Immigrant Chinese and American Start-Ups" (Ph.D. diss., University of Pennsylvania, 1996).

social and functional role can be difficult for a Westerner, even a sincere *attempt* to exhibit appropriate role behavior and recognize corresponding social expectations can help develop a flexible mindset and perspective—and go a long way toward improving communication in the Chinese context.

A Society of "Face" (面子)

Mianzi, or "face," is inseparable from the concept of social roles. In assuming a social role, one accepts a standard set of behavioral characteristics and social expectations. Quite literally, one's role becomes one's self-image—or *face*—which must be preserved to keep the social order intact.

In the West, the word *face* often carries the negative connotations of surface or superficiality. *Mianzi*, by contrast, is not a matter of dissembling or false pretense but an important element in the foundation of interpersonal relationships. It denotes a social standing based on one's character and reputation within a given social group. As Ambrose King remarks, "Having *mianzi* is like having good credit, so that one has a lot of purchasing power."[7] But *mianzi* is also reciprocal: It is a shared responsibility not to damage the standing or reputation of others. When you cause another to lose face, you damage not only their reputation but yours as well. It is an intangible form of social currency—"group credit"—that the whole community seeks to maintain.

In the Chinese context, causing someone to lose face is a mode of personal assault that can do serious damage to the relationship as well as to business opportunities. The maintenance of face is so important that people will sometimes lie to preserve it. **Yap** Pheng Geck, a Singaporean Chinese businessman, explains the complex sense of obligation Chinese people feel to maintain one another's reputations in the business community: "We do not like people with the same surname or people seen with us a lot to go down. If that person is a family friend, the community will say 'What sort of man are you to allow your friend to go down?' So I feel an obligation to assist him; otherwise it also reflects on me. We have this peculiar sensitivity that induces us to mutual assistance."[8] Although the practice of *mianzi* can cultivate a strong sense of social responsibility, it can also be an extremely conservative and sometimes paralyzing force. An exaggerated concern for others' feelings can limit entrepreneurial energy and business initiatives.

Mianzi extends beyond Chinese social circles to Chinese business dealings. Even where strangers are involved, the Chinese consider it important to maintain face, particularly if a future business or social relationship is envisaged. Respecting this practice can open up potential networks for the Westerner, while disrespect can create unanticipated problems and cause severe damage. In the 1980s, telecommunications giant AT&T turned down an offer from the PRC's then Ministry of Posts and Telecommunications to help develop the country's telephone network because at that time it was too busy with problems at home. Consequently, Chinese officials shut AT&T out of the Chinese market for a number of years because they felt they had lost face. AT&T not only lost 60 percent of the telephone switching market but also had to pay a higher price when it finally entered the market in the late 1990s.[9]

Finally, it is important to emphasize that *mianzi* often takes the form of symbolic gestures as well as substantial acts. When a Chinese businessperson says good-bye to a visiting associate, for instance, he or she will generally accompany a visitor of any importance to the outer door of the office as a sign of respect. A slightly more important visitor will be walked to the elevator. A very

---

Box 4-2: Cultural Dilemma: *Mianzi* versus Flattery

How do I give someone face without resorting to flattery? How can I be candid about problems and still prevent someone from losing face?

Options and Observations

- Pay attention to protocol. For example, observe hierarchy and seating order at the table and accompany a guest or visitor to the door or car at the conclusion of a meeting.

- Always defer to people older than yourself, regardless of their functional position.

- If you have a genuine compliment for someone and wish to give him or her face, pay the compliment in a public forum. However, before doing so, consider whether the compliment is for the individual or whether it applies to the group. If the latter, credit the group publicly, rather than the individual.

- If you must criticize someone and wish to prevent a loss of face, raise the issue with the person privately. Shaming someone in public is an extremely serious form of punishment in Chinese culture.

- Accept apologies readily and always downplay or minimize the offense.

- Insincere praise is no more acceptable in Chinese culture than in any other. In some instances, however, the Chinese may pay compliments that Westerners may perceive as excessive.

---

important guest may be accompanied to the front door of the building itself. Although the maintenance of face is a subtle practice, always tailored to take varying social roles into account, as a general rule it simply means finding a variety of ways to honor your associates and make them feel respected.

Reciprocity: The Source of Mianzi

Mianzi can exist only in relation to others; without relationships, there is no possibility of self-recognition, and no face. Consequently, the activating ingredient of any relationship is reciprocity, a princi-

---

Box 4-3: A Token of Appreciation

The importance of long-term reciprocity is beautifully illustrated in the best-selling novels of the late James Clavell: *Taipan, Noble House,* and *Gaijin.* Clavell lived much of his life in Asia and had a deep, firsthand understanding of Chinese values. In these three novels, Clavell follows the fictional Struan family and its company, loosely based on the famed Hong Kong conglomerate Jardine Matheson.

In the second novel of Clavell's trilogy, which tells the story of the modern-day Struans, the reader discovers that the company founder, Dirk Struan, had made a secret pact with four of his closest friends and business partners back in the mid-1800s. These friends had helped Struan so immensely that he decided to repay them in the following fashion: The four men secretly received one-half of an ancient Chinese coin, while Struan and his descendants kept the other half. If at any time in the future those friends or their descendants were in need, they could redeem one ultimate favor from the Struans with that half coin. The family leader of that time would be bound by this pact and by honor to grant that friend anything he or she might ask. In essence, Dirk Struan bound his descendants and the entire future power of the Noble House to ancient friendships and a code of reciprocity.

---

ple fundamental to all Chinese business and social interaction. Maintaining an ongoing give-and-take ensures that relationships develop and persist.

The principle of reciprocity also helps to assure that people will support one another in times of trouble. The Chinese sayings "When you drink water, remember from where it springs" and "A drop of water in a time of need will be reciprocated forever" convey the idea that help in times of difficulty will make a lasting impression and be generously repaid well into the future. Building a strong and enduring relationship with the Chinese, especially one that can survive adversity, requires a commitment to continuing and conscientious reciprocity.

Reciprocity is the norm at all levels of Chinese social interaction, from casual social gatherings to important business dealings. When Chinese people eat together in a restaurant, even if they have just met, they rarely split the bill. One person always pays the whole tab, after a noisy, good-natured argument to decide who will pay. The

---

Box 4-4: Cultural Dilemma: Gift-Giving and Reciprocity

I need to establish ties with prospective partners in China. My company, however, has strict limits on gift-giving and entertainment. What should I do?

Options and Observations

• If permissible, give small, thoughtful tokens of appreciation to your prospective partner.

• Spend time getting to know the partner, which is also a form of investment in the relationship and need not involve lavish entertainment.

• Recognize that in some instances the prospective partner will judge you by your generosity. Rigid controls on gift-giving and entertainment can work against you. This is especially true when your competitors have been generous to the prospective partner. If, however, gifts and lavish entertainment are so highly valued by the Chinese party, then not partnering with them might be to your long-term benefit!

---

unstated message is clear: "This time it's my turn and next time it's yours, and we'll be even over time." Although the Chinese are acutely sensitive to this kind of reciprocity, no one is keeping track of who owes whom. Instead, the assumption is that since everyone understands the principles of reciprocity, the details will generally balance over the long run.

In business, although the stakes are higher than the price of a meal, reciprocity is still carefully observed, and friends and relatives are expected to help each other in business endeavors whenever possible—with mutual support ranging from small, everyday favors to major investments. Sita Karnkriangkai, a Thai of Chinese descent, provides a good example of reciprocity in action. During the Asian financial crisis, Sita was able to help buoy his brother-in-law's floundering steel-supply firm, building it a new warehouse and asking for no payment for the project. Sita's first experience in business had come from working at his brother-in-law's company, and he remembered this well: "We have to help each other in business. Because when we make a profit, we get it from them. My business is based on trust."[10]

Treating the Business as a Family

Family relations, with their clear roles and accepted hierarchies, are the prototype for all Chinese social relations, including those formed in the workplace. ATI Technologies, Inc., a Toronto-based computer graphics company owned and operated by three ethnic Chinese partners, provides a case in point. The partners not only make all key business decisions together but also dine out every Saturday night with their wives and children and take vacations together.[11] Even in those businesses that are not family-based and not Chinese, the tendency is for Chinese employees to treat their business roles and relationships as a family affair.

Family titles such as *aunt* or *uncle* are often used to address non–family members in the business organization. A young Chinese man working at his first job in a traditional Chinese business will often call his elder supervisor "uncle," especially if the older man is a mentor figure. A female worker in the organization, more experienced and a few years senior to the young man, will be addressed as "elder sister." Younger colleagues entering the organization will be called "younger brother." By using family titles to name their colleagues, Chinese employees shape their business relations in terms of the well-known conventions and roles of the family and social structure.

Interaction between employers and employees also finds a basis in family-centered codes of behavior. For example, supervisors are often treated with the kind of respect and formality otherwise reserved for the family patriarch. In this capacity, supervisors will tend, in turn, to assume a more paternalistic role than their counterparts in Western companies. This mixing of business and private spheres may be considered unprofessional in the West, but the extension of family roles to the workplace can foster strong interpersonal communication, provide a supportive learning environment, and help to retain good employees.

In family-owned businesses—where *actual* family relationships exist—loyal, nonfamily employees may be "adopted" into the family

---

Box 4-5: Chinese "Siblings"

Family-like behavior in business is not limited to Chinese-owned enterprises. Western-owned firms that hire Chinese have to cope with family-like behavior among their Chinese employees. In the mid-1990s, one of the Big Five U.S. accounting firms had a few outstanding Chinese executives in its Hong Kong office at the level just below senior partner. These managers had worked together for years and had risen through the ranks of the company together. Each of them came to be in charge of one key area of the firm's business, and each was widely respected for his work. The senior partner, a Westerner, was ready to retire, and he wanted one of the Chinese managers to take over control of the business.

Although they were all qualified for the job, not one of the managers seemed interested in accepting it. The senior partner was baffled at this apparent indifference to a lucrative promotion. If the senior partner had only understood the Chinese family, he would have understood the reason. The Chinese managers considered themselves members of an extended family made up of all the employees of the firm, and none of them wanted to disrupt the company's existing relationships for individual gain.

---

fold. For example, a worker at one of Taiwan's leading construction companies had been a dedicated employee for four decades and had stood by the company's founder in times of adversity. Although not a member of the owning family, he was treated as such even after the patriarch died and control of the company was turned over to the patriarch's daughter. She had always regarded the loyal employee as her uncle and, in addition to putting him on several boards as the company's representative, made him the president and chairman of one of the company's major subsidiaries.

Westerners working for a Chinese company or with Chinese employees can be similarly part of the "family." Because the culture of relating to business associates as quasi-family members is so deeply ingrained, Chinese employees may assume that a Westerner will relate to them in a similar way. It is important to appreciate this tradition without, however, overplaying the adopted family role. The simplest and best approach is to be sensitive to the needs of your coworkers and to remember to keep their *mianzi*, or face, in mind at all times.

Box 4-6:   The Kingston Family, all 450 of them

John Tu and David Sun, who cofounded Kingston Technology Company, a California memory chip manufacturer, decided in 1996 to sell 80 percent of their company to Soft Bank for $1.5 billion. After the sale, the two executives established a $100 million fund for the company's 450 employees to share in the proceeds. Following the distribution of that cash in yearly bonuses, the cofounders decided to use their personal and corporate fortunes to help Kingston employees start their own ventures; they donated seed money, a majority investment, legal help, business advice, and even office space at Kingston. John Tu explained it this way: "David and I would rather help people find their own path—even if it's not at Kingston—than leave the Kingston family altogether."[a]

[a] P. J. Hoffstutter, "In Latest Bonus, Firm Helps Workers Become Own Bosses," *Los Angeles Times*, 28 December 1999.

Interorganizational Networks

In Chinese business, interpersonal relations provide the basis for interorganizational relations. When deals are made, they are considered to be agreements between people first and organizations second. The creation of responsibilities, roles, and obligations at the interpersonal level shapes and cements business transactions. From the point of view of a Chinese business considering a joint venture with another company, professional competence and a good track record are not enough, nor is the lure of an attractive deal. A bond of obligation that establishes a long-term intention to do business together must exist between the two parties.

The core of global Chinese business is made up of these interorganizational networks, which are often referred to as the "bamboo network." Chinese business networks are loosely connected groups of independent entities bound together by personal relationships. Unlike the highly centralized Japanese network, the *keiretsu*, Chinese networks are made up of organizations of similar size and status for which there is often no corporate leader or network head. The following section looks at network interactions in two areas: role expectations versus legal obligations, and financing among Chinese businesses.

Obligations—without Lawyers

As a consequence of their interpersonal approach to business, Chinese business dealings often bypass the key requirement of Western business: the legal contract. In an environment structured by the implicit rules of loyalty and mutual obligation, a contract is seen as unnecessary at best and offensive at worst. Historically, important deals have been executed among Chinese firms without legal contracts of any kind. Today, commitments are generally made informally, with only secondary recourse to a contract. One striking example is the construction of Asia's fourth-largest building in Hong Kong, which proceeded on a handshake instead of a formal contract.

Indeed, many Chinese businesspeople find the process of arriving at a Western-style contract counterproductive; in a culture that values the verbal agreement, a contract can symbolize suspicion and fear—a bad beginning for any relationship! Dhanin Chearavanont, the head of Thailand's CP Group, finds the negotiating tactics of U.S. lawyers meddlesome and believes they destroy the spirit of a pending deal.[12] Although the paper contract may be valuable as a symbol of both parties' commitment to an evolving partnership, it implies that the obligations and loyalty of partnership are not taken seriously, and it is rarely resorted to among Chinese businesses as a means of protecting the parties against each other.

Financing—without Bankers

The role of loyalty and reciprocity between Chinese businesses extends to financial matters. In this area, most Chinese businesses prefer not to rely on outside lenders, instead looking to one another to raise funds and finance new ventures. For the overseas Chinese, the importance of self-financing stems in large part from their position as a minority group in foreign countries. The older generation in particular, with its bags-packed-at-all-times mentality, is averse to becoming embroiled with institutional lenders. But the tradition of self-financing also has roots that lie deep in Chinese history. Given the state's historical emphasis on social (rather than legal) codes, Chinese families were asked to look to each other for support during times of need.

In the contemporary world, interbusiness financing can assume two forms. The first consists of short-term lending in the spirit of *biao hui* (loosely translated as "bidding consortium"); the second involves formalized long-term cross-holdings between business enterprises. In both cases, giving *mianzi* and respecting the rules of reciprocity are key to establishing and then maintaining a financing network.

Short-term lending is greatly facilitated by the fact that Chinese firms conduct the bulk of their business in cash. To a Westerner used to the complex financial services of long-established and powerful banks, this practice may be difficult to believe. However, a Chinese business network can serve as its own bank faster and more efficiently than almost any Western financial institution. Since debts are paid on time to avoid offending any member of the network (to avoid losing *mianzi*) a business in good standing can raise the capital for a new project in short order by simply calling on fellow members of its business network.

The self-reliant, mutually supportive nature of financing among Chinese businesses can be traced back to financing practices at the community level. The process known as *biao hui* illustrates the interplay of individual, commercial, and social roles. In this traditional practice, a group of personal associates or friends pools their cash to allow individual members of the group to access larger amounts of money in times of need. In a sense, the *biao hui* works like an informal bank: Each member agrees to contribute a fixed amount of money to the group on a regular basis, such as every month. Then, each time the group convenes, one individual receives all of the group's cash contributions. This kind of consortium is often initiated to meet one person's immediate financial needs, and it will continue to convene until each participant has had a chance to receive the pooled money. There is a high degree of trust involved in *biao hui* exchange (needless to say, for the practice to work, individuals must continue to contribute after they have taken their turn receiving). This kind of informal "community financing" promotes the establishment of bonds between lenders and borrowers.

This common practice extends into business dealings among Chinese companies. By enabling quick fund-raising through the mutual support of various organizations, *biao hui* shows reciprocity and loyalty in action and illustrates their business relevance. Indeed, *Fortune* magazine has attributed the success of the overseas Chinese to this unique financing system, particularly its use in Chinese communities in Taiwan, the Philippines, Thailand, and Indonesia.[13]

In addition to mutual lending on a short-term or project-specific basis, the Chinese frequently provide long-term support and investment by holding shares in one another's businesses—a way of formally endorsing and institutionalizing a friendship. In Indonesia, the social position of the Chinese as a minority group has further strengthened their economic network. To protect themselves against politically motivated attacks, the nine major Indonesia Chinese business owners cross-hold interests in each other's companies. In this manner, were the local government to take punitive action against a given business, all the members of the network would be affected.

Even Chinese bankers may often see money in the broader context of social and cultural capital. Mochtar Riady, whose Lippo Bank is one of the largest in Indonesia, might surprise Western bankers with his statement: "To me, banking isn't a business of buying and selling money. It buys and sells trust."[14] In the Chinese context, social capital counts for more than hard cash.

Conclusion: Knowing Their Place—and Knowing Yours

All Chinese business practices depend on a set of interpersonal expectations and obligations that perpetuate the network. Since a Chinese businessperson will never act without his or her network in mind, an efficient self-regulating system is set in place—one that requires little external reinforcement.

The danger of this system, though, is that when it runs perfectly, no one needs to think about what they are doing. Accustomed to acting in accordance with their roles, individuals can become more concerned with formalities than with the substance of their actions. Indeed, what Trompenaars, Managing Director of the Centre for International Business Studies in The Netherlands, notes about the British could also describe the Chinese: They tend "to do things right rather than do the 'right thing.'"[15] Common sense sometimes gives way to the obligations of hierarchy, and companies can suffer needless losses if associates refrain from criticizing each other for bad business decisions. In short, Chinese networks do not always run smoothly, and often require constant reassessment and readjustment.

Westerners need to understand Chinese social assumptions and expectations in order to position themselves in a role that the Chinese will recognize and respect. Indeed, the expectations that the Chinese have of one another inevitably color their dealings with outsiders, and outsiders do not fit into the traditional Chinese role-based hierarchy. Having an understanding of the Chinese social chain of command is therefore a necessary step in doing business with them.

There is a difference, though, between adopting a Chinese mindset and "becoming" Chinese. If the point of this chapter has been to examine Chinese role relations, this is by no means to suggest that Western businesspeople need to completely transform themselves. The most important advice for Westerners is to recognize and be sensitive to the fabric and intricacies of Chinese social and organizational concerns.

Having an understanding of your associates' assumptions and expectations, and being able to identify individuals who are socially in command, will give you an edge in doing business with the Chinese, helping you to understand the information flow and the decision-making process of many organizations. It will also give you a better idea of the extensive social networks and stakeholders with whom your Chinese partners may need to consult and, ultimately, to work more effectively *with* Chinese businesspeople.

5

THE MIDDLE WAY
A Holistic Perspective on Time and Performance

The notion of interdependent opposites is embedded in the Chinese language. A number of common Chinese words are made up of two characters that express opposing ideas: "many" and "few" combine to mean "how much"; "conflict" can be expressed by joining the characters for "spear" and "shield"; the characters "inside" and "outside" together mean "everywhere." Throughout the language, a balance of opposites creates a new whole.

ZHONG GUO (中國) is the Mandarin word for China. Literally translated, it signifies "middle kingdom" and is commonly understood as meaning that the Chinese see themselves at the center of the universe, as a privileged and superior people. Originally, however, "middle kingdom" had a philosophical meaning. It referred to the principle of being "in the middle"— of maintaining a balanced and integrated life and worldview. The word *zhong* encapsulates the essence of Confucius's prescriptions for adhering to the "middle way": avoiding extremes and holding a moderate and considered position. Lao Tzu, Confucius's immediate predecessor and the founder of Taoism, likewise counseled the middle way in his philosophy of enlightenment (see Appendix 4).

This Confucian-based philosophical orientation continues to have a pervasive impact on Chinese business. **Zhang** Ruimin, for example, CEO of the PRC's Haier Group, and one of the *Financial Times*'s "30 Most Respected Global Business Leaders" in 1999, acknowledges that his business philosophies and practices are deeply rooted in the philosophies of Lao Tzu, Confucius, and Sun Tzu.[1] **Chen** Feng, chairman of Hainan Airlines, one of the PRC's most profitable airlines, is a devoted Buddhist and Confucianist who gives philosophical "lectures" to his guests, including the Western consultants he hires. In the late 1990s, Ting Hsin, the PRC's largest instant-noodle company, built a holistically oriented executive training center in Tianjin where executives regularly participate in tai chi classes designed to balance and harmonize the flow of energy in their bodies.

This chapter will elaborate on two inseparable aspects of the philosophy of the "middle way"—holism and paradox—and illustrate their relevance to Chinese business conduct. With an understanding of holism, we gain an important perspective on Chinese ideas of performance. Similarly, an examination of paradox offers a means for comprehending some of the seemingly contradictory aspects of Chinese business behavior. As we will see, both holism and paradox are also closely intertwined with the Chinese view of time.

Valuing the Whole

In many respects, Chinese and Western worldviews are philosophically opposed. Since the pre-Socratic philosophy of Democritus (460–360 B.C.), by and large the occidental tradition has sought to break up, or atomize, the universe in order to understand how it works. The Western way of thinking is characterized by its analytic approach, which considers fragments of reality as independent objects of study (the Greek roots of the word *analysis*, in fact, denote "loosening" or "breaking apart"). This tradition is reflected in modern Western medicine, for example, which tends to analyze bodily organs in isolation to determine their functions; the body is broken down into parts in order to understand it as a whole.

Chinese thought, by contrast, adopts an "integrative" point of view, one that considers all things in terms of their relationships— be they social, economic, or biological. This point of view could also be labeled "holism": a consideration of individual elements as integrated, inseparable, and interdependent parts of a larger whole. Business writer Chin-Ning Chu explains, "In Asian cultures, there's no division between business, spirituality, personal relationships, the art of war. Every aspect of life is interconnected."[2] In contrast to Western methods, Chinese medicine attempts to look beyond the isolated ailment to rebalance all parts of the human body. In the traditional practice of reflexology, for example, different pressure points on the foot are considered to affect the head, the stomach, and the back. In the words of a Chinese proverb, "If you pull out one hair, you must rebalance the whole body."

Winston Chen offers a comprehensive illustration of how balance and holism can be applied to practical corporate affairs. An overseas Chinese living in the United States, Chen is the owner of Solectron, rated by *Business Week* as number three among global IT enterprises, with a market value of $24 billion in the year 2000 and $9.4 billion in sales in 1999. Chen attributes his success to his application of Sun Tzu's philosophies of balance to the management of his own company. For Chen, *tao* (the right way) means emphasizing employee relationships and common objectives. *T'ien* (Heaven or harmony) is equated with timely adaptation to the changing environment. Chen interprets *di* (surrounding) as strategic positioning, and *jiang* (leaders or leadership) as seeking the best possible managers. Finally, *fa* (law or method) points to the importance of implementing well-defined policies and managerial systems. Chen's translation emphasizes the interrelationships of all parts of the business and the need for a dynamic balance among these parts.

Another example of holistic integration comes from Hong Kong's Li & Fung, an exemplar of global supply chain management. Within its own operations and in its relations with its customers and suppliers, Li & Fung has achieved an almost seamless integration of its various functions. Originally a purchasing agent for Western retailers and wholesalers, Li & Fung now provides a wide range of services for its customers. In the clothing industry, it manages the entire procurement process for customers such as Warner Brothers and Wal-Mart. Although the firm itself does no manufacturing, it has extensive and close relations with small plants that handle each of the different production steps. Li & Fung's scheduling experts work with U.S. and European customers, assigning each customer its own "division manager," who is responsible for finding the best possible production flow for each of the client's orders and who oversees each job from start to finish. The company thus integrates the activities of many smaller agents within a complex production process. Both at its headquarters and in its hands-on customer service, *integration* (of information, connections, and know-how) has been a key factor in Li & Fung's success.[3]

Harmony (中和)

Zhong he, or "balanced harmony" (the equivalent of "holism" in Chinese), is what Confucian philosophy recommends for obtaining prosperity: "If balance and harmony are reached," Confucius writes in *The Book of Means*, "heaven and earth will be in place, and all things will grow." Chinese culture places a high value on the preservation of harmony, which is said to be not only at the core of Confucian principles but also at the origin of the world.[4] To attain harmony, individuals are expected to subordinate themselves to the good of the family (and, by extension, of the business) and adhere to the spirit of the "middle way."

In the Taoist sense, harmony is the product of *wu-wei*, which means "yielding." It is important to note that *wu-wei* does not encourage passivity but rather implies a pensive yielding to, or living in harmony with, the natural flow of events. The example of Taiwan's Wen-Long Shu is a case in point. Shu is a strong adherent of the ancient philosopher Lao Tzu's concept of *wu-wei*. Even before his company became the largest ABS (Acrylonitrile Butadiene Styrene) manufacturer in the world, Shu worked in the office only on Mondays, and he made a point of spending two days a week fishing in order to maintain a balanced and harmonious life. If *wu-wei* were truly passivity, or "nonaction," it would have been impossible for Shu to build his wealth and his business empire.

When a system is harmonious, it has achieved a *balance* between divergent tendencies. The Chinese understanding of balance is not "static" (an equilibrium that, once achieved, remains in place indefinitely) but rather "dynamic" (it requires constant readjustment and adaptation). Lao Tzu celebrated water as a symbol of flexibility and adaptability: Because the environment itself is in constant flux,

---

Box 5-1: The "Harm" in Harmony and the "Holes" in Holism: A Critical View

Particularly from a Western point of view, the Confucian idea of harmony can be less than ideal. An excessive deference to the group whole or the "natural" flow of events can mean that individuals may refrain from criticism of the group—even if it would prove constructive. Maintaining harmony may also mean that obedience to authority takes precedence over thoughtful questioning and reevaluation of the status quo.

Moreover, while much is made of holism in the West, especially in New Age discourse, it should be noted that for the Chinese, the whole may not be equivalent to all of society or to the world at large. Many critics have argued that the Confucian principles of harmony and holism apply only to a section of society to which the individual has strong attachments, that is, the family, the village, or the family business. Thus, holism does not necessarily indicate that Chinese businesspeople will assume a more ecological or compassionate view of the world than their Western counterparts. Unfortunately, the opposite is all too often the case. As Michael Backman, author and commentator on corporate Asia, writes: "Despite many claims to the contrary, egocentricity is a marked feature of Asian society. It's just that the focus of the selfishness is the family or the clan, rather than the individual."[a]

[a] Michael Backman, *Asian Eclipse: Exposing the Dark Side of Business in Asia* (Singapore: John Wiley and Sons [Asia], 1999), 18.

---

and any change demands a readjustment of the system, flexibility and openness to change are considered extremely important virtues.

The Chinese seek harmony and balance in all aspects of their lives. Confucian thinking teaches that a man who is capable of managing himself will also be able to run his family, his country, and eventually the entire world—in other words, the skills needed for all these management jobs are fundamentally the same. From a business perspective, personal growth at the individual level is expected to lead to greater success for the company; therefore, a well-managed business starts with a well-managed individual and family. This kind of thinking means that Chinese individuals will look for common threads connecting their social, personal, and professional roles, and success by Chinese standards means fulfilling the expectations of all these roles. David Ho, a *Time* magazine "Man of the

> **Box 5-2: A Generational Balancing Act**
>
> Throughout Greater China, a variety of innovations are signaling efforts at balancing old values with the demands of the modern world. One example is the growth of "five-generation apartments" in Taiwan—multistory buildings that provide a separate apartment for each generation of a single family, while allowing everyone to live under one roof. In this way, the modern Western idea of privacy is reconciled with the traditional moral obligation to take care of one's parents.

Year" for 1996, put it this way: "I may be a wise scholar, a famous businessman, or a good father and husband, but until I am all, I have not succeeded."[5]

The architectural practice of *feng shui*, increasingly popular in the West, is yet another manifestation of the Chinese practice of seeking harmony. Based on the idea of integrating the individual with the universe, *feng shui* was traditionally used by the Chinese to decide where to build their homes, what direction those homes should face, and how their furniture should be positioned. When railways and telegraph lines were set up across rural China late in the nineteenth century, many Chinese peasants protested that the harsh straight lines cutting through their villages and farmland disrupted the *feng shui*. *Feng shui* remains influential throughout Greater China today, and many Western firms in Asia have begun to take it seriously. According to a former executive of Chase Manhattan Bank, "*[F]eng shui* in Hong Kong is like an engineering survey. . . . you just do it."[6] Motorola, for example, has spent a great deal of money redesigning a factory on the mainland to correct its *feng shui*. Some companies even believe that errors in *feng shui* will damage business: "Chase Manhattan's Merchant Bank in Hong Kong floundered until a *feng shui* expert was consulted. . . . Hyatt Hotel in Singapore prospered only after alterations were made by a *feng shui* master."[7]

An Expansive View of Performance

Just as *feng shui* seeks harmonious relationships between inanimate objects, Chinese business prioritizes harmony and balance in social

---

Box 5-3:   *Feng Shui* **in the United States**

In the States, Donald Trump hired an expert in *feng shui* to consult on the layout and design of his Trump International Hotel and Tower in New York City. Among other recommendations, the expert suggested that the building's entrance face Central Park, in order to achieve balance with nature.[a]

According to *Fortune, feng shui* "seems to have worked for Ponderosa Homes, a developer in Pleasanton, California. Unable to sell five of fifteen $650,000 homes it built in a development in Freemont, California, Ponderosa consulted a *feng shui* specialist. At her suggestion, Ponderosa replaced straight walks with curved ones and turned rectangular front yards into rounded ones—and sold the homes in three months."[b]

[a] Enid Nemy, "Where the Room Is the View," *New York Times*, 22 September 1994.
[b] Sandra Kirsch, "Wind and Water as Business Builder," *Fortune*, 10 August 1992, 12.

---

and economic relationships. The Chinese believe that all things in the universe (the self, the family, a business, a nation) contain competing tendencies that must be balanced: an integrative tendency to seek assimilation into the greater whole and a self-assertive tendency to maintain individuality[8]. The emphasis on harmony has its roots in the Chinese people's historical need for cooperation in order to survive. In the words of Yunhu Dong, a young Communist Party member in the PRC who holds a doctorate in Western philosophy, "The West stresses personal and individual rights; we stress the need for harmony between the individual and the collective." From a business point of view, this means that any enterprise must assert its individuality in order to thrive, but it must simultaneously submit to the demands of the whole, or of society at large, in order to make the system viable.

This explains why Chinese businesses consider it vitally important to avoid upsetting the harmony of their extended communities. The son of one of the wealthiest businessmen in Hong Kong, with family assets in the billions, was asked about the business culture and inner workings of his father's business. He remarked: "If I were to spend $200 million (US) to acquire a company or make a business investment, I wouldn't have to get approval from my father. But if I wanted to sue someone, however insignificant they may seem, I would have to check with him first."[9] No one in a Chinese web of relationships is insignificant, and upsetting one member of the community—even someone you don't know personally—risks destabilizing the social network as a whole.

Recognizing this sensitivity to social harmony is key to understanding the Chinese attitude toward business performance. The big picture takes priority over the individual part, or, to draw an analogy with theater, the coordination between actors, director, and crew behind the scenes must be in perfect harmony, and all participants must share the achievement. In contrast to Western models of performance, the Chinese consider the "star" of the play not any individual actor but the whole production—the process and overall effect. Roles—which, beyond the theater, structure Chinese society at large—are written not for individual glory but for group stability and coherence. In business, the Chinese assess performance by taking a multifaceted view of a company, not analytic, piece-by-piece assessments and appraisals centered on individuals' achievements. In evaluating its business, a Chinese company is likely to ask, "Is there harmony among employees? Is everyone growing and developing along with the business? Do the members of the company see rewards being shared equally?"

By contrast, Western companies tend to stress hard indicators—net income or sales, profit margins, and earnings per share—when assessing performance. In evaluating management, Western businesses focus on factors such as employee turnover and job satisfaction. The results of such individual performance assessments have the advantage of being clear and objective, but they can reduce motivation for group harmony and cooperation unless proper reward systems are built in.

Because of its concern for social harmony, a Chinese business conglomerate will be much less willing than a Western corporation to jettison an unprofitable subsidiary. When such situations arise, the people running the conglomerate will consider their relationship to the people running the subsidiary. If the individuals who run the subsidiary have made substantial contributions to the company in the past, or have strong social ties to the company owner or leader, efforts will be made to save it. Alternatively, if the subsidiary offers the conglomerate useful positioning for future business opportunities, it will also be spared—even if this means losing money.

Similar patterns show up in relationships between companies. A firm may be willing to pay a higher price to a given supplier, for example, if that supplier is a member of its business network. Although the company may make less money on a particular deal, the understanding is that its support will be repaid in kind at a future date or in another (frequently nonmonetary) form. In other words, maximizing profits on absolutely every deal is not the highest priority for many Chinese businesses. According to Peter Woo of Hong Kong's Wharf Holdings, this means a worthwhile project won't always yield an immediate return: "You never sell things simply to dress up the profit-and-loss statement. It doesn't matter whether the payoff is coming this year or next year."[10] Indebting a partner keeps that relationship open and active well into the future.

A Holistic Time Perspective

The value of harmony in relationships is closely tied to another crucial element of the Chinese philosophical worldview—its "holistic" view of time. A long-term perspective allows events to be contextualized into a greater whole and emphasizes connections instead of isolated moments. The traditional Chinese conception of the birthday illustrates this point: At the moment of birth, a Chinese baby is already considered to be one year old because the time spent in the womb is included in a person's age. This expansive way of counting time is subtly related to a holistic, relationship-based sensibility: One's age, a component of "individual" identity, begins at a point of connection with—rather than separation from—the mother.

The Chinese holistic view of time stems in part from the country's long agricultural tradition, and the fact that until the Sun Yat-Sen Revolution of 1911, China still officially used a lunar/solar calendar to measure time. This traditional calendar is actually still in use, existing alongside the now official Gregorian calendar. Unlike

Table 5-1: Contrasting Perspectives

	Chinese	Western
Intellectual Paradigms	Holism	Analysis of parts
	Both/and	Either/or
	Paradox	Exclusive opposites
Time	Circular	Linear
	Correlation and coexistence	Causality
		Deadline-oriented
	Process-oriented	Efficiency
	Go with the flow	Future-oriented
	History and tradition	
Performance	Group harmony and shared accomplishment	Individual performance accomplishment
	Qualitative and subjective	Quantitative and objective
	People-oriented	Task-oriented
	Economic and social concerns	Economic indicators

the Gregorian calendar, which counts years in an infinite sequence, the traditional Chinese calendar measures time in 60-year cycles. This notion that time recurs was reinforced in China by the Buddhist teachings of reincarnation, according to which one may always achieve in the next life what has not been achieved in this one, and where the wrongdoings of a past existence may come to bear on the present.

From this perspective, events do not follow each other progressively, one leading to the other along a line (and each move leading *away* from the past). Rather, they unfold cyclically: Nothing is lost, gained, or surpassed, but only repeated. Success and failure occupy the top and bottom of the same cycle. The past is ever present, and the present is everything that has come to pass. The future, no matter how far away, results from actions in the present, no matter how small. In fact, in the Chinese language there are no tenses to express past and future. The three dimensions of time are always there and can be distinguished only through context.

In Chinese culture, where time is considered cyclical, events are often expressed as coexisting, rather than following each other in a

---

Box 5-4: What Time Means to the Chinese

Management researcher **Fan** Xing offers the following explanation of how the Chinese view of time diverges from the perspective taken in the West:

> Chinese are inclined toward tradition; their mindset and behavior are both significantly influenced by past cultural values. Americans, in a nation molded by change, view time as a scarce resource. They keep a daily schedule precise to almost every minute. Time to them means efficiency and movemental value, and therefore is carefully budgeted to achieve personal or organizational goals. The Chinese, based on their philosophy of life, look at time as a process of eternity. What is the point of keeping such a tight schedule? Rice will grow by seasons, not by minutes; the sun will rise day after day. What really matters is how life can be made natural and enjoyable each day. If one is always pressed by time where is the quality of life to be found? The Chinese look upon each experience as different and unique, not accumulative in a linear fashion. A frog on a lotus petal is a moment in time and beauty to contemplate and meditate upon, a thing not to be lost. According to the Chinese cultural values, the highest reward in life is the spiritual enrichment and serenity received from the contemplation of one's living environment. Time is valuable when it is used to achieve this ultimate human reward; time is flexible and repeatable regardless of how much present-day business wants to go against it.[a]

[a] **Fan Xing,** "The Chinese Cultural System: Implications for Cross-Cultural Management," *SAM Advanced Management Journal* 60, no. 1 (1995): 19–20.

---

causal chain of actions. When events are not causally linked, people have a greater consideration of possibilities because everything is, in a sense, "present." The downside of this attitude toward time is that it can, and often does, result in a lack of accountability.

Cultures that view time in a cyclical, elastic, and open-ended fashion also tend to be more group-oriented, stressing the development or preservation of relationships over task accomplishment. Since, in itself, economic success does not guarantee a comfortable social position over time, members of these cultures are rarely "single-minded," and they will pay as much (if not more) attention to personal matters as to professional ones. Business-wise, they will work simultaneously on a number of tasks, managing each one according to its own time requirements, as opposed to following a single agenda. Anthropologists have termed such cultures *polychronic*, or "many-timed," and have contrasted them with cultures that are *monochronic*, or "one-timed." The latter tend to be individualistic and analytic; their view of time is linear, compartmentalized, and deadline-based—it is taking one thing at a time.[11]

This difference has several broad implications for business. During any given workday, for example, it may appear that a Chinese manager is accomplishing less than an American counterpart. From the polychronic perspective, however, measuring performance in terms of pure output is reductive. Polychronic people will devote attention not only to the task itself but also to the people involved, the process of completing the task, and so on. If a Chinese employee is asked, "What have you accomplished today?" the answer is likely to include things other than the specific assignment at hand. For the Chinese, there can still be a target to aim at, but many targets exist at once.

From the Chinese point of view, timing and planning must remain open-ended and adaptable, especially because relationships have their own unpredictable requirements, which must be attended to as they arise. The amount of time allotted to casual and spontaneous conversations, for example, varies greatly between Chinese and Americans. Americans are less willing to improvise changes in their schedules to make time for unplanned discussions at work or in the street. The Chinese, by contrast, may arrive late for work or for a social meeting in order to accommodate such a situation. Indeed, a Chinese person may be deeply offended if a close acquaintance seems to be in a hurry to get off somewhere and cannot take the time to catch up on business and personal affairs. Schedules in the Chinese business world are therefore very different from the detailed, slotted calendars typical of American companies. It is not an exaggeration to say that while in the United States the flow of events must follow the schedule, in the Chinese context, the schedule must follow the flow of events.

Figure 5-1: Yin and Yang Symbol

The extreme of yin is yang, and the extreme of yang is yin; the combination of one yin and one yang is the way of nature and the seed of change, or "I."
—Confucius, *The I Ching, or Book of Changes*

Embracing Paradox

I learned to make my mind large, as the universe is large, so that there is room for paradoxes.[14]

—MAXINE HONG KINGSTON, *The Woman Warrior*

As the quotation from Kingston suggests, reconciling opposites can simply be a matter of taking a more expansive point of view. Indeed, the "holistic" and long-term time perspectives we have discussed so far are crucial underpinnings for another important element of the Chinese worldview: embracing paradox. As the yin and yang image reflects, the Chinese see opposites containing within them the seed of the other and together forming a dynamic unity (see Figure 5-1). For the Westerner interested in understanding the Chinese frame of mind, it is important to exchange an "either-or" framework for a paradoxical, or "and-and," framework, in which opposites are interdependent rather than mutually exclusive. The common complaint that Chinese behavior is baffling and indecisive is very often the result of misperceiving a frame of mind that embraces paradox.

When the PRC's Haier Co.'s legendary CEO **Zhang** Ruimin turned to classic Chinese texts to develop a personal and business philosophy, one of the central tenets he found in the writings of Lao Tzu was the idea of paradox: "Though all creatures under heaven are the products of Being, Being itself is the product of non-Being." The concept of paradoxical wholes is also essential in understanding Lao Tzu's joint use of *wu-wei* (yielding) and its opposite, *wu-bu-wei* (do it all); the common definition of *wu-wei* as "nonaction" overlooks this interdependence with its opposite, *wu-bu-wei*, which implies "in action."

Wei-ji (危機): *Danger-Opportunity*

Perhaps the most famous Chinese paradox can be found in the Mandarin word for "crisis," *wei-ji*. Composed of the characters for "danger" (*wei*) and "opportunity" (*ji*), *wei-ji* illustrates the profound connection the Chinese perceive between adversity and change. From the Chinese point of view, crisis appears not as an insurmountable problem but as an aspect of transformation, demonstrating how paradoxical thinking can lead to opportune action. In the late 1990s, *wei-ji* was noted by numerous economic analysts in the West as a perspective that allowed many Chinese businesses to quickly recognize and capitalize on the opportunities that surfaced in the wake of the Asian financial crisis.

The rapid business moves made by Hong Kong's First Pacific immediately following the Asian financial crisis are a case in point. Finding opportunities in the midst of danger, First Pacific refocused on its core businesses, moved into new high-growth sectors, and repositioned itself successfully as a leading Pan-Asian enterprise. Around the Asian Pacific region, scores of Chinese-owned firms— both large and small—made similar moves to take advantage of new opportunities. In Thailand, a company called United Auction found a booming new market auctioning cars that were repossessed during the crisis. United Auction has since tripled its size to become Thailand's largest auctioneer. One computer retailer saw a new opportunity in the used-PC market. During a period when the sales of new PCs dropped by 40 percent, the revenues of this company doubled in a mere seven months.[13]

K. K. Fong's I-One.Net offers another example of opportunity in the midst of crisis. In the 1980s and 1990s, Fong built a

---

Box 5-5: Hong Kong's "*Wei-ji* Hero"

Dr. Yu-Tang Cheng, head of Hong Kong's New World Development Group, has become known as the "*Wei-ji* Hero." Dr. Cheng is well known for making quick moves in times of uncertainty or economic downturn—moves that later turn out to give him tremendous advantage. During the real estate price slump of 1994–1995, Cheng moved into New York and paid the cash-poor Donald Trump $90 million for a large lot on the city's West Side, referred to as "the last piece of land in Manhattan." Cheng had seized a similar initiative in 1984 when plans for Hong Kong's repatriation to the mainland were announced. Amid fearful speculation about the island's future, Cheng purchased the site of the Hong Kong Convention Center, where the official turnover was to take place in 1997. Since then, he has made a fortune with the center and contributed to set up an Executive M.B.A. program for Canada's Richard Ivey School of Business at the University of Western Ontario. Cheng's boldness in the face of adversity has also earned him the respect of the mainland Chinese. His was the first company to reenter the PRC after the tragic events at Tiananmen Square. Today he is esteemed in Guangdong, the site of his business activities, as the nonmainland Chinese businessman who cared most about the PRC.[a]

[a] *China Times Magazine* (in Chinese), July 31–August 6, 1994, 12–16.

---

small printing shop, Xpress Print, into one of the world's largest printers of time-sensitive financial research reports. In the wake of the Asian financial crisis, however, research reports were one of the first costs that firms cut, and Fong's business fell by 50 percent. Rather than scaling back, however, Fong took the aggressive approach of reconceptualizing his business. Changing the company name to I-One.Net, Fong began spinning off into a variety of Internet businesses. His goal, he says, is to become the Asian version of Yahoo![14]

Taking Fast-Slow Action (快慢有節)

Articles covering East-West business interactions typically discuss perspectives on time as differences between "long-term" and "short-term" orientations, the former characterizing Chinese business dealings, the latter, Western. These terms are often associated with the idea of slow versus quick action. In fact, a long-term orientation can encompass both fast and slow action. The quick-thinking characteristic of *wei-ji* can only occur in the context of a more holistic, or long-term, view. This view could be summed up as acting when "the time is right"—whether this means waiting patiently or acting swiftly to seize opportunity. As Jack Ma, the CEO of Alibaba.com, the largest B2B Internet company in China, summarized: "One must run as fast as a rabbit, but be as patient as a turtle."[15]

Many Chinese businesspeople are practical and entrepreneurial and can act swiftly. One of the reasons they make cash transactions, for example, is to keep open the possibility of executing pressing deals and making fast decisions. Moreover, the flexibility and smaller size of many Chinese companies allow for opportunistic thinking and quick action, and thus set them apart from larger competitors. According to a spokesperson for a Taiwanese electronics company, "We are not in a position to set standards and take huge risks, but we have the capacity to develop leading-edge products faster and at lower cost than our competitors—here or overseas—once standards are set."[16]

Indeed, the ability to combine patience with speed is one of the greatest strengths of traditional Chinese businesses. Examples abound of companies that wait until a market ripens and then move in quickly to take advantage of opportunities. When Taiwan's Alex Hung founded Sunonwealth Electric Machine Industry in 1980 to build miniaturized cooling fans for computer-calculators, the big manufacturers of the day—IBM, Siemens, and Olivetti—could not be bothered with the savings he offered them. So Hung waited until the 1990s, when competition increased in the computer manufacturing business and manufacturers saw a greater need for the kind of savings Sunonwealth could offer. Hung moved back into the market quickly, and by 1997 Sunonwealth was posting $5.5 million in after-tax profits, up 92 percent from the previous year, and its fans were being used in most of the computers manufactured in Taiwan.

In the case of the Asian financial crisis, too, a *combination* of fast and slow action helped many companies find opportunities: The cyclical view of time allowed Chinese businesses to take a healthy perspective on the crisis and to see the event not in linear terms, as an "end-of-the-line" catastrophe, but as an inevitable part of a revolving cycle. At the same time, their patient perspective did not translate into resignation or complacency but instead generated short-term strategies for quickly seizing opportunity-in-crisis. The short-term capability of Chinese businesses is an important "opposite" to combine with their long-term view in order to gain a "holistic" perspective on Chinese business time and timing, and to help make sense of the seemingly paradoxical strategies of many Chinese businesses.

Conclusion: Keeping Your Balance

One of the key elements of the "middle way" philosophy is the search for a balance between the self and the other. The two are not diametrically opposed but are elements that combine to form a greater whole. This philosophy is also particularly useful for thinking about globalization and East-West relations, for unless one has a deep appreciation of one's own culture and tradition, whether it is 200 or 5,000 years old, one cannot fully appreciate and respect another culture. Indeed, when developing a global point of view, it is imperative to start from one's own perspective and beliefs before looking to understand the other.

The concept of self-other integration has broad implications not only because it is useful for understanding Chinese business behavior but also because it is an opportunity for self-reflection. We often overlook the generic truths that span time and bridge the multiple levels of life, as well as different aspects of our own lives and careers. We lose the ability to see relationships and to apply what we learn in one setting to another. This kind of fragmentation constrains our potential and unbalances our lives.

Indeed, overly narrow and real-time business and professional concerns can sometimes consume too much of our energy, and we begin to lose perspective on time and performance. As an antidote to this tendency, I like to keep in mind the story of the master who tutored me in Chinese philosophy and classics over twenty years ago. His balanced, holistic outlook grows out of his long-term view of time and performance—and thus provides a fitting conclusion to this chapter. A highly respected Chinese intellectual, my master has written several unpublished works that could offer significant contributions to Chinese literature and history. In spite of his personal and scholarly reputation and the promise of his work, this ninety-three-year-old teacher steadfastly refuses to allow his work to be published while he is still alive. His desire is to let history be the judge of his work, which, if it is published after his death, will have to stand or fall on its own merits. In his view, achieving professional recognition or glory during his lifetime is unimportant; the accomplishment of true value is that his ideas should stand the test of time.

6

PUTTING VALUES INTO PRACTICE
Competing Indirectly

American basketball teams usually start a game with their best players. The Chinese often adopt a different strategy. Depending on their opponent, they may begin a match with their second-string players and wait until later in the game to use their star athletes for advantageous mismatches or surprise attacks.

As UNDERDOGS or latecomers in global markets, Chinese businesses have often had to adjust their game plans to compete with their much stronger or more firmly established Western rivals. Chinese tactical and strategic choices, in many cases, have been strongly influenced by their competitors' relative economic strengths and market positions. Because Chinese companies have had to catch up with these stronger global players, they have quickly assimilated Western competitive concepts and analytical tools (such as Michael Porter's five forces model and Prahalad and Hamel's core competence[1]), and it may appear that, in the strategy sphere, traditional Chinese values and approaches are being completely displaced. But market contingencies are not the only determinants of Chinese competitive choices. Even in the midst of powerful global influences, Chinese businesses continue to rely on a few of their own core ideas about business competition.

Even when Chinese do adopt Western management and strategy practices, they are likely to apply their own style, one of the most salient features of which is low-key behavior. As we have seen in earlier chapters, the Chinese—who continue to be influenced by the ideas of Confucius and other ancient philosophers—tend to deflect attention from the self to preserve harmony and balance, whether this means finding subtle or less offensive ways of saying no, giving credit to others, or contextualizing individual accomplishments in a wider, long-term time frame.

If maintaining a low profile is a Chinese cultural value, the use of an indirect strategy is its manifestation in business competition. In fact, the indirectness that characterizes much of the thinking and practice in Chinese business might be seen as an attempt to balance the economic necessity of competition with the philosophical and social value of maintaining harmony. This chapter will begin by considering the Chinese preference for maintaining a low profile— in both personal and business spheres—and then move to some of the indirect strategies that characterize Chinese business competition.

Low Profile: From Personal Virtue to Business Practice

In *The Book of Means*, Confucius promotes modesty as a way to achieve personal growth: "The superior man acts in a way such that he conceals himself, yet every day gains in stature. The inferior man shows himself and every day loses stature." Holistic principles dictate that all things in life—goodness, success, failure, and so on—are inseparable from their opposites; accordingly, as discussed earlier, the Chinese consider the wisest path to be one that maintains a balance between extremes, or that follows a "middle way." Thus, modesty acts as a counterweight to success or, as an old Chinese saying grimly cautions: "The success of a general rests on mountains of soldiers' bones."

Following this line of thinking, the Chinese tend to deflect attention from themselves, a habit that contrasts sharply with some tendencies common in the West. The Chinese idea of one's birthday offers a telling example. "Birthday" in Chinese is often referred to as the "mother's extreme day of suffering"—an acknowledgment of the pain and labor the mother endured to bring the child into the world. Some traditional Chinese do not even celebrate their own birthdays;

Box 6-1: Tall Trees Experience Strong Winds[a]

Robert Kuok is a Chinese-Malaysian tycoon who runs the Shangri-La luxury hotel chain and the Hong Kong–based diversified company the Kerry
Group. While Kuok is clearly powerful and respected enough to be chosen as Coca-Cola's partner, his prominent status is belied by his low-key
style and demeanor. "I adapt like a chameleon to the particular society
where I am operating at the moment," he explains; and even his competitors note "he is a local everywhere he goes." Kuok's humble disposition makes him wary of many of the business egos he encounters. "When
I hear somebody's got an M.B.A. I have a feeling of dread," he remarks,
"because normally, they come to me with an overpompous sense of their
own importance." Kuok's skepticism of such attitudes comes from his
awareness of the pitfalls of a prideful and "successful" stature. One of his
favorite sayings is "Tall trees experience strong winds"—in other words,
"a highly successful man invites many problems and miseries."

[a] Andrew Tanzer, "The Amazing Mr. Kuok," *Forbes*, 28 July 1997, 90–96.

---

instead they make sure to call their mother on this day! In many
respects, the Chinese birthday is not a celebration of the individual
but an occasion for sharing credit with others.

While ostentation and materialism are certainly not unknown
among the Chinese, many (and especially the older generations) will
try to downplay affluence and business success through an appearance of thrift and frugality. (An old Chinese proverb says "The divine
dragon exhibits its head but never its tail.") Indeed, it is not uncommon to hear Western businesspeople comment that the people they
do business with look as though they have "slept in their clothes" and
have "a very humble demeanor." Despite "controlling 10,000 people
and 30 factories that do over a billion dollars a year,"[2] your Chinese
host might insist on carrying your bags and placing you in a limo,
while he rides in a minivan. Yue-Che Wang, the head of Taiwan's
Formosa Plastics Group, is a case in point. He actually has to be
tricked into getting new clothes. His wife waits until he is out of
town, sneaks an old suit out of the closet, and replaces it with a new
one before Wang comes home.[3]

The Chinese preference for a low profile—at both the individual

---

Box 6-2: The Invisible CEO

Foreigners entering Chinese markets will do well to remember that high
visibility may be perceived as arrogance or insensitivity. A more prudent
tactic may be to adopt a low profile, a route chosen by some informed
Westerners who have come to do business in Asia. A recent example is
John Olds, a New Yorker who became the first non-Singaporean to head
a major government-linked firm, the Development Bank of Singapore.
According to the *Far Eastern Economic Review*, Olds rapidly gained the
reputation of being a mystery man: "Though DBS has been making head-
lines with its regional acquisitions, its new head has assiduously avoided
publicity. In August, Olds tiptoed into town so quietly that two months
later some investors were asking whether he had arrived yet. He hasn't
held a single press conference, and has only recently begun to meet
investors."[a]

[a] Ben Dolven, "Offshore Ambitions," *Far East Economic Review*, 4 February 1999,
<http://www.feer/com/9902_04/p42banking.html> (accessed 20 December 1999).

---

and the enterprise level—has philosophical but also strong historical
roots. In the People's Republic, before the open door policy of 1979,
the communist government actively discouraged the accumulation
and display of wealth. During the Cultural Revolution of the 1960s
and 1970s, landowners were the target of purges conducted by
leftist forces, and were severely punished as the Red Guards looted
their houses and labeled them "right-wing" and "antirevolutionary."
Today, the 40,000-plus Taiwanese companies currently operating
within China remain especially discreet because of the political
tension between mainland China and Taiwan.

Elsewhere in Southeast Asia, the Chinese have faced persecution
and other difficulties, as ethnic minorities controlling vast amounts
of wealth in often-poor countries. Historically, the overseas Chinese
have been the target of racism and economic resentment—as the
anti-Chinese riots in Malaysia in 1969 and in Indonesia in the 1990s
tragically proved—and so it is clearly to their advantage to hide the
extent of their fortunes. In these economies, the low-profile approach
also confers a distinct business advantage since it enables the
Chinese to protect their wealth through tight and opaque family
holdings of assets. These complex networks of interfamily cross-

holdings protect the businesses from local governments and disguise the true extent of their wealth. Indeed, the low profile of many Chinese businesses may mean a "low transparency" to business outsiders. Kent Chan, an analyst at Salomon Brothers, is used to untangling webs of business subsidiaries, but he admits that most Chinese family businesses are too complicated to analyze and that the real value of a Chinese business is next to impossible to assess.

An emphasis on low profile means that the capital sources of Chinese firms also remain well hidden, and this concealment is facilitated by their widespread use of cash in business transactions. Cash is a convenient and circumspect financial vehicle well suited to the internal capital markets of *guanxi* networks. In the 1990s a group of Taiwanese investors highlighted this practice when it acquired several hotel chains in the United States—using $2 billion in cash.

The tradition of strategic concealment is coming under increasing scrutiny as Westerners demand standardization in local business practices. However, Westerners should not take every example of opacity as a sign of illicit concealment; they should remember that low visibility is a Chinese cultural preference based on historical experience. With respect to the sharing of information, there is a clear distinction between a low-profile company and a secretive company trying to conceal its activities. The former will make information available upon request; the latter will simply withhold it.

Another business manifestation of the Chinese tendency toward maintaining a low profile can be seen in the industries in which they have historically chosen to operate. Indeed, the Chinese have generally avoided mass-market, high-profile consumer goods businesses. Instead, overseas Chinese business families have historically focused on sectors such as land, banking, hotels, construction, textiles and finance. Land and property development accounts for more than 20 percent of the top 500 ethnic Chinese–controlled public companies.[4] Although this situation has changed somewhat in the wake of the Asian financial crisis (in which the property market was most severely affected), Chinese businesses still tend toward industries that require less sophisticated marketing and little brand promotion. Relative to their Korean or Japanese counterparts, Chinese companies have significantly fewer high-profile global brands. Taiwanese companies, for instance, now occupy a dominant—but

---

Box 6-3: Cultural Dilemma: Transparency

My company maintains very open relationships with shareholders. Our Chinese joint venture partner, however, is reluctant to be so open and forthcoming with outside parties. What should I do?

Options and Observations

Recognize first that the degree of transparency in communicating information to company shareholders (and other stakeholders such as the general public) is traditionally much more conservative among Chinese companies. Until recently, for example, it was not uncommon for a company to maintain several sets of accounts: one for internal use, one for taxation agencies, and a third for shareholders, following the advice of another Chinese proverb: "The sly rabbit hides in three lairs."

But attitudes toward transparency and the disclosure of information are changing in China and throughout Southeast Asia. Nonetheless, since your partner is likely to have a more traditional attitude toward the issue, you may consider several approaches to encourage the partner to be forthcoming:

- Cite examples where other domestic companies in China are holding themselves to higher standards of transparency.

- Reference the accounting and standards-setting organizations in China; they are actively seeking to promote high levels of transparency.

- Stress the business rationale for maintaining a high level of transparency. Resistance to a more open approach is often neutralized when the partner recognizes the correlation between investment risk, perceptions of the overall investment environment, and transparency.

The traditional Chinese method of assessing business risk has depended on *guanxi*: To know the partner is to know the risk. But this approach has been evolving over time, particularly as China enters multilateral organizations such as the World Trade Organization, and as openness promises a business benefit—especially when foreign investment is involved.

---

almost invisible—position in the global PC business. Instead of involving themselves in the heavily advertised and brand intensive PC market itself, they have concentrated on the lower-profile peripheral industries, manufacturing monitors, keyboards, scanners, and so forth. While there are several reasons for this disparity (smaller size, limited geographic focus, etc.), the Chinese tendency to avoid high visibility plays a role in explaining the scarcity of well-known Chinese brands.

Understanding the low-profile disposition may also shed light on the Chinese attitude toward market share. From the Chinese point of view, it is not necessarily desirable to seize the maximum overall market share. Rather, their goal traditionally has been to obtain and maintain a profitable share in a specific segment— one that does not attract too much attention. The reasoning is that if a company can maintain a solid profit margin or liquidity in a local, fortified market, there is little incentive to expand into the more visible (and hence more competitive) global market. The success of overseas Chinese business demonstrates, of course, that the Chinese do not object to becoming rich and powerful. However, in general, a Chinese company would prefer a smaller but reliable market to a larger and less stable one. In a way, this attitude stands the Boston Consulting Group's famed matrix on its head, since a Chinese business may pay as much management attention to its "cash cows" and "dogs" as it does to its "stars" and "problem children."

The "Invisible" Competitor

One Chinese company takes the low-profile market share strategy to what a Western business might consider an extreme level. Aware that the global giant Procter & Gamble (P&G) religiously tracks the top ten consumer products companies in the markets in which it competes, this Chinese company (which prefers to remain unidentified—even here) has made it an important strategy never to rise higher than number eleven in the rankings of PRC consumer products firms. This company's decision to deliberately avoid the top-ten list contradicts some deeply ingrained Western values. The very notion of a top-ten list, in fact, carries symbolic importance in the Western competitive mind-set. While the practical difference between a number ten or eleven ranking is often negligible, Americans tend to invest more prestige in such numerical cut-

---

Box 6-4: "We're Number Two": A Cross-Cultural Joke and a Western Ad with a "Chinese" Style

World-class chefs from different countries are asked to critique their own food. The American chef boasts, "My cooking is so good, it tastes as if it were made by the best chef in France." The French chef allows that his own cooking is "exquisite. Only a Frenchman could make something so perfect." The British chef admits, "We don't know how to cook. I recommend serving this meal with five or more warm beers." Finally, the Chinese chef evaluates his performance: "I am a terrible cook. People honor me by being willing to eat something so mediocre."

Avis, the number two car-rental company in the United States, behind Hertz, has a famous marketing slogan—"We try harder!"—a motto that would sit well with the Chinese mentality. Instead of emphasizing its high-ranking status, the Avis ad calls attention to the company's continuing humble efforts to improve.

---

offs (one need look no further than the deluge of top-ten rankings of everything from colleges to athletes to "most admired companies").

Of course, in many ways the Chinese are acutely conscious of ranking and status, and they will fight tenaciously for "number one," but it is precisely at the more arbitrary juncture between number ten and number eleven where cultural differences may influence competitive behavior. A top-ten ranking will attract attention and status, but it is also sure to attract competitors. Faced with a choice between a slight increase in symbolic prestige and a real competitive advantage, the Chinese will usually opt for the latter.

The number eleven approach exemplifies one of the ways in which one Chinese business has incorporated a low profile into its competitive strategy. The following sections will examine Chinese competitive strategy in more detail, on a continuum starting with modes of nonengagement and moving to Chinese alternatives to head-to-head conflict. To maintain a low profile and minimize conflict, the Chinese prefer to avoid direct competition; if competition is inevitable, they prefer to engage it indirectly.

Avoiding Head-to-Head Confrontation

The renowned Chinese military strategist Sun Tzu insisted, "The worst form of generalship is to conquer the enemy by besieging walled cities." He made "bloodless battle" (or "winning without fighting") the centerpiece of his strategies and argued that the optimum form of competition is "to conquer the enemy without resorting to war."[5] This line of thinking has continued to have significant influence on Chinese thought. Instead of courtroom litigation, price wars, and hostile takeovers—situations in which one or both parties suffer losses, and victory is achieved only at great social or economic cost—the Chinese tend to look for ways in which they can fly under the radar screen and avoid costly battles.

Unattended Niches and Unexplored Markets

One sure way of avoiding costly competition is to choose a market where there are no competitors.[6] The Chinese, both on the mainland and overseas, have been particularly adept at identifying, developing, and protecting profitable but underserviced niches. The PRC's Changhong Electronic Company, for example, established a critical foothold in a market no other company valued: the remote Sichuan Province. This area in the southwest of mainland China is far from the commercial centers in the East. While other businesses avoided the region, managers at Changhong used the location to their advantage, calculating that its geographic isolation would discourage competitors. Their strategy proved successful, and after it became a leader in the southwest, Changhong went on to become the largest manufacturer of televisions in China, with a 25 percent market share in 1999.[7]

Overseas Chinese businesses have also been known for their early exploitation of unattended markets, from the cement industry in Indonesia to the sugar market in Malaysia to the rice business in Thailand. Often, Chinese companies have taken advantage of untapped markets well ahead of their opponents, and they enjoy near monopolies as a result of these early initiatives. Many Taiwanese companies, which entered Vietnam in the early 1990s, were able to secure strong market positions before competitors arrived. In the late 1990s, for example, Taiwanese companies' cumulative invest-ments in Vietnam were 50 percent higher than those of all the European Union Countries, and three times higher than the total investment of either Japan or the United States.[8]

While many Western firms regard Africa as too politically risky to give satisfactory returns, PRC enterprises have been quietly estab-lishing footholds in several countries there. Huawei Technology, for example, is one of China's largest and fastest-growing manufactur-ers of fixed-line telecommunication switching equipment; it has attained this position by focusing on neglected rural areas in China and other developing countries. Huawei is already establishing itself on the African continent, having developed "integrated solutions that are modern, reasonably priced, and compatible with the African population."[9]

Converting Competition into Collaboration

Another way in which the Chinese have managed to avoid con-frontation is by turning potentially competitive situations into oppor-tunities for collaboration. Instead of seeing opponents in absolute terms, the Chinese look for ways that common ground can become part of competitive strategy. In the Chinese way of thinking, compe-tition and collaboration are simply two sides of the same coin—not diametrically opposed activities. The mainland's Legend Computer, a well-known local firm that has fended off much more powerful multinational corporations (MNCs) in the market, offers an example of a company that has taken advantage of the interests it shares with its rivals—even as it competes with them. Legend is the largest com-puter company in China, with a 26 percent market share in year 2000, well ahead of formidable competitors like Compaq, Dell, IBM, NEC, and Hewlett-Packard. But despite intense competition with these foreign companies, Legend is working with rivals like IBM to tailor that company's software to the China market, then prein-stalling it on Legend PCs.[10] It is also working with IBM to develop software for China's telecommunications, finance, and aviation sec-tors. In the words of D. C. Chien, general manager of distribution for IBM's Greater China Group, "On the one hand, we compete with Legend. But on the other hand they are our second-largest partner in

---

Box 6-5: Cultural Dilemma: How Close Is Too Close?

When partnering with a Chinese firm, how can we be sure we're not becoming involved in antitrust activities?

Options and Observations

Fair competition issues may arise in the context of traditional Chinese approaches to business relationships. Collusion, for example, is not usually perceived as a negative or illicit act.

It is important to be careful in forging alliances with competitors to ensure that the approach taken is consistent with global fair competition laws. Although legislation exists within China that declares such business practice illegal, enforcement is lax. Therefore, Western companies must be careful in the alliances they forge and must remain aware of the activities and strategies of their Chinese counterparts.

China."[11] For the Chinese, the ultimate good is a win-win situation, and this ideal receives more than lip service.

Because of their culture's emphasis on relationships and networks, the Chinese are more likely than their Western counterparts to "make peace" through cooperation. Of course, this close cooperation may contain troubling implications: What the Chinese see as collaboration, others may regard as collusion. Chinese companies' cooperation with their competitors in certain situations may raise regulatory concerns for a Western company. And just as they may avoid "bloody" confrontations (or capitalize on opportunities) with competitors, Chinese businesses tend to take a more conciliatory stance toward governments in the countries where they operate. They often seek to avoid conflicts with local officials out of a general respect for authority, and because the costs of conflict could be substantial. Again, what the Chinese call harmony, others may interpret as submissiveness. Indeed, certain Chinese businesses have been criticized for their unnecessary or unjustified compliance with local regimes or for uncritically accepting the policies and prohibitions of underdeveloped or restrictive governments. "Compliance" can periodically cross over into such misconduct as bribery.[12] For better or worse, though, the Chinese have traditionally deferred to local authorities for the same reasons that they often seek to team up with competitors—to avoid the casualties of head-to-head confrontation.

Redefining the Battlefield

In the business world, bloodless triumph is often difficult to achieve, and it goes without saying that Chinese companies engage in competition all the time. If they cannot fight on "enemy-less" battlefields like unattended niche markets or remain otherwise invisible to their competitors, the Chinese look for ways to redefine the battlefield or redirect the activities of their competitors. There are several ways in which the Chinese have been successful at shifting the center of conflict to their advantage. One method is to take a circuitous route to their goal. Rather than approach a target head-on, the Chinese may take incremental steps toward it, and look for alternative paths with less resistance—detours that will attract minimal attention. Another tactic is to redirect the energies of the rival company and then take advantage of the market left unattended by the diversion. Finally, by paying attention to the context of competition, the Chinese have found ways of capitalizing on their own strengths and setting the terms for competition.

Strategic Detours

A strategic detour is a way of approaching a target indirectly. The tactic requires small steps on a roundabout path toward a long-term goal; it is a more patient, more discreet approach, one without the immediate gratification, glory, and fireworks of a high-profile competitive showdown where the winner takes all.

Two Chinese companies—the Haier Group and Acer Computers—exemplify the strategic detour approach. The Haier Group, the PRC's largest home appliance conglomerate, is now taking a circuitous route toward its ultimate goal of establishing itself as the leader in developing countries. One of the nation's largest manufacturers of refrigerators and air conditioners, Haier has had remarkable success in the United States, capturing (by its own reckoning) 20 percent of the small-refrigerator market. Rather than competing

head-on against GE, Philips, and Matsushita, Haier carefully targeted the low-price, high-quality appliance market segment, which
has been unattended by the bigger companies. However, Haier's real
goal is not the mature competitive markets of the United States and
Europe. **Wang** Yingmin, a company director, explains: "[O]ur strategy is to sell first in developed countries and then developing ones.
If we can make it in mature markets against such well-known companies as GE, Philips and Matsushita, then we can certainly make it
in developing countries. . . ."[13] It is an unusual strategy, but the
lessons that Haier learns through competing in Western markets
will likely prove extremely valuable when it moves into the developing markets it covets.

Stan Shih, chairman and CEO of the Acer Group, follows the
same strategy but in the opposite direction. Acer first moved into the
Third World, then used its success there as a strategic platform for
penetrating the industrialized countries. Shih explains Acer's success with a military analogy: winning the countryside as a means for
surrounding and taking over the city. In this case the "countryside"
corresponds to the emerging Asian and Latin American markets
such as the Philippines and Mexico. The company became a dominant player in these countries and then used its position there to
attack the more Industrialized markets- the "suburbs," including
Germany and Australia. Finally, Acer penetrated the "city," or the
primary markets—including the United States. On the product
front, Acer followed a similar path, from original equipment manufacturer to assembler of mainline PCs.[14]

Misdirecting Competitors

Another military tactic recommended by Sun Tzu is to "Make noise
in the East and attack in the West." One of the more sophisticated of
Chinese competitive tactics is the shaping of competition through
the subtle, judo-like redirection of competitors' energies. Rather
than regarding competition as a game of checkers—in which players
exchange a series of sequential moves, anticipating and reacting to
one another's responses—the Chinese tend to regard competition as
a game of chess, beginning with a strategy that is intended not just

to anticipate but actually to influence the opponent's actions.[15] A variety of tactics can be used for this purpose. A firm may mislead its competitor about its interest in a given market by making highly visible moves in another market. It may also throw competitors off the scent by conspicuously retreating from a market in which it remains intensely interested, then, once its competitors have let down their guard, quietly but forcefully reentering that market, thereby staying one step ahead of opponents and keeping them off balance.

A recent case of competition in the Hong Kong grocery industry offers an example of redirected or misdirected competition. The two major players in the grocery business are Park'n Shop, which has a 35 percent share of the $2.4 billion grocery market, and is owned by Li Ka-Shing's Hutchinson Whampoa, and Wellcome (with a 30 percent market share, owned by Jardine Matheson's Dairy Farm Business). When Hong Kong–based adMart launched an attack on these two companies by offering an online grocery service, both rivals chose to respond, not by a direct counterattack on adMart's grocery business, but by taking aim at the newspaper business of Jimmy Lai (the owner of adMart), pulling ads from his publications business within the Next Media Group. This forced Jimmy Lai to divert his attention and resources from his initial attack on the grocery market and slow down his expansion pace to repair the damage in the other part of his business empire.[16]

Of course, influencing a competitor's action through redirection is not exclusively a Chinese business practice. It can be seen in any number of non-Chinese business examples as well. One Nike-Reebok confrontation offers an illustration. In the 1990s, Nike's "Air Jordan" shoe was a dominant player in the twelve- to seventeen-year-old age segment. When Reebok made a run at this market with the "Kamikaze Kemp," Nike directed its resources toward this market, introducing the "Air Jordan XI." Having diverted Nike's attention and resource commitment toward the twelve- to seventeen-year-old market, Reebok then effectively introduced the "Shaq Attack," which carved out a new niche in the eight- to twelve-year-old segment.[17]

While all business cultures occasionally indulge in attempts to misdirect competitors, Chinese business has formalized them into a series of competitive ploys, known as "The Thirty-Six Stratagems."[18]

Box 6-6: Competitive Asymmetry: A to B ≠ B to A

An important part of misdirecting competitors involves recognizing competitive asymmetry. What your competitors think of you may actually be more important than what you think of them.[a] Sometimes companies may even ignore rivals with whom they are in direct competition.

For instance, when Scott McNealy, the CEO of Sun Microsystems, was asked to name his competitors, he mentioned Digital Equipment, Hewlett Packard, and IBM. What about NCR? he was asked. "We never see them," he said.[b] At this time, NCR was the U.S.'s fifth largest computer manufacturer, twice the size of Sun Microsystems.

While actively misdirecting competitors can be an important strategic maneuver, sometimes your competitors may *already* be mis- or redirected due to their different perceptions of their rivals and/or their differing organizational structures and strategic concerns. Recognizing such asymmetries can expose vulnerabilities in a rival and open up opportunities for competitive exploitation.

The PRC's Legend computers may have gained some advantage from its Western rivals' "asymmetrical" assumptions: While Legend was clearly focused on its key competition, many of Legend's Western competitors initially did not acknowledge the possibility that a Chinese high-tech firm could compete at their level after such a short period of time. The were misdirected because they were still focused on who they perceived to be their key competitors: Western and Japanese firms. This asymmetry in competitive perception between Legend and Western firms gave Legend room to focus on important areas of the value chain (distribution, personal selling, service, and so on).

[a] Ming-Jer Chen, "Competitor Analysis and Interfirm Rivalry: Toward a Theoretical Integration," *Academy of Management Review* 21, no. 1 (1996): 100–134.

[b] J. R. Wilke, "Push into PC's: NCR Is Revamping Its Computer Lines in Wrenching Change," *Wall Street Journal*, 20 June 1990.

Competition in Context: Remembering Where You Are

A final way in which the Chinese have redefined the competitive battlefield is by emphasizing the context of a given engagement. Sun Tzu remarked, "Water retains no constant shape. In warfare, there are no constant conditions." Each competitive encounter, in other words, must be examined in its own right. Historically, Chinese busi-

---

Box 6-7:   The Importance of Context: Western MNCs in China

The experiences of two pairs of competitors in the PRC offer insights into the importance of a competitive strategy that accounts for local context.

Initially, Coca-Cola was not well accepted by Chinese consumers because it looked and tasted like a Chinese herbal medicine. Therefore, instead of pushing its cola product, the company focused on marketing its other soft-drink lines, Sprite and Fanta. Chinese women preferred Sprite to Coke, and Chinese people liked to mix it with beer or red wine. Once the company had established a foothold with Sprite, it was able to parlay customers' familiarity with its brand of products into greater sales of its cola. By the late 1990s, the Coke-to-Sprite sales ratio in China was four to three. By contrast, Pepsi's focus on its flagship cola product caused it to overlook the importance of Chinese customers' preferences—a factor that Coca-Cola accounted for and incorporated into its strategy.

Anheuser-Busch, the company that owns Budweiser, carefully studied the Chinese market before entering it, recognizing that Chinese consumers are very different than U.S. consumers. In China, 70 percent of premium beer is consumed in restaurants and bars, while only 30 percent is consumed at home. The main reason for this disparity is that Chinese are much more likely to order premium beer when they are out entertaining friends and businesspeople, and when they do, they prefer large bottles to share as a sign of courtesy and friendship. Furthermore, aluminum cans are twice as expensive as bottles in China. Accordingly, Anheuser-Busch produced Budweiser in twenty-two-ounce glass bottles, accommodating the needs of Chinese consumers. On the other hand, when Miller, the number two beer in the United States after Budweiser, launched its sales in China in 1992, the beer was available only in cans. The company discontinued its effort in 1994. In 1996, Miller reintroduced its product in large bottles, but it was still unable to compete with its by then well-established rival.[a]

[a] Rick Yan, "Short-Term Results: The Litmus Test for Success in China," *Harvard Business Review* 76, no. 5 (September–October 1998): 64–68.

---

nesses have understood that competitive advantage is relative and temporary, and that an individual business's strengths and weaknesses always depend on the competitive environment and on the other players active in this environment. Both the overseas Chinese and their cousins on the mainland have become accustomed to rapid, unpredictable political and economic change. Economic

Table 6-1: Contrasting Competitive Perspectives

Chinese	Western
Indirect competition	Direct competition
Low profile	High visibility
Incremental gains	Winner-takes-all
Finesse	Strength/force
Avoidance of destructive confrontation	Head-to-head combat
Competition and collaboration as two sides of the same coin	Competition and collaboration as opposed concepts
Niche- and local context–focused	Broad-based and overall market dominance
Risk-averse	Prone to take bigger risks
Privacy	Transparent flow of information

necessity and philosophical background have prepared Chinese firms to cope with such uncertainties, making them sensitive and adaptable to changing market conditions.

Very often, local companies' familiarity with the *guoqi*, or "ethos," of the locality can give them an advantage over a larger multinational firm. In a short period of time, for example, Legend overtook all its major global competitors in the PRC computer market. One important factor in its ascent was its successful marketing campaign, including a now well-known ad that appealed directly to the Chinese family-oriented sensibility: the commercial showed a Chinese *family* playing in front of a Legend computer! Similarly, Shanghai Jiahua outcompeted such global rivals as Procter & Gamble by appealing to local culture in its product development. The name of its perfume "Liushen," for example, refers to the "six spirits" that many Chinese customers believe determine the health of the body.[19]

Conclusion: A New (In)direction for Competitive Strategy

In many ways, the traditional Chinese penchant for maintaining a low profile is changing. As increasing prosperity erases memories of hardship, displays of materialism are no longer unusual for the Chinese living in urban centers, and they coexist with the more traditional emphasis on thrift. In Hong Kong and Taiwan, for instance, business tycoons and their families have few reservations about showing off their wealth by driving around in luxury cars, wearing designer jewelry and clothes, and throwing extravagant parties. Likewise, at the enterprise level, the necessary quest for marketing and promotion has brought a shift in the traditional low-profile approach to business. One symptom is the steady trend toward the creation of Chinese branded products—especially on the mainland, where Chinese consumers have shown a preference for local brands of certain consumer goods such as small appliances.[20]

Changing global dynamics are sure to put increasing pressure on traditional Chinese business theories and practices. In an increasingly globalized market, unattended niches will become rarer, Chinese and Western companies will continue to expand into each other's territory, and more and more Chinese businesses will be forced into head-to-head competition. While some Chinese companies will deviate from traditional business practices, many will continue to operate with traditional directives. Their approaches and values may clash with the demands of the new global reality, and may present Chinese business with unprecedented difficulties. Nevertheless, these businesses will continue to gain advantages by approaching competitive situations from an "outsider" perspective. As we have seen in this chapter, the benefits of competing "unconventionally" (by prevailing Western standards) can be numerous and unexpected.

For Westerners, understanding this "outsider" perspective may enable them both to anticipate the moves of their Chinese competitors, and to help them reap its benefits. As business interactions increase around the globe, Chinese outlooks can provide managers with valuable alternatives to their own long-held assumptions about business competition and strategy. Instead of the direct approach, which still holds powerful sway over the Western mind-set, managers might expand their own strategic repertoires by considering means of "indirect competition": winning without fighting, approaching goals sequentially, capitalizing on unattended opportunities, or lowering visibility. Understanding an "opponent's" strategic mind-set can also provide the flexibility for seeing a competitive engagement in a different light—and for turning a potentially damaging rivalry into a mutually productive opportunity.

7

NEVER SAY "NO"
Communicating with the Chinese

Traditional Chinese writing runs from the top of the page to the bottom, while the Western writing system runs from left to right. When Chinese people are reading traditional texts, it looks as though they are nodding their heads and saying "Yes, Yes." When Westerners are reading, they appear to be shaking their heads and saying "No, No."

COMMUNICATION PROBLEMS can ruin business deals even before they have reached the table, and Western expatriate managers working in Asia report that communication is their number one problem.[1] Similarly, Chinese managers have noted that "conflicts occur every day" with foreign managers because of different communication styles. In the Chinese context, where business is fundamentally a matter of building relationships, effective communication is absolutely critical to business success. While most Western business cultures treat communication as an exchange of information (and communication ends when the deal is over), Chinese business culture considers it an inseparable part of building—and maintaining—business relationships.

Understanding the role- and relationship-based nature of Chinese communication is essential to doing business with the Chinese, both overseas and in the PRC. This chapter aims to provide an understanding of Chinese communication in a broader social and cultural framework. The first part of the chapter draws attention to the highly contextual emphasis in Chinese communication: the importance of social roles, of nonverbal language, and of *mianzi*, or face. The second part focuses on the linguistic ambiguity of *yes* and *no* and offers some tips for understanding what the Chinese may *really* mean when they answer your questions.

Communication in Context

Communication is not simply a transparent exchange of information with pragmatic ends but a highly nuanced and culturally encoded form of interaction. Indeed, all communication takes place within a cultural context. In the business world, this means that having a translator present at meetings is essential for beginning a dialogue but not enough to ensure complete understanding. Behind every act of communication is a series of cultural codes that inflect, supplement, or even substitute for the purely verbal aspect of speech.[2]

The degree to which communication depends on its cultural context varies across societies. According to Hall and Hall, Chinese society is a "high-context" culture, where a message can be properly understood only in relation to its environment or "context," including a wide array of variables such as gestures, tone, social hierarchy, and background information. By contrast, the authors consider American society—and, to an even greater extent, German and Swiss societies—as "low-context": The main source of information in an exchange is the content of what is said, and not what is implied or suggested by other means.[3]

It follows, then, that American society would also be highly legalistic, since law epitomizes "low-context" communication in that it details only literal aspects of its message, leaving little to context. In North American business, this is reflected in the sanctity of the contract, without which it is virtually impossible to imagine negotiating and sealing deals. Chinese and other "high-context" cultures, by contrast, tend to be much less literal and much more personal. They are characterized by close relationships between family, friends, and business associates, which together form an extensive network of information that is used to interpret all events and communications.[4]

Among Chinese, the social roles and relationships that structure society inevitably influence communication events. Face and social harmony are safeguarded by conveying a message implicitly and indirectly, especially if bad news is being delivered. Indeed, indirectness can mean that the nonverbal dimension of communication may entirely override what is said explicitly. A gesture can say more than a thousand words.

Who You Know Is Who You Are

Establishing and reaffirming the social order is a central aspect of communication in the Chinese context. While businesspeople in the West aim to put people at ease (by telling jokes, for example), the Chinese want to ensure that everyone receives the appropriate respect. To this end, knowing the role that both you and your Chinese counterpart play is vital. In terms of language, this means that Chinese use different expressions to address and distinguish between people of varying social statuses. The members of a Chinese family, for example, are never addressed by their first names, but according to the position they occupy within the family structure. These forms of address can become quite elaborate, as illustrated by the differentiation among various kinds of uncles—"oldest paternal uncle," "youngest maternal uncle," "paternal older cousin/uncle" (the father's older cousin), and so on. Such precise social distinction in everyday communication provides an ongoing confirmation of everyone's place in the social structure. For Westerners, translating these kinds of linguistic social codes into English can be difficult, but simply thinking along these lines can be useful in improving communication.

To become established in the Chinese business world, you need to position yourself within a context that the Chinese recognize and are comfortable with. In other words, you must demonstrate that you are part of a network. When meeting people for the first time, for example, it is generally expected that you will situate yourself socially and professionally within the first few sentences of a conversation. This means mentioning the people with whom you associate, such as family, relatives, friends, classmates, or people from your home town. "You work for CITIC—do you happen to know Mr. Wei?" or

"I understand you went to Harvard; did you ever study with Professor Bauer?" are easy questions that help to contextualize, or establish a common ground between, new acquaintances.

Although this type of conversational pattern is not uncommon in the United States, for example, Americans are generally more reserved about immediately discussing their social, educational, and professional background (particularly if it is prestigious), perhaps because advertising one's social and educational connections can be perceived as "name-dropping" or bragging. In the Chinese context, however, it is an expected way of letting people know who you are, of establishing affiliations with a broader network and searching for common ground. Among strangers, especially, such exchanges serve as quick and inexpensive background checks, and they can provide information about possible channels for network expansion. Once such exchanges have been completed, conversation will often turn to focus on a third party—a mutual acquaintance, for example—rather than remaining centered on the two conversants. These discussions may sound like gossip, but they are not. They are a chance to demonstrate concern for others by drawing attention to the larger network.

There Is No "I" in Group

The tendency to downplay the self and deflect attention toward the group or toward a superior is even clearer in traditional forms of Chinese speech, which avoid the pronoun *I* and refer instead to the relationship between the speaker and addressee. A tradition-minded student talking to a teacher will say "your student thinks" rather than "I think"; a young man addressing his father would say "your son" rather than "I." In writing, too, traditional Chinese print words referring to themselves in noticeably smaller characters than the rest of their text, especially when addressing parental and authority figures. The same protocol applies to some government office settings, where subordinates will use smaller characters to write their own names than they use to write their supervisors' names. Another way the Chinese avoid the use of *I* is by referring to the group (*we*) when they are actually talking about themselves. This phenomenon is often called the "royal we" in English, but it has decidedly unaristocratic connotations in the Chinese usage, where it signifies deferral to (not presumptions about) others.

Finally, as in many languages throughout the world, there are two ways to say "you" in Chinese, one formal and one informal. The formal and more respectful *nin* is used with strangers, people who are older than the speaker, and people of a higher social status. The informal *ni* is used with peers, good friends, and family members. In English, of course, there are no built-in grammatical distinctions between formal and informal. When speaking English with the Chinese, then, finding other ways to differentiate or change one's language according to the status and social positioning of the addressee will go far in creating a good impression. Deferring to the addressee's experience ("you have much more experience negotiating with government offices than I") or mentioning third-party praise ("[our mutual friend] Elaine always spoke very highly of your creative business plans") can reinforce the social codes that are so crucial to communicating effectively with the Chinese.

Situations may arise, however, where roles conflict, and where the terms of address that should be used are unclear. A young female manager, for example, may have difficulty finding the appropriate form of address for an older but subordinate male employee. At stake are issues of gender, age, and professional hierarchy, and there are no steadfast rules regarding which should take precedence. If it is difficult to determine the social status of your interlocutor, remember that in any situation it is best to defer to the other person as though he or she occupied a higher social status, as long as you feel comfortable with your authority and position in the relationship.

Communicating Face to "Face"

The most important thing to remember about Chinese communication is that it aims at preserving the harmony of the group, even if this harmony rests merely upon surface appearances. In this context, face—either giving or saving—is a crucial consideration. Strong expressions of emotion, for example, can disrupt group harmony and should be replaced with more indirect comments. Public expressions of praise can also embarrass a Chinese person because such comments may disrupt the social balance by giving that individual

---

Box 7-1: It's Not Easy for the Chinese, Either

If you find Chinese language and communication overwhelming, you're not alone. Norman Fu of the *China Times*, one of the most respected Chinese news correspondents, has been based in Washington, D.C., for the past twenty years. Despite his fluency and eloquence in his native Mandarin, Fu once remarked that, when communicating with others, he would rather write in English than in Chinese. The social etiquette that must be accounted for in Chinese writing, he explained, can be so complex and delicate that he sometimes has a hard time moving his pen!

---

greater status than his or her peers. In the Chinese context, one should always be moderate in dealing with others and modest in presenting oneself. The Chinese tend to downplay personal misfortunes. In stark contrast to many circles in Western societies, where sharing complaints and/or criticism serves as a form of social bonding, the Chinese consider it bad form to draw attention to one's own problems.

Outright expressions of negative emotion are even more destructive and should be avoided if possible. The experience of an MNC general manager illustrates the damage that can be wrought by an inability to control one's temper. During a meeting of the senior people in his China office, the general manager actually screamed in anger at his financial controller for failing to have some desired information. The controller—who enjoyed a lot of support in the company—was shocked. He left the room and would have quit except that the general manager's behavior was well known in the organization. As it became evident that he would not change his behavior, people in the organization began withholding information from him until eventually everything had to be filtered through his senior management team. Because of his inability to control his temper, the general manager lost touch with his people; consequently, he lost managerial control and authority and ended up as little more than a figurehead in the organization.

Airing criticism and expressing praise are particularly delicate areas in the Chinese context. If criticized too directly or praised too openly a Chinese person will lose face, especially if others are present. The solution here is to take a more indirect approach. Showing appreciation through a personal, private gesture, rather than a public one, is a more tactful approach to praise. Similarly, if a person must be criticized it is better to do so privately and in a gentle, nonconfrontational manner. Giving a Chinese associate an "out," whether or not you feel they deserve one, will smooth communication in the long run. For example, it will help a Chinese associate save face if you acknowledge that your communication may not have been clear, even if you feel that it was. The person will take your point and appreciate the concern you have shown for his or her face.

One example from Hong Kong illustrates the potential pitfalls of aggressively direct communication. A young Western expatriate manager in a major global corporation had scheduled a meeting with a Chinese colleague on a Saturday. The colleague arrived an hour late to the meeting, and the expat, annoyed at losing weekend time, exclaimed, "You're wasting my time!" Her Chinese colleague was so offended that he withdrew his support from her entirely, and she received no cooperation from him for three years. In the West, her comment might have been regarded as an honest if undiplomatic statement of justifiable irritation. In the Chinese context, however, it caused deep offense because of its extreme negativity and directness. The manager's lack of cultural sensitivity caused her Chinese colleague to lose face.

In any situation, there are a number of ways to construct sentences and express the same ideas. While frankness may save words and seem to save time, it can come at the expense of respect and valuable business associations. Look for gentle, respectful ways of making your point. For instance, instead of saying, "You're wasting my time," ask, "Is everything fine at home?" Such a tactic would invite some explanation without hurting the other person's feelings. More important, it also shows your genuine concern for your counterparts.

Due to the social nature of face, conversations that occur in front of third parties can pose a great risk to an individual's reputation or status within his or her network. Among the Chinese, communication styles are carefully chosen to ensure that no one loses face, regardless of the content of the conversation. To maintain smooth relations with their Chinese associates, Westerners will do well to take similar care. Furthermore, the Chinese tend to be more reserved than Westerners (particularly Americans) in public or among people they do not know well. In the United States, where gregariousness is perceived as a strength, people often do more talking than listening. The Chinese, by contrast, equate wisdom with silence: According to a well-known proverb, the wise man does not say much.

Learning to be a perceptive listener and choosing words wisely and selectively can help enormously with interpersonal relations. In a recent survey conducted by Singapore-based Steve Morris Associates, forty chief executives of Asian-owned and Western multinational companies cited the inability to listen as a major limitation for leadership and management in the Asian context.[5] Indeed, listening carefully can bring you more power, and in the corporate setting, paying attention to employees or coworkers makes it possible to get more accurate feedback. Learning to listen more and talk less can also act as an advantage simply because there is less potential to say the wrong thing. Be conservative in your speech: If you fail to say something about yourself that your Chinese counterparts need to know, they will tactfully inquire about it.

When Words Are Not Enough

In almost all Western cultures, business interaction is expected to be direct and forthright. While nonverbal communication (a warm smile, a firm handshake, direct eye contact) inevitably plays a role, the verbalized message generally acts as the principal source of information. Chinese businesspeople, by contrast, pay a good deal more attention to nonverbal communication and will watch for signals from your manner of delivery to interpret a message. Since the meaning of nonverbal signs varies largely from culture to culture, it is important to have a basic understanding of Chinese gestures in order to communicate effectively.

Chinese people convey a large amount of information through gestures of courtesy and body language. Presenting your business card with two hands shows greater respect than presenting it with just one. Facial expressions are also commonly used to communicate an implicit message that may contradict and override the explicit verbal message. Frowns, for example, are to be taken very seriously and in Chinese business usually signal "no deal." Pursed lips communicate disapproval or anger, and sighs express dissatisfaction or unhappiness about which the other party should inquire.

Some forms of Western body language are absent in the Chinese context. For instance, Chinese never greet each other with kisses on the cheeks, nor do they exchange bear hugs. Similarly, the Chinese gesticulate much less than most Westerners when they speak. Flying arms or moving hands to express or emphasize points are perceived as ill mannered, as are physical displays of frustration and enthusiastic slaps on the back. Of course, most cosmopolitan Chinese will find it acceptable for outsiders to act according to their own cultural codes, as long as such behavior does not proceed from insincerity or criticism.

When done properly, communicating through action rather than words is a useful way to build and maintain relationships in the Chinese context. The seemingly minor details of a dinner meeting, for example, can be used to convey or derive information about a relationship. If the host receives the guest, it is understood that the host highly values the meeting and the relationship.

Gift-giving is another common form of nonverbal communication among the Chinese. In many situations, the recipient of a gift will politely and gently push it back. There will be a few moments of pushing the gift back and forth (as a ritual of modesty), but one should never openly or positively refuse a gift from another individual. Such a refusal could have strong implications in a business setting: During a pending business deal, refusal of a gift can signal that the deal will not be made and that the intended recipient does not care to be friends with the giver. On the other hand, acceptance of a gift can be used as a sign of forgiveness and a way of moving beyond a misunderstanding.

Speaking between Tongues

While Chinese styles of communication are generally indirect, the Chinese language itself is, in some ways, more "direct" than English and other Indo-European languages. Chinese has no grammatical structure equivalent to the English counterfactual mode; that is, statements that encourage the listener to put aside immediate real-

---

Box 7-2: Missed Communication in the PRC

John Sie, a Chinese-born American, is CEO of the cable conglomerate Encore Media Group. The company has gained a strong foothold in mainland China, where it has imported premium movie channels such as Encore and Starz. For Sie and his daughter Michelle, president of Encore's international arm, culturally sensitive communication is the key to success in China. Indeed, Sie attributes 80 percent of Western companies' problems in China to miscommunication or misunderstanding of Chinese business culture. Michelle points out that the potential for confusion in communicating with the Chinese is high, noting that when potential Chinese business partners say they "would like to research your proposal," they probably have no interest and will not get back to you. And then there are the perennial problems with translating English terms into Chinese: The term *pay-per-view*, for example, translates as "expensive television"—hardly the message a young cable enterprise wants to convey to its new customers![a]

[a] Leyla Kokmen, "American Cable, Telecom Firms Seek Chinese Market Share," *Denver Post*, 13 April 1999.

---

ity and enter an imaginary realm of events that did not take place ("If you had arrived on time for the meeting, we would have made the deal"). This grammatical difference between Chinese and English has important cognitive and communicative implications; namely, the Chinese show a remarkable resistance to counterfactual thinking. In the business world, this means that telling someone what they *should* have done, or what *would* have happened *if* they had done things differently, is an infinitely less effective form of communicating expectations than simply telling Chinese associates or partners in detail what they must do. For the Chinese, effective verbal modes should communicate a real state of affairs.

What do we mean, then, when we say that communication is more indirect in the Chinese context? Despite grammatical directness, the sociocultural *use* of Chinese is more indirect than most social uses of English. Because they must protect face and respect social roles, the Chinese may talk *around* the point and hedge their speech with softening modifiers such as *maybe, perhaps*, and *would you please*, even when making definitive statements or giving direct instructions. As a high-context culture, the Chinese assume that those involved in the exchange have the cultural and contextual background necessary to interpret a statement correctly. Frankness, in other words, is less important to the Chinese than smooth relationships, and therefore it is not uncommon to hear a Chinese person answer yes to an important question and then proceed to act as though they had said no.

Yes? No? Or Is That a Yesno?

The *yesno* is not a mysterious creature that haunts the Himalayas but a figure of speech lurking in Chinese business boardrooms. From the Western point of view, this figure of speech can be one of the most daunting obstacles in East-West communication.

In the Western context, answers to business questions are expected to be literal; indirectness can indicate dishonesty or secrecy. Metaphors are meant for poetry, not business. From the Chinese perspective, however, there are many reasons to be vague and evasive, principally because the question of saying yes or no is intrinsically tied to preserving face, and thus to building and maintaining relationships.

Since Chinese communication tends to be high-context, it is possible to say one thing while meaning another; in other words, both *yes* and *no* can carry a variety of meanings. The Chinese *yes* should be seen not as an absolute statement of affirmation but as existing on a continuum that runs from mere acknowledgment to strong endorsement. *Yes* may be used in a noncommittal way to indicate "I hear you; I understand your position." At the other end of the continuum, *yes* may express the strongest form of agreement in the traditional Chinese context: "You have my word." Without an understanding of the context of a communication event, it is impossible to know the meaning of these words.

Having to account for Chinese concerns such as saving face and preserving relationships can be a major source of frustration to a Western executive who relies on the literalness of a verbal message in making business decisions. Indeed, many Westerners doing business with Chinese companies find that Chinese partners will apparently agree to certain terms or conditions but then fail to follow through. In some cases, of course, this behavior is simply bad-faith bargaining or breach of contract. But frequently the problem will arise from considerations of face. In conversation, as in all Chinese social interaction, two or more faces are at stake.[6] The Chinese party will lose face if he or she fails to understand what has been asked or cannot supply what is being requested and must say no. At the same time, the Chinese are also concerned about protecting your face. If they deny your request with an outright no, you will lose face in their eyes, even if you yourself are not worried about face. The inclination to say yes (instead of a direct no) is even greater when the request comes from a party higher up in the social or business hierarchy. In such situations, a yes can save the higher-up's face.

How can Westerners cope with the *yesno*? One solution is to listen carefully for cues. Highly noncommittal language may convey strong signals. If a Chinese person tells you, "It is difficult for me to say I am comfortable with those terms," you should probably take that as meaning no. Similarly, the use of such adverbs as *maybe* and *perhaps* can be a sign of negation. Answering a question with a question—sometimes an apparently irrelevant one—is also a way of saying no, as is criticizing your question ("Your question is difficult to answer").[7]

Other ways the Chinese avoid an outright no is by changing the subject or repeatedly putting off a discussion of the project at hand. Phrases such as "Let me look into this further" or "We will take that under consideration" may simply be ways to avoid a direct no. Sometimes the Chinese may simply remain silent about an issue—a clear indication that you should move on to another topic. Finally, bringing up the potential disagreement of a third party, particularly that of a higher authority, is a way of saying no. "My boss is very conservative, and I'm not sure how he would react to this proposal" is typically a no politely disguised as a deferral.

As a Westerner, you, too, can use these techniques to modify how you communicate negative statements to Chinese counterparts. Be aware that the way you phrase questions—either openly or rhetorically—affects the position of the other party. Try to avoid direct yes or no questions, which allow your counterparts no face-saving way out and may leave you with a misleading, face-saving yes. Instead, focus attention on developing a context or atmosphere that will

---

Box 7-3: Ways of "No"-ing: A Philosophical Perspective

To say that the Chinese never say no may sound like an exaggeration, but it is very close to the literal truth. For a Chinese, saying no goes against the grain of affirming the other people around them and strengthening the social web that joins them. For a Westerner, however, the idea of never saying no seems alien. The Western worldview begins with the individual's right to self-assertion—an idea rooted in Western philosophy. The Cartesian practice of "radical doubt" suggests the negation of the entire universe to arrive at a principle of certainty based on individual consciousness. The French philosopher Jean-Paul Sartre (1905–1980) even argued that human dignity and human freedom stem from the ability to say no.

---

permit the true answer to be revealed through communication. Humbling yourself, for instance, and minimizing the other party's social "cost" is a good way to bring truth closer to the surface. If you are managing others, for example, you may be able to ease the anxieties of status-conscious Chinese by sharing stories of your own past mistakes or by using self-deprecating humor. Of course, securing a strong relationship over time is the best assurance of obtaining real answers.

What on Earth Does That Mean?

The difficulty of translating idioms across languages is especially apparent between Western and Asian languages, where important cultural differences make the context or background of slang or metaphoric expressions particularly difficult to grasp. Therefore, in general it is better to avoid using such expressions as "*We missed the boat,*" or "This venture is a *cash cow* for our company, and we would like to *milk it,*" or "*What's the game plan for today?*" or "*Let's brainstorm.*" Although your Chinese associates may be familiar with such English expressions, the idioms present greater potential for confusion or even insult.

Sarcastic humor and even seemingly inoffensive jokes are also often misunderstood and may unintentionally cause someone to lose face. While a witty exchange of deadpan remarks, for instance, may

---

Box 7-4: Advertising Culture

Advertising is one form of communication that poses special challenges in the PRC and other Chinese-speaking countries. Culturally specific, idiomatic expressions are difficult to translate into Chinese, as one Pepsi ad comically illustrated: in Taiwan, the translation of the Pepsi slogan "Come Alive with the Pepsi Generation" carried the meaning "Pepsi will bring your ancestors back from the dead"!

Beyond language translation, advertising can run into conflicts with local cultural mores. In 1999, McDonald's ran a television ad in which a woman hits a man in the groin with her shopping bag after he takes her fries away. The commercial was deemed too violent for Chinese culture, and touched off complaints that it had a bad influence on young people.

On the other hand, Coca-Cola found success with the nonverbal component of one of its ads. In an attempt to realistically convey a local feeling, the Coke ad team traveled through snow and bitter cold to film a commercial in a small village celebrating Chinese New Year. The effort was successful, and feedback on the ad was positive.[a]

[a] Shawn Choi, Daniel Mizrachi, and Linda Yeh, "Chapter 8: Review and Application" (student paper, The Wharton School, February 2000).

---

be an indirect form of social bonding in certain Western contexts, such humorous verbal exchanges require too much cultural context to be useful as communication.

Chinese E-Communication in English

The Internet is steadily becoming an important communication vehicle for Chinese language and culture, as a wide variety of software options have opened up for Chinese-speaking users. Several computer companies have already released programs with Chinese-language input and display. The pinyin romanization system and display software for Chinese characters make possible online communications in Chinese, and specialized digital pens allow users to write Chinese characters directly into computer applications. In response to the development of a Chinese-language version of the Internet-oriented Linux operating system, Microsoft released a Chinese version of its Windows 2000 software. Furthermore, sev-

Box 7-5:   Advice from the Outside In

The lessons learned by expatriates living in Asia and working with the Chinese provide a valuable primer for newcomers. Melanie Hayden, a former vice president of organization development and communications at Citibank Asia Pacific, consulted her network of American and European friends and colleagues in Asia to find out what advice they offer to Westerners for communicating with the Chinese.[a]

- Use "softening" words: "Maybe it could be looked at this way" instead of "I think"; "Could be" instead of "Should be."

- Use groups to elicit better participation; in a training session or meeting, employees are more willing to speak for the group than for themselves.

- Where possible, use oral (preferably face-to-face) rather than written communication.

- Balance criticism with confidence-building; it never hurts to give others credit.

- Always start with a positive statement.

- Showing anger is a no-no.

- Often the "real" story comes from an uninvolved third party.

[a] Frank Lavin, formerly of Bank of America in Singapore; Maura Fallon, Honeywell (formerly AlliedSignal International) Asia Pacific; Valerie Hayden, of ABN-Amro Bank in Singapore; Mary Frances Bellman, of *Business Week* Magazine/The McGraw-Hill Companies in Hong Kong.

eral major online sites are finding success adding Chinese-language versions of their existing content. Charles Schwab online, for example, added a Chinese version of its site, and investors of Asian heritage now represent Schwab's fastest-growing ethnic market.[8]

Despite these efforts to accommodate Chinese users, however, approximately 85 percent of all Internet material is currently available only in English, making it the language of choice for online communications.[9] The use of English as lingua franca puts a cybertwist on more traditional forms of networking. Joe Cheon, chief executive of Click2Asia, considers English one of the most powerful tools in connecting those of Chinese descent all over

Table 7-1: Contrasting Chinese-Western Communications: Concerns and Practices

	Chinese	Western
Concerns	Saving face	Frankness or "honesty"
	Respect and politeness	Assertiveness
	Compromise and flexibility	Self-assurance
	General feeling or "spirit"	Specific terms
	Social status	Task at hand
	Patience	Time efficiency
Styles and Practices	Reserved	Extroverted
	Tentative	Firm
	Personal	Impersonal
	No body contact	Hugging and backslap-ping acceptable
	No pointing	Index finger used to point

the globe—people of common ethnic heritage who may speak different dialects or languages. "Offline they might have a problem communicating," he says. "but the online community all understands English."[10]

Since the English found on the Web is generally more informal—and much more straightforward—than that used in print, Internet use is challenging the indirectness that has characterized traditional Chinese communication (see Table 7-1 for main differences between Chinese and Western communication styles). It is not unusual today, when exchanging e-mails with some Chinese, to find them communicating much more explicitly and openly. Nonetheless, this "casual" mode is not yet the norm, and it does not generally carry over into face-to-face communication.

Conclusion: Read My Lips . . . and My Eyes and My Hands and . . .

Learning to communicate effectively with the Chinese should not entail a loss of self. For the most part, there is a middle ground in communication that is acceptable in almost any cultural context. Politeness and diplomacy are traits that at the very least are respected

---

**Box 7-6: Communicating with the Chinese:
Some Quick "Translations"**

Here are some common English phrases, with suggestions for diplomatically expressing them in the Chinese context.

Western	Chinese
Do you understand?	Am I being clear?
Pardon me? (Certain intonations of this phrase can embarrass the Chinese, especially those who may be insecure about their English language skills).	Could you please repeat that? I don't quite understand.
Is the project acceptable?	What do you think of the project?
Please stop what you are doing.	Could you perhaps wait and do that a little later?
We cannot do that.	That may be a little difficult for us to do.
What's the problem? Your office says they sent an e-mail, but I never got it.	There must have been a problem with the server, because I never received an e-mail from your office.

---

in all business cultures and that do not require you to compromise your integrity. Likewise, learning the basic cultural values of the people with whom you are doing business will help to smooth over communication wherever you go.

Let me offer an example from the point of view of a Chinese learning to communicate in the Western context. When I first came to the United States, and for years afterward, whenever anyone complimented me I would respond with dead silence. I was embarrassed and puzzled by my instinctive reaction, and struggled to figure out why I did this. One day I realized that in Chinese culture people are expected to respond to a compliment by simply denying it or attributing it to luck. I was aware that this might not be appropriate in American culture. So I learned to respond to compliments with "It is very kind of you to say so." In this way I am able to make a culturally appropriate response while still deflecting the compliment enough to be true to my Chinese roots.

Remember that there is always a middle ground between saying yes or no, and that this is the ground of cultural accommodation. You, too, can find a balanced way to be yourself even as you integrate and adapt to difference. The crucial point is that different communication systems are constantly in "dialogue." Interestingly enough, the more popular form of Chinese writing now is not from top to bottom but from left to right!

8

Negotiating from Start to Finish . . . and Beyond

Chinese business executives commonly complain that the Western approach to negotiation is like signing an elaborate prenuptial agreement, a contract that could doom the relationship to failure before it starts. From the Chinese perspective, detailing a commitment in ink spells the death of the relationship, since it dissolves the need for continuing gestures of trust and loyalty. All close relationships, from marriage to healthy business partnerships, evolve through an ongoing dialogue between the parties involved.

THE CONCEPT OF NEGOTIATION is a foreign import into Chinese culture. In fact, there is no word for negotiation in traditional Chinese. The term used today, *tan pan*, translates the Western concept through a combination of two characters: tan (discussion) and pan (making judgment). The second character is only vaguely defined, and the emphasis thus falls on the first: discussion. This compound word does not have the connotations of bargaining, conflict resolution, and final agreement implicit in the Western term *negotiation*. Indeed, when two Chinese people who want to negotiate say "Let us talk," they literally mean what they say. The term *negotiation* defined in a strictly Western sense is used only as a last resort. In the Chinese context, negotiation is not a euphemism for debate; rather, it indicates an ongoing dialogue.

With all their emphasis on informality, the Chinese are nevertheless known to be shrewd negotiators. One reason for this perhaps lies in recent Chinese history. Over the last twenty years the mainland Chinese have been actively courted by the West, first for political, then for commercial reasons. As the second-largest Asian economy, and the world's most populous nation, China has been in the privileged position of choosing with whom it wanted to deal, and under what conditions. Historically, too, the Chinese have had a strong sense of self-sufficiency and maintaining face. As **Deng** Xiaoping once boasted to Henry Kissinger, "China has never asked for favors from others."[1] The country's unique position has meant that the Chinese on the mainland could always drive a hard bargain, and, to a large extent, they still can.

This philosophical background also contributes to the uniqueness and strength of the Chinese approach to negotiating. Stressing hierarchy and social harmony, the Chinese attempt to minimize direct confrontation.[2] As a result, they are considerably more patient than Westerners, and, when faced with the possibility of disagreement, they will tend to defer. The cultural preference for social harmony accords with the Chinese translation of *negotiation* as discussion or talking rather than direct debate and problem solving. In the business context, this means that the Chinese will place as much emphasis as possible on the social context that informs the negotiation at hand, stressing the more informal, relationship-building interactions of the pre- and postnegotiation periods rather than the formal negotiation itself. In this way, the focus is taken off the moment of potential conflict and diffused into a more personal and long-term view of the process. This chapter explains the basic features of negotiating in the Chinese context and provides cultural insights necessary for understanding Chinese negotiation goals and tactics.

What's the Deal?

Cultural elements such as role relationships, time perspectives, and communication styles all come together in the practice of negotiation. The Latin etymology of the word negotiation (*neg-otium*, or "not at leisure") reminds us that, from a Western perspective, negotiation and leisure tend to be regarded as mutually exclusive categories. The Chinese, however, with their personalism and long-term attitude toward business, may seem to Western eyes to introduce a measure of "leisure" (or at least an informal, more social element) into the negotiation process. In negotiation—as with the other aspects of business behavior we have discussed in this book—the Chinese emphasize the social and interpersonal dimension and take a long-term perspective. The following sections will take a closer look at how cultural differences inform three major categories of negotiation: the process, the negotiation teams, and the context.

A Beginning, a Middle, and No End

While for analytical purposes we describe Chinese negotiation in terms of clearly defined stages (pre-, formal, and post-), in fact such boundaries often vary from case to case. The Chinese see the negotiation process as a continuum, based on repeated social and business interaction.

The primary focus for most Western companies is the formal negotiation period—when two parties sit down to review the proposed deal item by item. For the Chinese, however, decisions made during formal negotiations are no more sacrosanct than the understanding developed before and after the formal deal. In fact, the prenegotiation and postnegotiation phases may actually be more important for the Chinese, because the relationship is built and commitment is secured during these phases. Rather than emphasizing the content of the deal and the final outcome, the Chinese take a more expansive view, seeing negotiation as a *process* that goes beyond the life of the deal.

For this reason, negotiation success with the Chinese depends in large part on the quality and the duration of *guanxi* relationships. As unknown parties, Westerners need to show personal commitment to the working rapport from the outset, and the prenegotiation phase is the critical time to do so. This is not achieved by simply performing in-depth evaluations of the business deal but rather by establishing common ground with your counterparts. A study looking at the strategies Hong Kong businesses use when dealing with PRC counterparts found that 73 percent of Hong Kong businesspeople had

---

Box 8-1: Cultural Dilemma: Gift-Giving versus Bribery

I was recently advised that for my company's project to move forward in China, a small payment to a high-level provincial official is necessary. What should I do?

Options and Observations

You should not make the payment. Corruption is an enormous problem in Chinese societies; too many such payments have been made in the past. It is important to realize, however, that the PRC government is now taking this issue very seriously, and that there can be severe penalties for those who are caught. Additionally, the bribery of foreign public officials is prohibited under the domestic laws of many countries, such as the U.S. Foreign Corrupt Practices Act.

---

held intensive prenegotiation social functions, such as meetings in restaurants with the PRC representatives, and 68 percent had sent gifts for social reasons.[3] These interactions often do not involve business discussions, but rather establish a foundation and obtain commitments to principles that negotiators can later invoke. Prenegotiation bonds serve a purpose similar to the contract in the West—solidifying a working relationship by defining the obligations of each party.

One of the greatest surprises—and a major source of frustration—for Western companies doing business with Chinese partners arises from the two sides' differing attitudes toward the role and authority of the legal contract. "We saw that we had a contract, [but] we saw our partner try to change the rules every day,"[4] lamented Juergen Hubbert of DaimlerChrysler. The fact is that the Chinese do not view "postnegotiation" as simply the time to implement an agreed-upon deal. To some traditional Chinese, signing a contract to show commitment can even be considered an insult ("Why can't you trust my word?"). For others, a contract may not always be considered the binding document denoted in the Western legal sense; rather, it is seen as an agreement between two parties on the general principles and "spirit" behind a deal. Because relationships evolve and situations shift, the Chinese perceive contracts as too rigid to take new circumstances into account. Hence there is no stigma attached to changing the terms of an agreement after it has been signed, and Western businesspeople can expect to renegotiate or reinterpret points of the contract during their entire working relationship with the Chinese party.

Just as in a marriage, the signing of a contract does not mark the end of the business relationship, but rather the beginning of an ongoing process. According to Ernest De Bellis, former managing director of international ventures for the Foxboro Company, "Everything in China is a negotiation. When you come right down to it, the negotiation process continues after the joint venture agreement is signed. To be successful, you have to make a continuing commitment to negotiation. . . . Even though you have signed an agreement, you still have to continue to reaffirm what was originally decided on."[5] The experience of Morgan Stanley (now Morgan Stanley Dean Witter) in China illustrates the importance of postnegotiation as a means of solidifying a working relationship. According to John Mack, Morgan Stanley's CEO, the company's controlling power in its Shanghai joint venture (35 percent equity ownership on paper) "might as well be 1%" in terms of real influence.[6] It is an ongoing challenge for any business partnership to translate a signed contract into business reality. The successful translation of equity control into operational control is, however, particularly difficult—especially in the Chinese context. One could invest a lot with minimal reward or, conversely, one might invest only a little but gain a substantial reward.

Around the Table: The Players and the Game

True to their Confucian tradition, the Chinese are extremely sensitive to and respectful of role and rank. Around the negotiating table, company titles and social status are an important part of projecting authority and gaining respect, and the Chinese will quickly assess the power and authority of the Western negotiating team. Sending someone with rank and title conveys the message that you value both the company and the potential deal, thus giving face to your Chinese partners. If your senior officers cannot attend the negotiations, you can find creative ways to increase the perceived status of the negotiators assigned to the job. Placing a phone call from a high-ranking company executive or assigning prestigious titles to the negotiators for this particular task would be effective ways of addressing the Chinese negotiators' concern for status. Such moves are also more likely to counter the strategic use of rank by the Chinese, who may send senior company officials to the negotiation table simply to pull rank and obtain new concessions—and sometimes may even demand that a higher-ranking Western official join the negotiations.[7]

The Chinese tend to involve more people in negotiations than Westerners do, though only a small part of the Chinese team—those present during the prenegotiation phase—will normally remain throughout the entire deal-making process. This core group, made up of specialists, company managers, interpreters, and, to a growing extent, lawyers, merely operates as a front for the officials who are really in charge—either senior executives, family members (often among overseas Chinese), or government authorities (as is common in the PRC). The negotiating team present around the table often does not have actual final decision-making power. Its main task often is to gather information and insights for those behind the scenes. It is extremely important that you determine early on where the power lies and how the negotiators fit into the larger scheme of authority and networks.[8]

Given the slower, more patient approach to negotiation taken by the Chinese, Westerners should attempt to keep the same negotiating team in place throughout. If this is not possible, it is important to ensure that the complete negotiation history and the *guanxi* network are passed on to the new negotiators, and also to the people who will execute the deal or operate the venture once the contract has been signed. In this way, the benefits of the personal connection continue into the implementation phase. Indeed, many of the problems encountered by large Western companies occur simply because their complete separation of the roles and responsibilities of deal negotiator and project manager goes against the grain of *guanxi*.

According to one Western executive, "Professional negotiators are focused basically on the concept of negotiations rather than what is best for the partnership itself. . . . They always try to change the structure of the agreement for what they perceive to be better [terms]. . . . Their training is primarily on the negotiation process and not on the actual project."[9] Separating the roles of negotiator and executor may also mean that the big-picture issues do not receive appropriate attention. Indeed, it makes little sense to fight over the details of a contract that is subject to change —especially since an aggressive, adversarial attitude during the negotiation process detracts from a strong relationship, which is the best guarantee of a deal's success in the long run. Compromise and diplomatic communication may not win the negotiating battle, but will secure you a solid position in the actual operations war.

As we saw in chapter 7, Chinese communication is highly context-dependent; this is especially important to keep in mind during all phases of the negotiation process. In formal negotiations, where you might most expect an explicit use of language, body language is in fact often the clearest sign of agreement or disagreement. When in disagreement, for example, a Chinese negotiator may rapidly fan a hand before his or her face, refuse to make eye contact, offer a blank, neutral face, or simply remain silent.[10] While these gestures can have strategic purposes, they may be a way to downplay overt conflict, through either avoidance or delay.

From the Chinese point of view, indirect communication is a form of cooperation. Chinese negotiators value harmony and consensus over the specific resolution of particular details, believing that if the parties can reach a general agreement, the details will fall into place. This attitude may appear oddly casual and even suspicious to Westerners, who might wonder why their partners will not get down to business. For the Chinese, however, social harmony and general agreement *are* the business issues. They strive to maintain smooth interpersonal relations throughout all phases of negotiation, and often expect their Western counterparts to do the same. Even if negotiations fail and the deal falls through, it is important for the Chinese to part on good, face-saving terms. For Westerners, the opportunity to do business in the future with the same company, or with the company's business networks or partners, will be greatly facilitated if they have taken care to preserve the relationship.[11] "For a Chinese negotiator," comments John So, "his 'face' (*mianzi*) is his future."[12]

An old Chinese proverb warns: "It is better to die of starvation than to become a thief; it is better to be vexed to death than to bring a lawsuit."[13] Among the Chinese, disputes—including contract disputes—tend to be resolved through ongoing negotiations and out-of-court settlements. This approach can be extremely frustrating

Box 8-2: How to Sell Another Billion Hamburgers

In the West, legal action is often the first and last approach to resolving major conflict. In the Chinese context, other forms of conflict resolution are preferable, and some of them may preserve the long-term ties that a legal battle could undermine.

In 1992, after ten years of market research and infrastructure development, McDonald's opened its flagship restaurant in Beijing, two blocks from Tiananmen Square. The outlet was the largest McDonald's in the world, serving 20,000 customers per day and as many as 50,000 on holidays. Suddenly, in 1994, just two years into its twenty-year land-lease agreement with the city of Beijing, the chain was ordered to vacate its premises to make room for a major commercial development. The eviction notice sent a shock through the foreign investment community in the PRC, and some firms reconsidered their business investments.

McDonald's set about defending its position in a firm but cooperative and face-saving way. The restaurant chain first issued a conciliatory public statement: "McDonald's looks forward to working in close cooperation with the Beijing municipal government to resolve the future of the Wang-Fujing McDonald's to our mutual satisfaction and benefit and in a spirit of understanding and cooperation." McDonald's remained in its location and undertook closed-door negotiations with the Beijing government. In late 1996, agreement was reached: Beijing agreed to pay McDonald's U.S.$12 million to compensate for the move; McDonald's moved into a new restaurant 150 meters down the road and was granted permission to open more restaurants in the city.

While some Western businesspeople criticized the company for making too many concessions to the Chinese government,[a] McDonald's did take a culturally sensitive path: It chose nonconfrontational negotiations, a decision that helped to save the government's face, and built upon an already-established relationship. The company's patience paid off with increased business and goodwill.

McDonald's choice of action stands in sharp contrast to Lehman Brothers's highly publicized litigation of 1994, in which the company filed suit against three of China's biggest trading companies for allegedly failing to pay U.S.$100 million in debts arising from foreign-exchange

[a] McDonald's thirty-four Beijing outlets were paying on average thirty-one fees to municipal authorities, including such seemingly gratuitous fees as $5,000 for local "river cleaning," in a city that can boast only a few streams and lakes! For the full story on covering these fees, see Ian Johnson, "Fees, Fines to Go? McDonald's Is Hit in Chinese Capital," *Wall Street Journal*, 5 September 1997.

Box 8-2:   How to Sell Another Billion Hamburgers (continued)

trading. The lawsuit received an enormous amount of attention in the Chinese investment community, severely embarrassing the PRC government. Lehman did recover its money, but it has since lost a tremendous amount of business in the PRC.[b]

[b] "McDonald's Amicable on Dispute over Beijing Site," *South China Morning Post*, 10 December 1994, and Simon Holberton, "Lehman Sues Chinese Companies for Dollars 100 m," *Financial Times*, 17 November 1994.

---

to Westerners, for whom changes in a signed contract are tantamount to breaking the law. While the common Western procedure in these cases is to sue, this is still not so in the PRC. Undoubtedly, the legal climate in the PRC has improved substantially over the last decade; nevertheless, there remains a cultural preference for keeping disputes private, unless recourse to the law is absolutely necessary.

Behind the Curtain

In Chinese negotiations, there are often many unseen parties operating behind the scenes, representing layers of governmental agencies (in the PRC) or important family members. Western negotiators are often not aware of these "phantom stakeholders," whose interests can make or break a deal. Chinese negotiators always work very hard to ensure that these diverse parties are consulted and well served.

Western negotiators should also be aware of the complex feelings mainland Chinese experience in dealing with the rest of the world. A long history of colonialism, combined with a relatively late entry into the world of global business relations, sometimes makes them suspicious of foreign business, although certainly the situation has changed substantially over the years. The challenge for Western business negotiators is not to appear as the successors of the late colonialists, imposing economic or cultural imperialism.

In the PRC, foreign companies must pay very close attention to government regulations. All deals must be approved by various independent agencies of the government, and it is sometimes unclear which policies are in force. Government policies not only differ from one region to another (Beijing and Shanghai, for instance, may have entirely different business regulations) but also can change quickly, negating the terms of any business deal. According to one Western executive, "There is not only the central government with its 'go' or 'no go' decision, but [also] a provincial government and a municipal government. All forms of government . . . are involved [with approvals] . . . and I'm not talking about 'one stop' agencies."[14] In the PRC, jurisdictional conflicts arise frequently. The country's two major telecommunications companies, for instance, are sponsored by two different ministries.

Overseas Chinese differ substantially from PRC businesspeople in their greater familiarity and comfort with the Western negotiation style. Nevertheless, they often retain traditional Chinese family business values, which strongly influence their goals and attitudes in the deal-making process. Indeed, overseas Chinese negotiators tend to be family members or trusted managers who play a day-to-day role within the business. These people have attachments to the company that go beyond a purely professional and contractual affiliation. They have a deep involvement in and understanding of the firm, its business partners, and its other deals. In negotiating, this means that they can take a less urgent approach to deal-making than that taken by Western professional negotiators, who are under intense pressure to sign a particular contract.

Government plays a much less influential role in overseas Chinese negotiations than it does in PRC negotiations. The overseas Chinese tend to have good relationships with local Southeast Asian governments, although they usually do not involve themselves directly in politics. Historically, overseas Chinese businesses have faced drastic changes of regime and consequently have become adept at staying out of politics while remaining in favor with local authorities. Westerners will usually be more comfortable in dealing with overseas Chinese in countries like Indonesia, Malaysia, and Thailand because they have the option of signing the contract in Hong Kong or Singapore, where more developed and Western-style legal systems are in place.

Tactics around the Table

The fact that Chinese culture emphasizes social harmony and conflict avoidance does not translate into passivity or a lack of strat-

---

Box 8-3: Cultural Dilemma: What Is Fair Play?

Our Chinese counterpart on the negotiation team uses tactics that I believe are unfair. Do Chinese have fundamentally different conceptions of fairness?

Options and Concerns

As a society the Chinese also believe in fair play though like all societies there are those who don't play by the rules. Before concluding that your partner falls into this category, however, consider that there are some respects in which Chinese conceptions of fairness might differ.

Given the importance of harmonious social dynamics among Chinese, the emphasis is often placed on receiving fair treatment during the negotiation process itself. Aspects that the Chinese consider important when defining fair treatment during negotiation include: receiving due respect, sharing control of the agenda, and saving face.

In contrast, there is often less attention paid to the specific terms of the final contract. This stems from both differing conceptions of the role of a legal contract and the sense of trust associated with *guanxi*-based relationships. Business associates, for example, who share strong *guanxi* ties often assume that the outcome or contract will be favorable and beneficial to both parties.

"Mutual benefit" is a highly valued concept among Chinese. To the extent that your Chinese partner is inflexible and keeps pushing for what you believe is a "winner takes all" approach, you may need to reevaluate the partner and the strength of your relationship with him.

---

egy at the negotiating table. As we saw in chapter 6, Chinese strategies are often based on classical war tactics.[15] The following sections will examine important Chinese negotiating practices, many of which take an indirect and nonconfrontational form, following Sun Tzu's strategy of "winning without fighting."

Exploiting Strengths and Weaknesses

To gain ground, the Chinese will generally choose to throw an opponent off balance rather than pin him down, following the theory that an opponent's strength is also his major weakness. In judo, for example, fighters learn to turn an opponent's own weight and momentum against him. In negotiations, the Chinese might flatter Western counterparts excessively and portray them as all-powerful, hoping to blind the Western party to the Chinese party's strengths and make the Westerners more disposed toward conceding "small" Chinese demands. In essence, they aim to convert the Westerners' strength (economic dominance) into a liability (overconfidence). By casting themselves strategically as the weaker party, the Chinese can play upon a *guanxi* pattern where the stronger party has greater obligations to the weaker. The expectation that the stronger party will shoulder more responsibility partly explains some of the unusual demands made of foreign companies in PRC negotiations, such as covering the costs of employee training programs, housing expenses, and other social welfare concerns.

The Chinese almost always show a willingness to compromise if your negotiators accede to some of their requests, although it is important that you hold on to some key concessions and points of renegotiation for the "last-minute" demands that characterize Chinese deal-making. Throughout the negotiations, the best solution is to find a middle way between making concessions to the Chinese (and saving the negotiator's face), while keeping a firm eye on your company's goals and principles.

Another way that foreign businesses can deal with the "stronger West/weaker East" tactic is to demonstrate an active interest in local affairs: sociopolitical, economic, and even cultural. At the same time, Western companies can share valuable experience about global business practices, since they have a longer history of doing business in the global marketplace. The Chinese will appreciate this sharing of knowledge, which can develop into a deeper relationship and lay the groundwork for future cooperation. If the aim is to influence the Chinese into following the rules of the global marketplace, an effective approach is to engage them and show interest in their local concerns. Education can thus be a key part of the negotiation process, as long as the Chinese feel they are not being treated with condescension and that you are also willing to learn from them.

The Home Court Advantage

Exploiting situational weaknesses is another tactic employed by PRC Chinese, who frequently insist on holding negotiations in China. The mere fact that the Western party has traveled to China for business forces it to function in a foreign cultural and legal environment and hence places it in a weaker negotiating position. Chinese negotiators often will make reference to the infamous *neibu* regulations— unpublicized laws the Westerner has no way of knowing, except through an insider or a good Chinese lawyer. The *neibu* regulations can be conveniently "remembered" at key moments during the negotiation, and their existence cannot be easily validated.

Eastern Negotiating Time

Chinese negotiators are well known for using time to their advantage. Aware that Westerners are apt to feel deadline pressure, they frequently use delay tactics—referring to outside authorities, "phantom stakeholders," or *neibu* regulations. These tactics, in combination with the different perspective on time, mean that everything takes longer than you think it will during negotiations with the Chinese. A good rule of thumb is to double the time you expect to spend during the deal-making process, and not to share your schedule with your Chinese counterparts. Also, expect negotiations to take more than one visit. Finally, making the point that you are not in a rush for a quick agreement can work to your advantage. As one American negotiator recounts, "When I knew that negotiations had reached an impasse, and I couldn't compromise, I returned to the U.S. I never stayed in China more than three weeks. I told them 'if you have new opinions on the issue, please let me know, and we will talk.' Sometimes we had no contact for 4 months. But at last I received from them a new draft . . . in which there was generally some compromise [and] . . . I would compromise on non-principle issues as well."[16]

Directing Information and Attention

Guanxi relationships must not be treated lightly; they carry with them high expectations and obligations that influence the partnership during and after the negotiation. For this reason, the Chinese will ask questions throughout negotiations, both to deflect attention from themselves and to seek the information necessary to judge trustworthiness and determine intentions.[17] And it is important to remember that while casual exchanges are a necessary part of

Box 8-4: CNTC versus Celanese: Time, Patience, and Tow

China's National Tobacco Corporation (CNTC) needed to upgrade its cigarette production with filter tips. Its problem was "tow," the fluffy fibers from which cigarette filters are made. Not having any, the company had to pay to import it, draining scarce foreign reserves. Furthermore, it could only afford to import tow for a mere 10 percent of its total production of a trillion and a half cigarettes per year.

No one would sell CNTC the tow-making technology (tow makers were suffering from excess capacity), so it invited the U.S. company Celanese Fibers Corp., one of its tow suppliers, to discuss a joint venture to build a tow-making plant in China. Celanese examined the CNTC proposal and decided not to negotiate: CNTC was asking for too big an investment with too little profit potential.

Enter Steven Perry of the London Export Company, who asked for three months to use his long experience dealing with both parties to formulate terms of a joint venture. Three months later, Perry had hammered out a win-win deal. Celanese was to be a "preferred supplier" of tow to CNTC—which meant sure payment up front—while the Chinese plant was being built. CNTC received not just technology but also engineering assistance in building a modern plant, and Celanese guaranteed the plant's operating efficiency. CNTC's future tow output was to serve only its domestic market, saving Celanese from competing against CNTC in the international market. Finally—and most significantly—Celanese was protected from the notorious (in the West) "never-ending contract." The deal agreed on was the final deal.

Five years after CNTC began its search for tow-making technology, it began producing the product in its new plant. Its output exceeded its rated capacity the first year, and soon after another joint venture agreement between the two parties, a raw materials plant, was under construction.[a]

The success of these negotiations rested on three crucial factors. First, they approached the negotiations patiently, which allowed the two companies to find a time that was right for both of them. Second, they balanced this long-term view with a "Western-style" agreement not to defer commitments or delay decisions. Finally, the partners adopted a

[a] A much fuller description and analysis of the launching of Nantong Cellulose Fibers Company are given in W. H. Newman, *Birth of a Successful Joint Venture* (Lanham, MD: University Press of America, 1992).

Box 8-4: CNTC versus Celanese: Time, Patience, and Tow (continued)

"holistic" consideration of the diverse stakeholders involved—agreeing, for example, to set 5 percent of profits aside for a Welfare Fund, and to provide assistance to the city of Nantong in handling clean-up of drainage into the Yangtsi River.

Box 8-5: Negotiating with the Chinese: Some Tips

- Showing excessive emotion of any kind is frowned on in the Chinese context; "antisocial" emotions such as anger or frustration are considered even more unseemly.

- Learn to see adversity in a positive light. Even a failed negotiation can be a good investment for the future. Don't leave bad feelings behind.

- Cultivate continuing support from the corporate office. Remember that Chinese value relationships of all kinds, and that they will view you in the context of your own network. An important part of that network or "family" is the corporate office at home.

- Use nonbusiness opportunities to enhance intercultural ties. To give your Chinese counterparts an appreciation of the American cowboy and frontier spirit, take them to Texas!

- Be sensitive to timing, and be prepared to compromise.

- Think beyond the short term. Avoid the "car buyer mentality," where the goal of negotiation is to get the best possible deal for now, given that the car can be sold or replaced in a few years.[a] Instead, think in terms of "investing" in a relationship.

[a] This analogy was suggested to me by negotiation expert Thomas Reed.

---

building *guanxi* relationships, the Chinese may use them to their advantage by reminding you of an opinion you voiced or a promise you made casually over dinner.

The best counterstrategy is to arrive well prepared with your own questions, both to show interest in your partners and to ensure that information flows both ways. It is also important to double-check any

Table 8-1: Major Differences between Chinese and Western Approaches to Negotiation

	Chinese	Western
Negotiation is focused on:	Process	Content
	Means	Ends
	Generality	Specificity
	Prenegotiation and post-negotiation phases	Formal negotiation phase
	Trust	Legal contract
A contract is:	A summary of discussion	A binding legal document
	A snapshot of the relation-ship	
	Open to change	
Assessment of fairness is based on:	Procedure	Specific outcome

information you receive with several independent sources, especially when legal and political issues are at stake. Information sources you can call on include Western expatriates in the region who may have experience with similar deals or trusted local confidants who can help gather information and interpret events. Remember, too, that interpreters do make mistakes and that even accurately translated words may lose certain nuances in translation. You should conduct information checking quietly and subtly, to avoid appearing suspicious and distrustful. Finally, because negotiation can take years in China, keep a summary of the key points of consensus at the end of each meeting and have both sides agree to them in order to move the process forward more efficiently. Given the Chinese reservation about contracts, asking them to literally sign a copy of the agreed terms could imply a lack of trust. But there are other, more tactful ways to assure that you and your partners are "on the same page." You might, for example, send a copy of a meeting summary (in the more casual form of a friendly "update") both to the Chinese negotiators and to a mutually trusted third party as a subtle, relationship-based way of "documenting" business negotiations. For your quick reference, Table 8-1 summarizes the key differences to remember between Chinese and Western approaches to negotiation.

Conclusion: Recipes for Negotiation

The chicken says to the pig, "Let's get together for a business break-fast. I'll supply the eggs and you can supply the bacon."

The disturbing thing about this joke is that sometimes negotiators do act like the chicken—unaware of or, worse, indifferent to the plight of the pig. Such a win-lose mentality, as the Chinese know, is bound to destroy harmony in negotiations. From the Chinese point of view, business should be a "tie" in order to proceed. This is not exactly the same as a "win-win" mind-set; rather, the "tie" refers to the bond established between business partners throughout—and as a result of—the negotiation process.

Establishing relationships as the basis for business deals is not a completely foreign notion in the West. Increasingly, Western business thinkers are stressing the value of building relationships in the negotiation process,[18] in large part because more and more ventures between Western companies end up in arbitration courts after unexpected issues were not dealt with in the original contract. With this in mind, the Chinese disregard for such formal documents makes sense; since the details of a deal cannot anticipate implementation issues, a working relationship capable of taking changing circumstances into account is essential to the deal's long-term success.

While the Chinese tendency to employ protracted and indirect negotiating has clear benefits, it also has its drawbacks. Using deferral and delay tactics often means that decisions are never made, or that forward-looking plans are neglected. Consequently, many Chinese business people are now relying more heavily on Western negotiation handbooks and learning from the Western style of making firm commitments to action, confronting obstacles head-on, and so forth. For the Westerner, however, the Chinese outlook can offer valuable ways of utilizing deep, long-term relationships—"ties" that can bring benefits during the negotiation process, and beyond.

9

TRADITION IN TRANSITION
Doing Business in the PRC

What is happening in China today is unprecedented, but there are analogies.... The American West in the nineteenth century, with some areas functioning in an orderly fashion and some utterly lawless; France in the Fourth Republic; Italy today; a yacht race before the gun goes off.

—RICHARD MARGOLIS,
Managing Director of Smith New Court (China)[1]

THE AIM OF THIS BOOK has been to explore the common cultural principles behind Chinese businesses, whether they are in the PRC, Southeast Asia, or North America. One must recognize, however, that significant differences exist between Chinese businesses around the globe, and this is especially true with respect to the mainland and the overseas Chinese. On a general level, there are some very basic and tangible differences between the two. Most notably, PRC businesses are much more subject to government involvement and control than overseas Chinese enterprises. In the latter, the family is a more prominent and pervasive influence than the state. On the mainland, government involvement often means that PRC enterprises are huge bureaucracies, while overseas companies tend to be small to medium sized. Finally, while the overseas Chinese have tended to operate transnationally, PRC firms have been much more limited in their geographic scope.

Underneath these basic differences, though, lie a host of historical and cultural factors that have shaped PRC attitudes and perspectives. This chapter begins by concentrating on some of the historical events of the past two centuries that have shaped China's attitudes toward the West. We then analyze the unique transitional state of the PRC business environment and, finally, provide some guidelines for developing a *balanced* strategy that can effectively manage the challenging conditions that characterize the business environment in China.

A Brief Overview of China's Recent History

While the West has only recently become sensitive to the potentially imperialistic connotations of the term *globalization*, the word's implications for the Chinese can be downright hostile, especially in view of China's colonial past. As **Yuan** Ming, a professor of international relations at Peking University, explains, "Our political leaders don't use the term 'globalization.' We prefer 'modernization.' There is a cultural reason for this. . . . China was forced into the international community in the last century by gunboats—so globalization represents something that China doesn't pursue but rather something that the West or America is imposing. Modernization is something we can control."[2] It is important for Westerners to have a basic understanding of China's history with the West, in order to realize why current Western "interest" in China may still be met with wariness or skepticism.

China and the West

In 1759, European powers began trading with China on a regular and regulated basis at Guangzhou (the port of Canton). Although the British were keen for Chinese tea, silk, and porcelain, the Chinese did not have a great demand for British woolens. The only desired British import was opium, brought from the neighboring Indian colonies. As the drug trade grew, a crisis in the silver currency used for trade payments developed alongside an epidemic of social problems brought on by the spread of opium addiction. In response, the Qing emperor suppressed all opium imports, sparking a massive smuggling operation backed by the British. The Opium Wars broke out in 1839 and ended three years later with Britain's triumph. The Chinese were forced to sign a series of humiliating trade agreements requiring them to open their ports to all comers, and concede the island of Hong Kong to the British (see Appendix 4). In England, William Gladstone, Secretary of the Colonies and future prime minister, commented, "A war more unjust in its origin, a war more calculated to cover this country with permanent disgrace, I do not know."[3]

During the decades following the Opium Wars, China's internal affairs, already in disorder due to a weak and corrupt dynasty, were taken over by European powers, who demonstrated little concern for the Chinese population or culture. Hundreds of thousands of Chinese transport workers, for example, lost their jobs and died of starvation as the Europeans replaced traditional Chinese transportation systems with railroads. In 1898, the Boxer Rebellion in Beijing—a peasant uprising against foreign occupation—led to Chinese deaths in the thousands and to the destruction by the Europeans of some of China's most precious ancient buildings, treasures, and libraries.

The traditional Chinese sense of superiority over other cultures made this period of colonization all the more difficult to accept. This blow to China's pride continues to influence contemporary attitudes toward the West. (Needless to say, our Western focus here is leaving out the large and complicated story of the Japanese invasion of China from the late nineteenth century to World War II.) As the world powers once again clamor at China's gates, the PRC government has often adopted a seemingly uninterested, "take-it-or-leave-it" attitude to foreigners, hesitant to make concessions or extend invitations to Western investors. This approach accords with an ideology that inhibits Beijing from speaking or acting in an openly capitalist manner. Nevertheless, China recognizes its need for foreign technology and capital in order to advance economically and have access to current technological breakthroughs. Albeit slow and equivocal, China's movement in the direction of globalization (or "modernization") marks an abrupt shift from past policies and a revolution in its attitude toward both trade and the West.

A Latecomer to the Market System

As we described above, Confucian tradition recognizes five basic relationships. The merchant-client relationship is not among them and therefore has never been especially valued in China; instead, merchant-client transactions remained subject to governmental control and bureaucratic obstacles—factors that do not encourage an entrepreneurial spirit. As Fairbank explains, "The tradition in [Old] China had been not to build a better mousetrap but to get the official mouse monopoly."[4] In 1979, however, three years after Mao's death, **Deng** Xiaoping reversed Marxist-Leninist and Maoist dogma by announcing plans to reform China's economy and open it up to foreign investment. These reforms represented an entirely new course for the country: **Deng** Xioaping's oft-quoted statement, "To get rich is glorious," would have been unthinkable in China ten years before the reforms began, when the country was still mired in the anticompetitive practices of a planned economy. Change has been rapid and dramatic since the beginning of Deng's "open-door" policy, and many free-market mechanisms that the West takes for granted—stock and security markets, corporate law, or the distinction between management and ownership, for example—had to be developed from scratch in a mere two decades (see Appendix 5).

Cross Currents in China's Business

Despite recent reforms, China is still not a free-market economy. One of the prevalent myths about doing business on the mainland is that market forces have taken over.[5] In reality, the Chinese economy is driven by complex social and political forces that go far beyond simple market imperatives. To be sure, the recent moves toward market-driven economics have been drastic, and many more changes are sure to come. But China is still in a transitional state, and it is important to understand the forces at play in a few key areas that will continue to be most relevant to doing business on the mainland. As the following sections explain, the government remains the largest—and most variable—influence on Chinese enterprise. And just as the government's influence on business is mixed and evolving, the country's newly adopted free-market policies have had an uneven impact on the nature of the PRC business enterprise, and an inconsistent influence across different regions of the country and among different segments of the population.

The Changing Role of the Government

The People's Republic of China is still a socialist or communist country, and foreign business people forget this at their peril. The centralized Communist Party continues to exert a strong conservative influence, especially at the national level, and is often a major player in policy decisions affecting business. A network of party representatives still operates—formally and informally—within government and business organizations.

Under the former strict communist system, the national government was involved in all activities. It was supplier, distributor, information controller, housing provider, and so on. With the reforms, government involvement in business was the first factor to change, although this varied from industry to industry. Indeed, the national government is not uniformly interested in all business activities. Certain "pillar industries" such as petrochemicals, auto manufacturing, and telecommunications are still under direct national government control or supervision. In these industries, leading companies receive support from the state but are required to check back with governmental authorities for major decisions. Other industries are less regulated. Shipping, for example, has developed virtually unnoticed by the PRC government, and remains relatively independent today.

Figure 9-1 presents the complex web of internal and external parties, as well as government agencies to which a typical enterprise operating in China is accountable. The role that these various units play in a business's operation is tremendous. A global consulting firm's study of PRC executives found that they spent, on average, 5 percent of their working hours on strategic issues, 5 percent on human resources issues, 20 percent on operating issues, and 60 *percent* dealing with various governmental supervisory agencies![6]

Box 9-1: Cultural Dilemma: Who Should I Know?

My firm is establishing an enterprise in China. How do we establish the government relationships necessary to make sure that we get the appropriate approvals and that we are in compliance with the applicable laws?

Options and Observations

Companies operating in the PRC must deal with a wide range of stakeholder groups, many of which are linked to the approval process. You can take several steps to minimize legal risks.

- If you have local partners, involve them in the process. They are likely to know the political geography and can provide important introductions.

- Consider involving a local "agent" who is familiar with the industry and has personal credibility to work with you throughout the process. Also, some U.S.-based consultancies specialize in assisting companies in entering the China market.

- Hire reputable lawyers in China—but make sure they have the right experience, preferably in your industry.

China's Enterprise Types

The PRC government is not a monolithic entity, and neither are PRC enterprises definable by a single type. China's economic reform is being carried out in incremental steps, resulting in a wide range of business enterprises, all with varying levels of government involvement. Some of these enterprises are themselves in a state of transition. Regardless of the type of enterprise, the general trend is toward a clearer definition of ownership, greater separation between owners and managers, and a movement away from a purely social organization toward a socioeconomic or largely economic entity.[7] The main types of enterprise found today in the PRC can be loosely arranged into four groups: state-owned, local collective, private, and foreign-invested.

State-owned enterprises (SOEs) are slow-moving and highly centralized bureaucratic organizations with a reputation for inefficiency.

Figure 9-1: **The Internal and External Relationship Network (Web) in a Typical Chinese Enterprise**

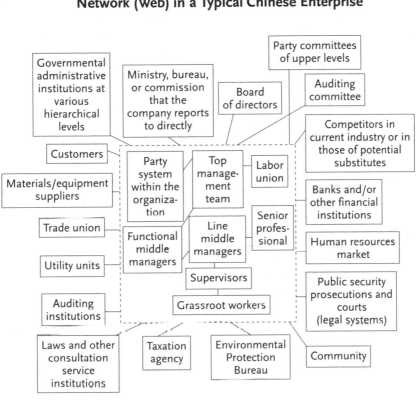

Their functions tend to extend well beyond those of the average business enterprise. According to a Chinese estimate, SOEs own or operate nearly one-third of the country's schools and hospitals, and social welfare expenses consume on average more than 45 percent of their overhead. But this social role is changing as SOEs face growing market pressure to sharpen their competitive edge and realize profits: Once the most important business players in China, SOEs laid off 8 million people in the first half of 1999 alone. The government is carrying out major reforms to rescue what is left of these ailing organizations, privatizing some and limiting the social functions and benefits of most. SOEs no longer provide guaranteed housing for workers, for example, and other services such as education and transportation are being separated from these organizations as well.

Another traditional form of business enterprise that has been undergoing major restructuring and consolidation is the *collective*, an enterprise owned jointly by a group of people who live in the same town, village, or community. The future of such businesses is in fact quite questionable. In July 1999, it was reported that almost half of the country's 300,000 collectives were facing bankruptcy due to lack of competitiveness and rising debt.[8] Nevertheless, one particular type of collective, known as the "township" enterprise, is experiencing growing popularity: Its employment figures have increased from 1.5 million in 1978 to more than 30 million at the end of the century. Considerably healthier than the SOEs, township enterprises are firms created by former agricultural communes. Investments in them may come from town governments, village committees, families, or individual farmworkers. The township enterprises' style of operation varies widely: Some are run like SOEs, with heavy government influence, while others are merely thinly disguised private firms. Following the reforms initiated under **Deng** Xiaoping, the objective of such firms is to maximize profits. Most pay hourly wages and, unlike SOEs, have the ability to recruit and fire as the organization deems necessary. Although township enterprises suffer little intervention from the national government, their success is generally enabled by a symbiotic a relationship with the local community and government, as well as by the effective leadership of the top management.

Private enterprises constitute a growing proportion of China's businesses. These tend to be small-scale firms, often family-owned and family-managed, with simple, centralized organizational structures. In this regard, they are similar to the typical overseas Chinese business: They make decisions quickly, are sensitive to cost, have low debt-to-equity ratios, and are linked to similar organizations across the country through interpersonal networks. In the southern coastal areas, and increasingly in other parts of the country, many private enterprises have become low-cost, labor-intensive processing plants for Hong Kong–based and Taiwan-based manufacturers of products such as toys and consumer electronics. These small private enterprises will play an increasingly important role as their size and numbers grow nationwide.

Foreign-invested enterprises (FIEs) include both joint ventures between Chinese and foreign companies and wholly foreign-owned

---

Box 9-2: Kelon, China's Refrigerator King

In 1983, the town government of Rongqi in Guangdong decided to form a company to manufacture refrigerators. With a grant of $11,500, nineteen staff members visited a number of refrigerator factories, learned what they could, and, in September 1983, built the first Kelon refrigerator by hand under the leadership of **Pan** Ning. After further government investment, a factory was built; by the end of 1984, it had produced 3,000 refrigerators. By 1985, annual output had reached 30,000 units. Major investments throughout the 1980s, in addition to joint ventures with Hong Kong companies, expanded the company's production capacity and enabled it to begin producing air conditioners. In 1993, the company went public, offering $49 million worth of shares on the Hong Kong exchange. In 1996, Kelon established a research institute in Japan, entered into a joint venture with Sanyo to develop freezers, and acquired another factory in Chengdu. From humble beginnings, this township enterprise has grown into one of China's most successful domestic brands. Its head, **Wang** Guoduan, was the highest-paid CEO in China in 1999, and Kelon has successfully fended off formidable global competitors such as Whirlpool.

Although Kelon is a collective and partially government-owned enterprise, the company's growth has successfully kept pace with the dramatic rate of change that often occurs in China's transitional economy. In 1999, a group of consultants recommended that the company restructure its top management within three years to make it more market-oriented. Kelon adopted the consultants' advice but implemented the suggested changes in less than one year![a]

[a] Garry D. Bruton, Hailin Lan, and Yuan Lu, "China's Township and Village Enterprises: Kelon's Competitive Edge," *Academy of Management Executive* 14, no. 1 (2000): 22–24.

---

entities. Investors from over 180 countries and regions have set up about 350,000 enterprises in China with a contracted worth of over U.S.$630 billion. By the end of 1999, the number of Chinese working in FIEs was 20 million, accounting for about 10 percent of the country's total labor force in urban areas. These enterprises made a huge contribution to the PRC's export trade in the eighties and nineties. In 1998, FIE exports amounted to U.S.$80.96 billion, accounting for 44.1 percent of the country's total export. However, the business plans of most of them were based on low-cost production labor. Technology, equipment, marketing, and finance were provided by the foreign partner. Today, very low labor cost in and of itself is a fading competitive advantage—especially in Southeast Asia. Therefore, the PRC is encouraging higher value-added enterprises wherever it can. China hopes that foreign investment in its pharmaceutical industry, for example, will extend from the production sector into research and development, with the government encouraging this growth by exempting foreign-funded research centers from tariffs and surcharges on the import of equipment, supporting technology, and spare parts not available in China.[9]

Types of FIEs have been divided until recently into the joint venture and the wholly owned foreign enterprise (WOFE).[10] The PRC government, of course, has traditionally favored the joint venture; in fact, in many economic sectors and industries foreign investors have been prohibited from using the WOFE structure. In any case, a government-sanctioned WOFE is still subject to certain formal limits and receives comprehensive "guidance" from government authorities.

In the last few years, as the Western world has shown more interest in China, its leaders have been experimenting with the legalization of new ownership structures. These new systems include holding companies (permitted by law as early as 1995), joint stock companies, partnership arrangements, and joint trading companies. Foreign companies have begun using the new formats, which, while still restrictive regarding ownership and operation, provide a platform for future expansions as China's economic reforms keep pace. Unilever, as reported, "seeks to become the first listed foreign company."[11]

Uneven Development

While China's economic development has been proceeding rapidly, and its economic reforms have led to unprecedented levels of opportunity for Chinese businesses, the economic reforms have simply not had enough time to touch the lives of the vast majority of the nation's people. The reforms have principally targeted urban areas, leaving the countryside untouched. In 1999, 44 percent of the urban population had heard of the Internet, in contrast to only 6 percent of the rural population. Among city dwellers, 42 percent had heard of stocks; in rural areas, only 9 percent. And with all the attention the West has been lavishing on fast-food chains in China, 49 percent of the urban population—but only 1 percent of rural Chinese—had tried fast food.[12] In cities such as Guangzhou and Shanghai, professionals work in high-rise office buildings, drive cars, and shop for the latest fashions at the mall. In less developed regions, however, some Chinese live essentially as their ancestors did a hundred years ago, scraping out a meager living working on family farms and living in houses with no indoor plumbing. The overall Chinese standard of living has risen substantially in the last twenty years. Nevertheless, widespread poverty persists, particularly in the rural and remote areas of the country.

The widening gap in social and economic development is manifest across the country's provinces and is reflected in the pattern of foreign direct investment (FDI), which has focused almost exclusively on the coastal belt, virtually excluding the heartland of the country. Over 27 percent of China's FDI is concentrated in the southern coastal province of Guangdong, and 83.4 percent in the coastal provinces as a whole. In contrast, the vast inland provinces of Sichuan, Anhui, and Hunan benefit from only slightly more than 1 percent each. The publication *Yazhou Zhoukan* ("Asia Week") annually surveys the top 100 PRC companies ranked by market capitalization. The geographic distribution of these companies demonstrates the economic disparity across different provinces and the concentration of major enterprises in coastal provinces. As Figure 9-2 illustrates, 40 percent of these top enterprises are located in the two coastal areas of Guangdong (23 percent) and Shanghai (16 percent). Although development is now spreading aggressively into the western inland territories, the regional disparities are likely to continue well into the future.

Such uneven development has created immense social problems, as millions of workers migrate to urban areas in search of greater opportunities. In 1992, the government estimated that there were 100 million migrants roaming China looking for work. In the first six months of 1999, there were 7.4 million unemployed in the

Figure 9-2: Geographic Distribution of the PRC's Top 100 Enterprises

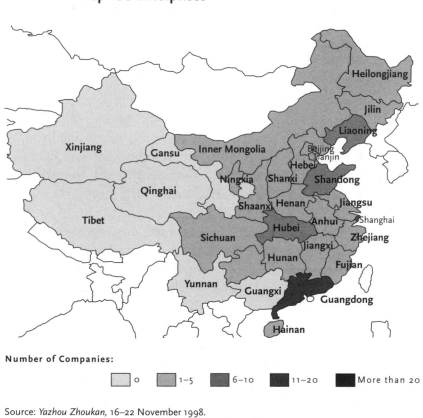

Number of Companies:

0	1–5	6–10	11–20	More than 20

Source: *Yazhou Zhoukan*, 16–22 November 1998.

cities, unemployment for the country as a whole was estimated at 16 to 18 million, and the total number of people affected by unemployment was approximately 120 million.[13] The government's concerns about social instability and unrest are significant factors in both the recent reforms the state has instituted and the tight controls it strives to maintain.

Three Generations, Three Attitudes toward Reform

The reforms of 1979 represented a fundamental challenge to the old economic ideas, and among the Chinese population there is by no means a uniform understanding of (nor uniform support for) what the government is hoping to achieve. Only one segment of the Chinese population, those under forty years of age, grew up in the era that introduced capitalism and competitive markets. The previous generation, aged forty to seventy, was strongly influenced by the Cultural Revolution and anticapitalist campaigns, and it tends to be wary of radical change—but equally unwilling to go back to the old ways. Because of the educational and social disruption of the Cultural Revolution, this generation missed its chance for a college education; nonetheless, these people form the core of middle- and even upper-tier management today.[14] The oldest generation (aged seventy and above) grew up during the time of civil war and communist expansion in China and consequently has little context for understanding modern market capitalism.

China's employment market has also suffered from a "brain drain," with many of its most talented people seeking higher education outside the PRC and choosing to remain in their new countries. Western-style M.B.A. education only became available in the PRC in 1991, and there is a severe dearth of good business schools in China. According to an article from early 1999 in the *China Business Review*, "Chinese universities produce fewer than 1,000 M.B.A. graduates per year, though many senior Western managers in China estimate that 20,000 are needed to meet the growing demand of businesses."[15] Moreover, many Chinese M.B.A. programs lack the hands-on class assignments, company internships, and joint research initiatives with industry that provide Western business students with valuable experience.

Get-Rich-Quick Mentality

Like many other rapidly developing markets, the PRC has its share of Wild West–style profiteering and questionable business practices. One of the most noticeable and troubling results of the PRC's transitional status is a newly developed appetite for instant prosperity. This approach to business success differs radically from the practices common among the overseas Chinese, who typically favor a long-term approach to business.

**Box 9-3: The Greatest Challenges of PRC Business:
The Word from the Managers**

A survey of senior executives from multinational corporations with substantial experience in China (BASF, IBM, PricewaterhouseCoopers, among others) offers insight into the challenge of doing business in the PRC.[a]

The managers' top concerns stemmed from governmental, cultural, and human resources problems. Bureaucratic delays, legal barriers, and political uncertainty were identified as the main government-related concerns, with the respondents emphasizing that strong relationships and a long history in the market conferred competitive strengths. The executives repeatedly pointed out that a thorough understanding of cultural factors (e.g., the importance of social networks in business activities) was essential to their PRC operations. Finally, in the human resources area, the respondents cited localization of management and developing employee skills as their main managerial challenges and pointed to the need for making training investments in the local labor force.

It is important to note that human resources also tops the list of concerns for Chinese senior executives in the PRC, far outweighing the challenges presented by competitors or government policies.[b]

---

[a] Ming-Jer Chen, "The Risks and Rewards of Doing Business in the People's Republic of China," Global Chinese Business Initiative, The Wharton School, 1997.

[b] Whenever I consult with senior Chinese executives, I always ask them to identify their top three domestic and global concerns. Human resources consistently ranks number one, far outweighing all other factors.

While in part this get-rich-quick mentality may be a backlash against the communist policies that preceded the era of reform, it may also be rooted in the mainland's history as a "society of shortage" or a "survival economy." Paul Jensen, an American consultant working in Shanghai notes that "what might be termed 'ethical dislocations' . . . are perhaps an inevitable side effect of very rapid but disproportionate economic growth."[16] With famines commonplace throughout rural China's history, and with the added disruption of communist programs, some Chinese entrepreneurs ignore Confucian guidelines and instead think primarily and exclusively about their individual profit.

Box 9-4:   Prominent Voices on China

Some people call them losses [in China]. I call them investments.[a]

—ROGER ENRICO, Chairman and CEO of PepsiCo, Inc.

China will be one of the great economies and political forces of the next century. And it can only be good that China . . . shares the responsibilities of international leadership [and] has the confidence to evolve politically as well as economically.[b]

—TONY BLAIR, British Prime Minister

[The success] has nothing to do with who we know and everything to do with what we do.[c]

—MAURICE GREENBERG, Chairman and CEO, AIG

It's the most fascinating country—it's changing the most; it will have the most impact on what goes on; there's the most uncertainty about exactly how things will proceed.[d]

—BILL GATES, Chairman and Cofounder, Microsoft

We don't walk into a country with an ideology, saying here's what the Internet can or should do for you. We try to find out what the [country's leaders] want from the Internet, and what role they think it can play in their country. We try to work with that.[e]

—JERRY YANG, Cofounder, Yahoo!

When you go into a marketplace like China . . . [it's] not about taking American culture and pushing it around the world. It's really about trying to take the ethnic diversity we have in the world and give it expression.[f]

—GERALD LEVIN, Chairman and CEO, Time Warner

---

[a] *Asiaweek* Forum, "China's Prospects: In Shanghai, a Conference of Capitalists Ponders the Country's Future," 15 October 1989, <http://www.japan.cnn.com/ASIANOW/asiaweek/magazine/99/1015/forum.html> (accessed 3 July 2000).

[b] Speech by the British prime minister, at the British Chamber of Commerce dinner, "The International Economic Crisis: The Urgent Need for an International Response," Peking, China, 7 October 1998.

[c] "Maurice Greenberg Reveals a Little Too Much," *Financial Times*, 22 May 1998.

[d] "Interview: Bill Gates on Microsoft's 'Only Sin' and Other Subjects," interview by Don Tennant, *Computerworld Hong Kong*, 19 December 1995, <http://209.1.23.51/javaworld/jw-03-1996/idgns.java.1995/idgns.java.1995.195.html> (accessed 3 July 2000).

[e] *Asiaweek* Forum, "China's Prospects."

[f] Brian Palmer, "The View from China," *Fortune*, 8 November 1999, 214.

Box 9-4: Prominent Voices on China (continued)

In China, you cannot just duplicate what you have done in other markets. We have given Chinese characteristics to our phones. China is different from the rest of the world.[g]

—JORMA OLLILA, Chairman and CEO, Nokia

An entrepreneur in China faces so many psychological pressures. You need to have a special strength and endurance to succeed. Initially, we couldn't borrow from the [government] banks, so we had to raise capital on our own. We built our business, our brand and our image. Then the banks came looking for us, offering loans. Entrepreneurs in China should not count on help from the government; otherwise, they won't be able to grow quickly.[h]

—LIU YONGHAO, Chairman, New Hope Group

[g] *Asiaweek* Forum, "China's Prospects."
[h] Ibid.

Navigating the PRC's Transitional Economy

The PRC's constantly changing environment has led many companies to debate whether or not China is a "lost cause." But even if the Western scorecard in doing business with China shows as many losses as wins, China's market and political clout still make it a force to be reckoned with in the world economy.[17] The following sections offer a set of strategic guidelines for approaching business in the PRC with a balanced integration of global practices and local contexts.

Enthusiasm Meets Reality

Writing in *Fortune* magazine, Louis Kraar brought down to earth the fanfare that has long surrounded the promise of doing business in mainland China. Kraar attacked what he calls the "five Chinese myths" including the notion that the PRC is a huge market, that China will become the world's largest economy, that the key to modernizing China is foreign investment, and that market forces have taken over the country's economy.

The reality of doing business in China is much more complex. China is not a single market but rather a vast collection of unevenly developed markets. Although China's economy is growing, its pace is slowed by social and economic factors that cannot be resolved overnight. Simply throwing investment money at these problems is not the answer; a deep understanding of social and historical realities can be immensely more valuable than cash. China's political and business systems do make it vulnerable to the same problems that contributed to the Asian financial crisis. Finally, the Chinese economy is driven by complex social and political forces that go far beyond simple market imperatives.[18] To succeed in the PRC, Western companies need more than enthusiasm—they must take a balanced view of the real opportunities there and do their basic homework on business and sociopolitical concerns. The streets of China are not paved with gold, and the key to success there is understanding and preparation.

Drawing the Line

The typical advice offered to companies doing business in the PRC is to be flexible—about expectations, negotiations, time, and the behavior of Chinese partners. In general, this advice is sound, and this book has frequently made the same recommendation. However, it is equally important that Western firms identify certain areas in which they *cannot* be flexible, and determine the minimum conditions (product quality, consistent global corporate behavior, conformation to WTO standards, etc.) required for their continuing presence in the PRC. If these conditions cannot be met, it may simply be better to not get involved in Chinese business. Thus, it is important to recognize which elements of doing business are, in fact, essential to your company's "identity," as well as those business routines that might benefit from a rethinking and an adaptation to the PRC environment.

Balancing the Executive Team

Human resources issues are particularly important for MNCs operating in China, whose memory of foreign colonialism and

---

Box 9-5: Is China a Lost Cause?

As this book was nearing completion, a pair of editors at the *Harvard Business Review* approached me with a proposal for an article on the current state of the PRC market. After some discussion, we agreed on the provocative title: "Is China a Lost Cause?"

Soon thereafter, I began floating this question to Western and Chinese executives. As I expected, the two groups' responses were split along cultural lines: The Westerners were truly fascinated by the question, and found it perfectly appropriate and timely; the Chinese (even those who had worked for Western companies or who had been educated in the West) were puzzled by the proposal, and had trouble understanding why one would ask such a seemingly pessimistic question.

The two groups' respective answers to the question are highly suggestive. Given the history of Western companies' often disappointing involvement in PRC markets, I had expected that the Western respondents would see the logic of such a question. The surprised reactions from the Chinese, on the other hand, indicated a high level of comfort with China's market environment as well as a strong confidence in its future prospects—a confidence that, one could argue, has been in place since the PRC's opening to the West in the late 1970s.

One tangible sign of the optimism expressed by the Chinese executives is the grassroots momentum for economic reform. Additionally, an increasing number of native Chinese are returning to their homeland after receiving degrees in the West. This movement reverses a trend of departure that had persisted into the late 1990s. Now, with the country's imminent entry into the WTO and with a host of Internet markets promising great opportunities, the PRC is starting to lure more managers who were educated overseas back home.[a]

In short, while the answers to the question "Is China a Lost Cause?" were not conclusive—depending very much on the assumptions and experiences of the executives I asked—it was the question itself that elicited the greatest diversity of response.

[a] Brook Larmer, "China: Home at Last for a Group of Harvard M.B.A.s, Returning to China Means a Chance to Serve the Country—and Get Rich. The Tiananmen Generation is Back," *Newsweek International*, 31 July 2000.

---

whose population diversity can present special challenges to non-locals. It is vital, for instance, to have someone on the team who understands the regional dialects and customs; simply knowing Mandarin may not be enough. Furthermore, a local will have an

---

Box 9-6:   Cultural Dilemma: Dealing with T&E

A group of potential Chinese customers will be visiting my company in the United States. I've noticed that their travel itinerary includes non-business stops, including Las Vegas. My company balks at that kind of entertainment expense. What should I do?

Options and Observations

Before making your final decision about the excursion, your company should consider the following:

- Chinese customers may reasonably expect to combine business and pleasure, which affords an opportunity for each party to get to know the other better.

- Business might be adversely affected if the company does not show its visitors proper hospitality, especially if your competitors are willing to do so.

Nevertheless, if it is against the policy of your company to engage in such practices, it is vital that you explain the situation with all the diplomacy necessary to allow a face-saving way out for the customer.

---

immediate understanding of *mianzi,* or face issues and may be able to interpret confusing signals from the government or put seemingly incoherent or inconsistent policies in perspective. Beyond the language barrier, foreigners will encounter among the Chinese a complex mix of feelings of inferiority (linked to the colonial past and relative inexperience with global business practice) and superiority (born out of cultural heritage and national pride, including recent economic successes and market potential). Strong and committed local people can help an organization recognize and handle this mix of factors skillfully and effectively.

Segmentation

While China's vast size may provoke business dreams of equally vast markets, a more realistic and productive approach will acknowledge the segments within a given market rather than seeing China as an undifferentiated, exploitable whole. Market segmentation and

---

Box 9-7: Global Training: A Two-Way Street

Familiarizing your Chinese partners with your own ways of doing business should go beyond simply transplanting your corporate culture into the Chinese context. Chinese partners will be looking to become associated with your network just as you are looking for access to theirs. If possible, bring your Chinese associates to visit the headquarters in the country where your company is based so that they can meet the people in your organization and begin to feel a part of your community. Most companies are reluctant to spend money on these kinds of visits or to extend their associates' trips to include cultural or social excursions. Such expenditures, however, are generally a sound investment in the long run and may be the cheapest and most effective way to help your Chinese partners understand your national and corporate culture and practices.

---

targeting have particular relevance in China due to the uneven development discussed earlier.

The case of agribusiness provides a useful example of segmentation. With a population that represents one-fifth of the world and which increases by 16 million people each year, the demand in China for grain and other agricultural products is staggering. China's size, however, means that dietary preferences and farming practices differ greatly by region. Moreover, farming operations in China tend to be small and local. For these reasons, U.S. agricultural products and machinery (equipment typically geared for large-scale farming), are not of equal value to all of China, where only 55 percent of the country's arable land is plowed by machine, and less than 20 percent is sown and harvested mechanically.[19]

In agriculture, as with many other seemingly vast markets on the mainland, the key is to first recognize and then tailor an approach appropriate to the characteristics and needs of individual market segments. Trading powerhouse Mitsui & Co. learned this lesson the hard way. As its CEO Ueshima Shigeji explained, "Our biggest failure in China was in marketing. In the 1980s we sold our products to China as a single, unified market—and lost a lot of money. We learned that China consists of segments—the coast vs. the hinterland, urban vs. rural. Each segment has a different culture, tastes, and history. So we developed a strategy of 'tailored' marketing."[20]

Balancing Culture and Geography

As many companies have come to realize, the overseas Chinese, as partners or as employees, can greatly facilitate business interactions in the PRC. Many overseas Chinese have family or social ties on the mainland, maintain connections in their hometowns, and still speak local dialects. Despite their cultural differences with their mainland cousins, to the overseas Chinese the PRC is not the "foreign" place that it often is to Westerners.

The deep financial and cultural connections between the overseas Chinese and mainland China point to a potential weakness in the typical MNC approach to China operations. Adhering to strict geographic divisions in their global strategy, most Western firms draw a distinction between regions like "Southeast Asia," the "PRC," and "Greater China," for example. There are, of course, many sound business reasons for taking such a regional approach. But a more flexible and creative perspective might consider a "China division" as a cultural (rather than a regional or national) unit, and draw on the commonalities and networks that *connect* Chinese businesses across geographically distant areas.

Profit—Plus Service

Though most PRC firms exist to make a profit, they also remain driven by socialist-era and traditional Chinese community service–related imperatives: providing jobs, assuring the well-being and stability of the community, and maintaining face within the community and to the world at large. The strong service component of doing business on the mainland, while it may pose challenges for some foreign businesses, also presents benefits. In fact, the best long-term strategy for any business operation in the PRC may be to find an approach that combines service and profit. Given the memory of Western intervention it is wise to earn your welcome.

The experience of Motorola, the largest foreign company in the PRC, provides an instructive example. Although the reasons for its success are many, the company's (and in particular its former CEO Robert Galvin's) skill in building relationships with government

---

Box 9-8: Inside PRC Business: Some Tips

- China is not just one market. There are substantial differences among regions, communities, and generations, and socioeconomic conditions are changing rapidly. Success in one area does not necessarily translate to success in others.

- The diversity of types of businesses within the PRC requires a flexible mind-set. The American distinction between "for-profit" and "nonprofit," for example, simply does not apply in the PRC.

- Goodwill at the *personal* level is critical. Strong reputations and relationships with Chinese employees or partners provide valuable assets, especially in times when relationships between countries' governments become strained.

- An annual "cameo" appearance by a senior executive who has otherwise been uninvolved in the relationship is not the way to do business with the Chinese.

- Learn Chinese business geography. The best path to mainland Chinese business may be through overseas Chinese partners: the shortest route from Denver to Shanghai might actually be through Vancouver or Hong Kong. Conversely, the quickest route from Paris to Malaysia could be through the connections established in the PRC.

---

entities, business partners, academic institutions, and local communities has been instrumental in its positioning in China. For instance, Motorola has been very active in promoting environmental protection, a growing concern in the PRC. The company has also made significant investments in higher education, founding "Motorola University" to offer training and other educational opportunities to local employees, and is among the largest donors to China's Project Hope (a program that promotes literacy among children in remote areas). It has built goodwill in the communities where it operates by seeking local sourcing for parts, assisting local suppliers in exports, and providing housing for its employees. As a result, Motorola has received accolades and awards from the PRC government for its responsible corporate citizenship.

Box 9-9:   Taking the "Service Road"

American businessman D. Bruce McMahan has taken a long, indirect, and unexpected route to business success in the PRC—one that started with service. McMahan is the founder of the nonprofit National Cristina Foundation (NCF), which brings technology's benefits to the disabled. (The NCF was named for McMahan's daughter Cristina, who was born with cerebral palsy.) While serving on President Reagan's National Advisory Board on Technology and the Disabled, McMahan received a letter from **Deng** Pufang, the son of then-premier **Deng** Xiaoping. During the Cultural Revolution, the younger Deng was crippled when Red Guards threw him out a window. When his father returned to power, **Deng** Pufang was appointed to lead an organization to help the disabled of China. He had seen an exhibit at a trade show about using technology to help the handicapped, and he wrote to the United States to find an American organization that could share information about this topic.

   McMahan responded by drafting a proposal to create a National Cristina Foundation in China. Within ten days, he was invited to China. McMahan led a group of eleven members of the NCF's board of directors on their first trip to China, where they spent three weeks setting up and manning a demonstration center. By 1988, McMahan had become well known in Chinese business and political circles. Despite initial suspicion on the part of the Chinese, he was eventually taken into the inner circles and invited to make investments in Chinese business ventures. In 1994, he was given the opportunity to take a comanager's role in a major Chinese stock offering—a $333 million deal on a new Chinese power generation company. One of the three underwriters on the deal was tiny McMahan Securities Co. Although his title as comanager is largely honorary, it is worth upward of a million dollars; in terms of McMahan's *guanxi* with the Chinese, it is priceless.[a]

[a] Philip Mather, "A Chinese Puzzle," *Investment Dealers' Digest*, 15 August 1994.

The Motorola experience is a reminder of the importance, especially in the Chinese context, of finding a balance between civic-mindedness and profit—a balance that could be decisive in the ongoing success of MNCs in China. As the country continues to develop on an uneven course, the gap between Chinese haves and have-nots is likely to increase. It is therefore crucial that foreign MNCs do not become the scapegoat for such uneven development. Should civil unrest occur, a record of serving China and of respecting the public good is perhaps the best protection a foreign firm can have.[21]

Conclusion: The Middle Way Is a Global Way

Throughout this chapter, we have used the word *transitional* to describe the state of the economy in China. In the PRC context, though, *transition* does not necessarily imply a direct and inevitable road to a Western-style market economy. It is unrealistic to expect that in the next twenty years China will become a market like Japan—which has thrived through its adoption of American-led Western capitalism. Instead, it is likely that the PRC will take a few decades to find a balance between Western free-market enterprise and the historical influences of communism, nationalism, and Confucianism. This transitional character will surely continue to challenge many Western businesspeople, but it may also provide the opportunity for developing a new conception of business enterprise, one that is suited to the global reality of the twenty-first century.

It was precisely this possibility that I presented to a group of 300 Asian-based senior executives and business leaders during my keynote speech for the World Economic Forum's China Business Summit 2000, and which I provide now as a summary for this chapter and more largely, this book. The market-driven, finance-focused Western free enterprise system has made substantial contributions to the global economy, but it is less compatible with societies where business enterprises have traditionally played greater social and noneconomic roles. Alternative types of business—from overseas Chinese business families to China's mixed forms of enterprise—do not always make sense from a profit-maximizing point of view. As disparate kinds of business come into more frequent and closer contact, we will have an increasing need for a common language at the enterprise level—a language that fully recognizes institutional and cultural differences even as it draws on their respective strengths.

Epilogue:
Toward the Globe as a Whole

AROUND THE TIME I was completing this book, I met a British businessman with extensive experience in Asian business transactions. When I prompted him to give me his impressions of Asia, and the PRC in particular, he repeated a common complaint about Chinese businesspeople. "They do not follow any ethics," he protested. "They're only looking to make a quick profit. And when dealing with foreigners, their main concern is how much extra money they can cheat out of them!" What the British businessman said next, however, was revealing. He told me that he had been offered a high-paying job in Hong Kong but had turned it down. His reason? "I just didn't understand the [Chinese] guy I'd be working for. He was too shrewd." Hearing this, I realized that his impression of "shrewdness" was most likely caused by cultural differences—the exact differences that this book has attempted to explain in detail.

Adverse reactions toward Chinese business behavior are fairly common, for we often feel an instinctive dislike for cultures and methods foreign to our own. But we must remember that if we show no knowledge of another culture, its members will have little incentive to establish ties of trust with us (especially when distrust has been the norm historically) and may seek only profit. All of us have learned that when we travel abroad, learning to speak the country's language guarantees a more enjoyable vacation. In the same way, a person with cultural knowledge of the Chinese not only will receive a better welcome but also will have an entirely different business experience. It is my hope that this book will help produce such an experience.

It is tempting here to take this book's discussion of Chinese philosophy one step further—in the direction of the West. In the world today, global business thinkers and practitioners are unsure which path global business will take. One path leads toward the "melting pot" model of global business—a model where all practices will resemble each other and all cultural colors will blend into a uniform gray. The other path leads to the still undefined model of multicultural business practices—a model that many praise and many critique, but that still requires much more study and development.

Chinese philosophy may bring new light to this global dilemma. Where the West has historically valued self-knowledge as the ulti-mate goal (Socrates set "Know thyself" as his fundamental lesson), Chinese philosophers added to this pursuit the ideal of knowing others. Confucius taught: "The pursuit of ultimate truth requires first introspection, and then love for others. It is only when these two are combined that perfection can be achieved." Sun Tzu stated: "Know yourself and know the opponent, and you will win 100 battles." Placing the other on equal terms with the self is perhaps the only way to conceive of any effective model of multiculturalism—in society as in the business context.

Since in Chinese philosophy the individual exists only through role relations, knowing oneself is ultimately impossible without a knowledge of others. In fact, knowing one's role requires knowing one's relation to others. This is not as abstract as it sounds. For instance, viewing one's investments in a developing country as pure profit for oneself—which would be an extreme form of Western individualism—is ignoring the reality of social interaction as fundamental to human existence.

The Chinese concept of *zhong he* (holistic integration) brings the self and other into an even tighter relation. In line with yin and yang symbolism, self and other are perceived as complementary rather than opposing. Therefore, in business terms, competition and coop-eration are merely flip sides of the same coin, and competitors are perceived as collaborators rather than opponents. (Many Western firms, particularly high-tech ones, have already begun to adopt this practice under the name of "coopetition.") A recent example of the potential pitfalls of disregarding the other can be seen in Microsoft's dealings with its competitors. Through intimidation, Microsoft managed to secure a monopoly in the software business, only to see its empire come under general attack for its overly individualistic, anti-competitive conduct. Whatever the outcome of its antitrust trial, Microsoft's conduct has alienated most other players in the business and may do serious damage to the company's business in the long run.

Microsoft's is an extreme case that, like many extremes, casts a harsh but instructive light on business ethical practices. As one of the cornerstones of Western business ethics, antitrust guarantees that self and other in business remain balanced. In the final analysis, competition, that most revered Western idea, can happen only when there is someone to compete against. Ironically, competition rests not on pure individualism but rather on the knowledge and acknowledgment of others—a lesson Chinese philosophy has taught for 5,000 years.

Competition is but one area where Chinese thinking can offer valuable lessons for Western companies. Chinese ideas on performance—having the patience to wait for returns in an uncertain environment—may also represent an important adaptation for Western firms driven primarily by the bottom line. Recognizing that some things simply cannot be sped up, even though the pace of business is ever increasing, can be an important corrective to the "make-a-killing" mentality that warps some firms' goals.

One of the strengths of Chinese business—the ability to recognize and meet the needs of a wide variety of different stakeholders—is also likely to be an increasingly important skill for global businesses in the twenty-first century. In this sense, integration will be the main challenge of the future. Globally, business enterprises will need to establish a program for coping with such demands as infrastructure development and providing for various basic human needs. Meeting the needs of a diverse array of interests and parties, managing relations with suppliers and customers, dealing with demands for flexibility from employees, and developing marketing strategies for local markets will all be part of the success of a global enterprise.

Chinese thought can offer models for responding to these concerns. Indeed, Chinese culture is not the exclusive privilege of the Chinese, but rather a way of thinking that can be learned by all. One does not have to be Chinese to benefit from Chinese ways of thinking!

APPENDIX I
Definition of Geographic Terms

1. *Greater China*: geographic term relating to mainland China, Hong Kong, Taiwan, and Macau (but nominally).

2. *Southeast Asia*: geographic area containing Singapore, Malaysia, Indonesia, Thailand, Cambodia, Vietnam, Laos, Brunei Darussalam, Philippines, Myanmar.

3. *Far East*: geographic term coined during the British Empire pertaining to mainland China, Taiwan, Hong Kong, Japan, North Korea, South Korea, Singapore, Malaysia, Indonesia, Thailand, Cambodia, Vietnam, Laos, Brunei Darussalam, Philippines.

4. *Asia Pacific*: new term that pertains to a more eclectic East-West area including North and South America, East and Southeast Asia, and Australasia. Countries and regions include China, Taiwan, Hong Kong, Japan, North Korea, South Korea, Singapore, Malaysia, Indonesia, Thailand, Cambodia, Vietnam, Laos, Brunei Darussalam, Philippines, Australia, New Zealand, Canada, United States, Mexico, Panama, Peru, Ecuador, Chile, Colombia, Costa Rica, Nicaragua, El Salvador, Guatemala.

5. *ASEAN*: Association of South East Asian Nations. Officially includes Singapore, Malaysia, Myanmar, Indonesia, Thailand, Cambodia, Vietnam, Laos, Brunei Darussalam, Philippines.

6. *Oriental*: adjective, can be considered derogatory, of or pertaining to the people or culture of China, Hong Kong, Taiwan, Japan, North Korea, South Korea.

Migration Patterns of Ethnic Chinese Billionaires

FROM FUJIAN PROVINCE	
Family	**To**
Wonowidjolo	Java
Liem Sioe Liong	Java
Eka Tjipta Widjaja	Java
Sampoerna	Java
Sutanto	Java
Riady	Java
Nursalim	Java
Francis Yeoh	Malaysia
Robert Kuok	Malaysia
Vincent Tan	Malaysia
Wee Cho Yaw (UOB)	Malaysia
Lim Go Thong	Malaysia
Khoo Kay Peng	Malaysia
Lee Seng Wee (OCBC)	Singapore
Ng Teng Fong	Singapore
Khoo Teck Puat	Singapore
Kwek	Singapore
George ly	Manila
Henry Sy	Manila
Yuchengco	Manila
Lucio Tan	Cebu
Go (kongwei)	Cebu
Tiong	Sarawak

FROM SHANGHAI	
Family	**To**
Peter Woo	Hong Kong
Tung Chee-Hwa	Hong Kong
Run Run Shaw	Hong Kong

FROM GUANGDONG PROVINCE	
Family	**To**
Kwok	Hong Kong
Lee Shau-Kee	Hong Kong
Li Ka-Shing	Hong Kong
Cheng Yu-Tung	Hong Kong
Hsu Yi-Ziang	Taipei
Lamsam	Bangkok
Chearavanont	Bangkok
Sophonpanich	Bangkok
Rataranak	Bangkok
Tejapaibul	Bangkok
Phornprapha	Bangkok
Shinawatm	Thailand
Willam Cheng	Singapore

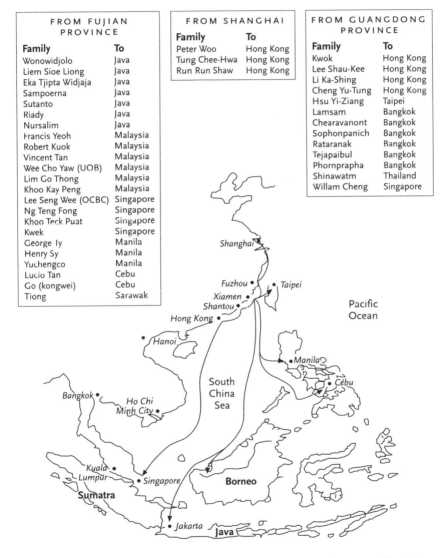

Source: Geoff Hiscock, *Asia's Wealth Club: Who's Really Who in Business—The Top 100 Billionaires in Asia* (London: Nicholas Brealey Publishers, 1997).

Main Events in the History of Mainland China, Taiwan, and Hong Kong

	Hong Kong	Mainland China	Taiwan
1800		1839–1842 Opium War. Britain forced China to open five treaty ports and relinquish Hong Kong.	
	1843 Treaty of Nanjing. Cession of Hong Kong island to Britain.		
			1858 Four ports were forcibly opened to foreign trade.
	1860 First Convention of Beijing: Cession of Kowloon Peninsula to Britain.		
			1884 French forces invaded northern Taiwan.
			1885 French withdrew.
			1895 China ceded Taiwan to Japan in perpetuity after Sino-Japanese war.
1900	1898 Second Convention of Beijing: a ninety-nine-year lease of the New Territories to Britain. The lease expired on 30 June 1997.	1898–1901 Boxer Rebellion against Western presence in China.	
		1911 Sun Yat-Sen revolution, which ends the Qing dynasty and imperial rule in China.	
		1915–1920 *May Fourth Movement* sought to resist foreign imperialism by revo-	

Hong Kong	Mainland China	Taiwan
	lutionalizing Chinese culture. It led to the reorganization of Sun's Nationalist Party, the Kuo Min Tang (KMT).	
	1921 Chinese Communist Party (CCP) founded. Mao Zedong is one of the organizers.	
1926 A Chinese appointed to the Executive Council for the first time.		
	1928 Chiang Kai-Shek became president of the Republic of China (ROC).	
	1928–1937 Nanjing Era. KMT retained power for a decade.	
	1934–1935 The Long March. The CCP sought shelter from KMT.	
	1935–1947 Yan'an Era. Civil war raged between CCP and KMT.	
1941 Hong Kong fell to the Japanese.	1937–1945 Sino-Japanese War.	
		1943 Chiang Kai-Shek's request that Taiwan be "returned to China (ROC)" was agreed to by Allied powers.
1945 The British reoccupied Hong Kong after the unconditional surrender of Japan.		1945 Nationalist soldiers arrived in Taiwan and took over from the Japanese.
1949–1950 750,000 Chinese fled to Hong Kong, many of whom were Shanghai industrialists, bringing capital and labor to Hong Kong.	1949 The Peoples' Republic of China (PRC) was established.	1949 Chiang Kai-Shek and ROC government with almost 2 million Nationalists fled the mainland for Taiwan.
1950s Hong Kong expanded its role from an entrée port to include manufacturing.	1953–1957 China's first five-year plan. Establishment of the Chinese socialist economy.	1950 U.S. sent naval forces to protect Taiwan from China.

Hong Kong	Mainland China	Taiwan
		1960s Great Economic Development: export-led growth.
	1966 The Cultural Revolution. An unstable period for the Chinese economy and politics.	
1967 Cultural Revolution fueled political tension in Hong Kong, causing riots.		
	1971 PRC was admitted to the UN.	1971 ROC was expelled from the UN. The seat of China was given to the PRC.
1972 China indicated at the UN that it regarded Hong Kong as part of its territory.	1972 Richard Nixon visits China.	
		1979 The U.S. terminated its relationship with the ROC and outlined its new relationship in the Taiwan Relations Act. It allowed the U.S. president and Congress to take appropriate action against aggression toward Taiwan.
	1980–1981 China was admitted to the IMF and World Bank.	
1982 British prime minister Margaret Thatcher met Chinese leader **Deng** Xiaoping and agreed to launch talks on Hong Kong's future.		
1983 HK pegs HK$ to US$ at the rate of 7.8.		
1984 Margaret Thatcher and Premier Zhao Ziyang signed the Sino-British Joint Declaration, agreeing on the transfer of Hong Kong in 1997. It stated that Hong Kong would become a Special Administrative Region, which conferred a high degree of autonomy and allowed capitalism to evolve.		
	1985 **Deng** Xiaoping supports capitalist techniques for building "socialism with Chinese characteristics."	

Hong Kong	Mainland China	Taiwan
1986 The United Stock Exchange opened, enabling disparate exchanges under one rule. The Hong Kong Commodities Exchange introduced Hang Seng future contracts.		
		1987 The end of martial law was declared in Taiwan. Nongovernment civilian contacts between Taiwan and the Chinese mainland were allowed.
1989 A million Hong Kong residents protested against the Tiananmen Square incident.	1989 Tiananmen Square student demonstration.	
1990 China published the "Basic Law," Hong Kong's post-1997 miniconstitution.	1990 Shanghai stock market reopened after nearly forty years.	
	1991–1996 Renewed economic liberalization.	
	1992 **Deng** Xiaoping emphasized the need for an acceleration in economic development.	1993 Taiwan and China held preliminary talks to normalize relations.
		1996 China launched "military exercises" in the ocean near Taiwan on the eve of the first free presidential elections.
1997 Handover of Hong Kong to China.	1998 Zhu Rongji became premier and contributed to economic reform.	
	1999 Sino-U.S. WTO agreement.	
2000	2000 The U.S. Senate voted to extend permanent trading relations with China.	2000 First non-KMT president elected in Taiwan.
	2000/2001 China enters WTO	

Three Chinese Thinkers

Confucius

Confucius was a minor figure in his day, but his importance to Chinese culture since cannot be overstated. Confucianism became the official state philosophy in the second century B.C. and has survived almost intact to remain the principal blueprint for Chinese society today.

Confucius, named K'ung Ch'iu, was born to a family of lesser aristocracy in 551 B.C., in the province of Lu (present-day Shantung). Later in life he was called K'ung Fu-Tzu ("Master Kung"), latinized by the Jesuits into Confucius. He began his career as statesman, and rose quickly in the ranks of officialdom. But his goals to implement peace, order, and stability into society brought him disfavor, and he fell almost as quickly as he rose from his political posts. After a turbulent career in politics, Confucius finally resigned and became a teacher, exerting what was to be a much more powerful influence on the younger generation of scholars and future leaders through education.

It is during this period that Confucius produced most of his best-known writings, although his most famous work, the *Analects*, is thought to have been recorded by his students and published after his death. Like Lao Tzu, Confucius's goal was to reestablish order and harmony in the anarchic society of his time. Contrary to Lao Tzu's rejection of scholarly pursuits, however, Confucius's lessons were based on the idea that human beings are perfectible through the study of history and philosophy. Confucius believed that order and social harmony could be achieved by studying the model of earlier Chinese dynasties, which had come to represent a Golden Age in China's history. Accordingly, he promoted traditional values of virtue—humaneness, benevolence, and goodness—which he united under the concept *jen*, a "state of grace" to be attained only by following the correct rituals (*li*) prescribed for the conduct of everyday life.

Though Confucius retained the religious practices and rituals of the ancients, he brought their ethics down to earth, advising followers to care more for man and society than for the supernatural. Instead of maintaining cosmic order, Confucian rites (often as simple as how to sit properly on a mat) aimed at the harmonization of man's social and emotional life. In this sense, what most distinguished Confucian rituals from those of the ancients was the element of benevolence that should accompany prescribed behavior, a virtue that translates into something akin to the Christian "Love thy neighbor."

Throughout its history, Confucianism always had a strong influence on government, and in fact virtually replaced it. As a philosophy conceived to restore social order at a time when a strong central authority was missing, Confucianism aimed at the self-government and self-regulation of the people. This was achieved through its prescription of a hierarchy of fixed moral and social roles that determined all levels of social interaction and behavior. When asked by the ruler of Chi what the best form of government was, Confucius is said to have replied, "Let the ruler be a ruler, the subject a subject, the father a father, and the son a son." When everyone acted according to their role, "rule of law" was no longer of consequence since "rule by man" intervened.

Lao Tzu

Lao Tzu ("Old Master" or "Old Philosopher") is thought to have been an older contemporary of Confucius, born to the name Li Erh. Though historical documents make little mention of him, legend holds that Lao Tzu was an archivist in the Imperial Library at the ancient capital of Loyang. As the story goes, Lao Tzu, disheartened by the social disorder of his times, set out alone for the desert but was stopped at the Han-ku Pass on the western border of China by a guard named Yin Hsi. Knowing of Lao Tzu's reputation for great wisdom, Yin Hsi asked him to record his teachings before leaving the country. There at the border, Lao Tzu is reputed to have spent a night composing the 5,000 characters of his major work, the *Tao Te Ching* (The Way and its Power, The Law of Virtue and the Way).

Whether the legend is true, or whether the characters of the *Tao Te Ching* were penned by a number of anonymous authors under the collective name of Lao Tzu, remains uncertain. What is certain, however, is that the figure of Lao Tzu and the writings attributed to him were of fundamental importance to the development of Taoism which, along with Confucianism, has shaped Chinese society and culture for more than 2,000 years.

Taoism is both a philosophical and religious tradition. However, for the sake of understanding Lao Tzu's original teaching of Taoism, it is important to differentiate between them. Taoism developed around 150 A.D. as an organized religion, with formalized rituals and institutional hierarchies. Its philosophical branch, on the other hand, is as old as Lao Tzu himself, and explicitly rejects social convention, ritual, and hierarchy in favor of the individual's search for spiritual self-fulfillment.

Lao Tzu believed that doctrines corrupt by teaching names that create distinctions (good and evil, beautiful and ugly, high and low, being and non-being) in an otherwise undivided and perfect reality. These distinctions create false desires (to be beautiful, for example) which give rise to "unnatural action." In Lao Tzu's view, it is man's "unnatural" activities and his excessive need for material things that mar the perfect natural order. Unlike Confucius, who sought social order and harmony through the implementation of rigid hierarchies, role-relations, and moral principles, the Taoists urged people to find harmony and stability by turning away from received wisdom. In their view, harmony and self-fulfillment were to be found by conforming to the natural way of things, by living in accord with *Tao*. In keeping with Lao Tzu's teachings, *Tao* itself is an ambiguous term, one which can signify nature, the eternal way, the path, or the absolute reality from which everything arises and to which everything returns.

Sun Tzu

Approximately 100 years after the birth of Confucius and Lao Tzu came a treatise on war and military science that was to be one of the most influential books on strategy ever written. *The Art of War* (or the *Bing-fa* in Chinese), was probably written by a general named Sun Tzu, who served the State of Wu toward the end of the Spring and Autumn period (770–476 B.C.), although as with the *Tao Te Ching*, the work's exact origin and authorship have been debated.

The parallels with the *Tao Te Ching* extend beyond its uncertain authorship. Many of *The Art of War*'s strategies and tactics are in fact based in the philosophical and spiritual tradition of Taoism. From its prescriptions for strategic assessment to those for the actual waging of war, the *Bing-fa*'s thesis centers around one basic principle: how to accomplish the most by doing the least (akin to the Taoist principle of *wu-wei*, or "nonaction").

"To win without fighting is best," says Sun Tzu, and to this end he tellingly underplays the role of weaponry in warfare. Instead, the tools he emphasizes are psychological: how to outwit and deceive opponents, how to turn weakness into strength, how to maintain the cohesion and loyalty of the group. The path to success that Sun Tzu recommends is indirect: It is the path that is least predictable (intelligence, deception) and most adaptable to the ever changing environment of the battlefield (surprise, speed, and flexibility). In sum, militarists must maintain an "invisible" profile, knowing others without being known themselves.

The Art of War remains as relevant today as it was during the Warring States period over 2,000 years ago. The treatise's philosophical underpinnings have lent it the flexibility to be translated into successful strategic lessons for a whole array of disciplines ranging from modern military tactics and political psychology to the art of competition in business and in professional sports. It is perhaps this broad application of the *The Art of War*'s lessons to a range of nonmilitaristic fields that best illustrates Sun Tzu's famous theory of the bloodless battle: that warfare is an art form which, when perfected, allows one to achieve the pacifist ideal of winning without ever fighting.

Major Events in the People's Republic of China, 1979–1999

Date of Event	Event
September 1979	The beginning of a new policy of reform and opening to the outside world.
1979	Issuance of law governing joint venture operations.
1980	Three foreign-invested enterprises are established in China.
Early 1980s	Urban areas undergo comprehensive enterprise-centered reform measures.
Mid-1980s	Opening of several economic and development zones.
1987	China introduces a high-tech research plan to keep abreast of the latest scientific achievements.
March 1988	A visit to Washington by then minister of foreign affairs Wu Xueqian has salutary effects on bilateral relations. China makes assurances that it will cease Silkworm missile sales to Iran, and the United States pledges to continue to make desired technologies available to China.
3–4 June 1989	Tiananmen Square student demonstration.
1990	Shanghai Stock Exchange is established.
January–February 1992	**Deng** Xiaoping completes a five-week journey through southern China, where he exhorts local officials to accelerate economic development and to "deepen" market-oriented restructuring.
October 1993	**Deng** Xiaoping issues a brief but potent declaration: "Slow growth is not socialism."

Date of Event	Event
Spring 1997	General Secretary **Jiang** Zemin sets forth his plan for the reform of state enterprises in a speech to senior party leaders: "Most enterprises were to be privatized or at least partially denationalized. Under the slogan *Zhua da, fang xiao* (Grasp the big, let go of the small) all but the largest and most essential enterprises were to be turned over to various forms of non-state ownership at a more rapid pace than hitherto had been the case."
July 1997	The Hong Kong handover heralded "one country—two systems."
Summer 1998	Clinton's visit, with a retinue of more than 1,000 people, proves surprisingly productive for Sino-American relations.
November 1999	Sino-U.S. World Trade Organization (WTO) agreement.

APPENDIX 6

Suggested Readings

Chapter 1

Chen, Min. *Asian Management Systems: Chinese, Japanese and Korean Styles of Business.* New York: Routledge, 1995.

East Asia Analytical Unit. *Overseas Chinese Business Networks in Asia.* Canberra, Australia: Department of Foreign Affairs and Trade, 1995.

Far Eastern Economic Review. *China in Transition towards the New Millennium.* Hong Kong: Review Publishing Company, 1997.

Haley, George T., Tan Chin Tiong, and Usha C. V. Haley. *New Asian Emperors: The Overseas Chinese, Their Strategies and Competitive Advantages.* Oxford: Butterworth-Heinemann, 1999.

Lever-Tracy, Constance, David Ip, and Noel Tracy. *The Chinese Diaspora and Mainland China: An Emerging Economic Synergy.* London: Macmillan, 1996.

Lu, Yuan. *Management Decision-Making in Chinese Enterprises.* London: Macmillan, 1996.

Pan, Lynn, ed. *The Encyclopedia of the Chinese Overseas.* Cambridge, MA: Harvard University Press, 1999.

Wang, Gungwu. *The Chinese Overseas: From Earthbound China to the Quest for Autonomy.* Cambridge, MA: Harvard University Press, 2000.

Chapter 2

Bruun, Ole. *Business and Bureaucracy in a Chinese City: An Ethnography of Private Business Households in Contemporary China.* Berkeley: Institute of East Asian Studies, University of California, Berkeley, 1993.

Cho, Lee-Jay, and Moto Yada, eds. *Tradition and Change in the Asian Family.* Honolulu: East-West Center, Distributed by the University of Hawaii Press, 1994.

Lim, Linda Y. C., and Peter L. A. Gosling, eds. *The Chinese in Southeast Asia.* Vol. 2. Singapore: Maruzen Asia, 1983.

Limlingan, Victor Simpao. *The Overseas Chinese in ASEAN: Business Strategies and Management Practices.* Manila: Vita Development Corp., 1986.

Redding, Gordon S. *The Spirit of Chinese Capitalism.* New York: Walter de Gruyter, 1990.

Schlevogt, Kai-Alexander. *Inside Chinese Organizations: An Empirical Study of Business Practices in China.* Dissertation.com, 2000.

Seagrave, Sterling. *Lords of the Rim.* London: Corgi Books, 1996.

Yeung, Henry Wai-Chung, and Kris Olds, eds. *Globalization of Chinese Business Firms.* London: Macmillan, 1999.

Chapter 3

Hamilton, Gary G., ed. *Business Networks and Economic Development in East and South East Asia.* Hong Kong: Centre of Asian Studies, University of Hong Kong, 1991.

Luo, Yadong. *Guanxi and Business.* Singapore: World Scientific Publishing, 2000.

Slote, Walter H., and George A. De Vos, eds. *Confucianism and the Family.* Albany: State University of New York Press, 1998.

Tu, Wei-Ming. *The Living Tree: The Changing Meaning of Being Chinese Today.* Stanford, CA: Stanford University Press, 1994.

Yan, Yunxiang. *The Flow of Gifts: Reciprocity and Social Networks in a Chinese Village.* Stanford, CA: Stanford University Press, 1996.

Yang, Mayfair Mei-Hui. *Gifts, Favors, and Banquets: The Art of Social Relationships in China.* Ithaca, NY: Cornell University Press, 1994.

Chapter 4

Bond, Michael Harris. *Beyond the Chinese Face: Insights from Psychology.* Hong Kong: Oxford University Press, 1996.

Lee-Wong, Song Mei. *Politeness and Face in Chinese Culture.* New York: P. Lang, 2000.

Pan, Yuling. *Politeness in Chinese Face-to-Face Interaction.* Stamford, CT: Ablex, 2000.

Tu, Wei-Ming. *Confucian Thought: Selfhood as Creative Transformation.* Albany: State University of New York Press, 1985.

Tu, Wei-Ming. *Confucian Traditions in East Asian Modernity: Moral Education and Economic Culture in Japan and the Four Mini-Dragons.* Cambridge, MA: Harvard University Press, 1996.

Weidenbaum, Murray, and Samuel Hughes. *The Bamboo Network: How Expatriate Chinese Entrepreneurs Are Creating a New Superpower in Asia.* New York: Free Press, 1996.

Chapter 5

Cleary, Thomas, trans. *Thunder in the Sky: Secrets on the Acquisition and Exercise of Power.* Boston: Shambhala, 1993.

Hall, Edward Twitchell, and Mildred Reed Hall. *Understanding Cultural Differences.* Yarmouth, ME: Intercultural Press, 1989.

Hartzell, Richard W. *Harmony in Conflict: Active Adaptation to Life in Present-Day Chinese Society.* Vol. 1. Taipei: Caves Books, 1988.

Huang, Chun-Cheih, and Erik J. Zurcher, eds. *Time and Space in Chinese Culture.* New York: E. J. Brill Academic Publishers, 1995.

Lip, Evelyn. *Feng Shui for Business.* Singapore: Times Books International, 1995.

Munro, Donald J., ed. *Individualism and Holism: Studies in Confucian and Taoist Values.* Ann Arbor: Center for Chinese Studies, University of Michigan, 1985.

O'Hara-Devereaux, May, and Robert Johansen. *Globalwork: Bridging Distance, Culture and Time.* San Francisco: Josey-Bass, 1994.

Tang, Michael C. *A Victor's Reflections and Other Tales of China's Timeless Wisdom for Leaders.* Paramus, NJ: Prentice Hall, 2000.

Tu, Wei-Ming. *Centrality and Commonality: An Essay on Confucian Religiousness.* Albany: State University of New York Press, 1989.

Xu, Chenggang. *Different Transition Path: Ownership, Performance, and Influence of Chinese Rural Industrial Enterprises.* New York: Garland, 1995.

Chapter 6

Chow, Irene, Neil Hobert, Kelley Lane, and Julie Yu. *Business Strategy: An Asia-Pacific Focus.* Singapore: Prentice-Hall, 1997.

Chu, Chin-Ning. *The Asian Mind Game: Unlocking the Hidden Agenda of the Asian Business Culture—A Westerner's Survival Manual.* New York: Rawson Associates, Macmillan, 1991.

Cleary, Thomas, trans. *The Illustrated Art of War by Sun Tzu.* Boston: Shambhala, 1998.

Foo, Check Teck, and Peter Hugh Grinyer. *Sun Tzu on Management: The Art of War in Contemporary Business Strategy.* Singapore: Butterworth-Heinemann Asia, 1995.

Griffith, Samuel B., trans. *Sun Tzu: The Art of War.* London: Oxford University Press, 1963.

McNeilly, Mark. *Sun Tzu and the Art of Business: Six Strategic Principles for Managers.* Oxford: Oxford University Press, 1996.

Wee, Chow-Hou, Lee Khai-Sheang, and Bambang Walujo Hidajat. *Sun Tzu: War and Management; Application to Strategic Management and Thinking.* Singapore: Addison-Wesley, 1991.

Chapter 7

Draine, Cathie, and Barbara Hall. *Culture Shock! Indonesia.* Singapore: Times Books International, 1986.

Engholm, Christopher. *When Business East Meets Business West: The Guide to Practice and Protocol in the Pacific Rim.* New York: Wiley, 1991.

Hu, Wenzhong, and Cornelius L. Grove. *Encountering the Chinese: A Guide for Americans.* Yarmouth, ME: Intercultural Press, 1993.

Irwin, Harry. *Communicating with Asia.* St. Leonards, NSW, Australia: Allen & Unwin, 1996.

Kim, Young Yun, and William B. Gudykunst, eds. *Theories in Intercultural Communication.* Thousand Oaks, CA: Sage Publications, 1988.

Schneiter, Fred. *The Joy of Getting Along with the Chinese: For Fun and Profit.* Torrance, CA: Heian International, 1992.

Ting-Toomey, Stella, and Felipe Korzenny, eds. *Language, Communication, and Culture.* Thousand Oaks, CA: Sage Publications, 1989.

Chapter 8

Blackman, Carolyn. *Negotiating China: Case Studies and Strategies.* St. Leonards, NSW, Australia: Allen and Unwin, 1997.

Bucknall, Kevin Barry. *Chinese Business Etiquette and Culture.* Raleigh, NC: Boson Books, 1999.

Fang, Tony. *Chinese Business Negotiating Style.* Thousand Oaks, CA: Sage Publications, 1999.

Goh, Bee Chen. *Negotiating with the Chinese.* Brookfield, VT: Dartmouth, 1996.

Lee, Tahirih V. *Contract, Guanxi and Dispute Resolution in China.* New York: Garland, 1997.

Mann, Jim. *Beijing Jeep: The Short, Unhappy Romance of American Business in China.* New York: Simon and Schuster, 1989.

Pye, Lucian W. *Chinese Negotiating Style: Commercial Approaches and Cultural Principles.* New York: Quorum, 1992.

Seligman, Scott D. *Dealing with the Chinese: A Practical Guide to Business Etiquette.* London: Mercury, 1990.

Solomon, Richard H. *Chinese Negotiating Behavior: Pursuing Interests through "Old Friends."* Washington, DC: Institute of Peace, 1999.

Chapter 9

Brown, David H., and Robin Porter. *Management Issues in China.* Vol. 1, *Domestic Enterprises.* London: Routledge, 1996.

Child, John. *Management in China during the Age of Reform.* Cambridge: Cambridge University Press, 1996.

The Economist Intelligence Unit. *Multinational Companies in China: Winners and Losers.* Hong Kong: EIU, 1997.

Engholm, Christopher. *Doing Business in Asia's Booming "China Triangle."* Englewood Cliffs, NJ: Prentice Hall, 1994.

Guthrie, Doug. *Dragon in a Three-Piece Suit: The Emergence of Capitalism in China.* Princeton, NJ: Princeton University Press, 1999.

Jones, Stephanie. *Managing in China: An Executive Survival Guide.* Singapore: Butterworth-Heinemann Asia, 1997.

de Keijzer, Arne J. *China: Business Strategies for the '90s.* Berkeley: Pacific View Press, 1995.

Lardy, Nicholas R. *Foreign Trade and Economic Reform in China, 1978–1990.* New York: Cambridge University Press, 1992.

Levy, Gina. *Moving China Ventures Out of the Red into the Black: Insights from Best and Worst Performers.* Hong Kong: Andersen Consulting, 1995.

Lieberthal, Kenneth. *Governing China: From Revolution through Reform.* New York: Norton, 1995.

Lu, Qiwen. *China's Leap into the Information Age: Innovation and Organization in the Computer Industry.* Oxford: Oxford University Press, 2000.

Overholt, William H. *The Rise of China: How Economic Reform Is Creating a New Superpower.* New York: Norton, 1993.

Rosen, Daniel. *Behind the Open Door: The Foreign Enterprises in the Chinese Marketplace.* Washington, DC: Institute for International Economics, 1999.

Schlevogt, Kai-Alexander. *The Art of Chinese Management.* Oxford: Oxford University Press, 2001.

Walder, Andrew G. *Communist Neo-traditionalism: Work and Authority in Chinese Industry.* Berkeley: University of California Press, 1986.

Wang, N. T. *China's Modernization & Transnational Corporations.* Lexington, MA: Lexington Books, 1989.

Wang, Luolin, ed. *Report on Foreign Direct Investment in China* (in Chinese). Beijing: Economics and Management Press, 1997.

Relevant Web Sites for Global Chinese Business Issues

Asian Business: http://web3.asia1.com.sg/timesnet/navigatn/text/ab.html

Asian Development Bank Homepage: http://www.adb.org/

Asia Media: http://www.asiamedia.ucla.edu

Asiamoney: http://www.asiamoney.com

ASIANOW: http://cnn.com/ASIANOW

Asia Pacific Management News:
   http://www.apmforum.com/news/apmm.htm

Asia Wall Street Journal: http://www.awsj.com

Asiaweek: http://cnn.com/ASIANOW/asiaweek/

AsiaBizTech: http://www.NikkeiBP.AsiaBizTech.com/

AsiaSource: http://www.asiasource.org

Asia Society: http://www.asiasociety.org/

Australian Financial Review: http://www.afr.com.au

Businessweek (in particular the International *Business* section):
   http://www.businessweek.com

China Business Review: http://www.chinabusinessreview.com

China Business Times (in Chinese): http://www.cbt.com.cn

China Diaspora Studies: http://www.huaren.org/diaspora

ChinaOnline: http://www.chinaonline.com

China To Go: http://www.china2go.com/

China and the World (in Chinese): http://www.chinabulletin.com

CICC News Wire (Taiwan news):
   http://www.taipei.org/teco/cicc/news/english/index.htm

CNN In-Depth Specials—Visions of China:
   http://cnn.com/SPECIALS/1999/china.50/

Daily New Sina.com (bilingual): http://dailynew.sina.com

DRC net (in Chinese): http://www.drcnet.com

The Economist: http://www.economist.com

Far Eastern Economic Review: http://www.feer.com

Financial Times: http://www.ft.com

Forbes Global: http://www.global.forbes.com/

Fortune: http://www.fortune.com

Global Chinese Electronic Daily News (in Chinese): http://www.gedn.com

Homeway (in Chinese): http://www.homeway.com.cn

Inside China Today: http://www.insidechina.com/

International Herald Tribune: http://www.iht.com

Macao Daily (in Chinese): http://www.macaodaily.com

McKinsey Quarterly: http://mckinseyquarterly.com

Ming Pao News (in Chinese): http://www.mingpaonews.com

National Bureau of Asian Research: http://www.nbr.org/

National Committee on United States–China Relations:
  http://www.ncuscr.org/

Newsweek International:
  http://www.newsweek.com/nw-srv/printed/int/front.htm

New York Times: http://www.nytimes.com

Outlook: http://www.ac.com/overview/Outlook/outlook.html

People's Daily/Renmin Ribao (in Chinese):
  http://www.peopledaily.com.cn

Singapore Business Times: http://business-times.asia1.com.sg

Sohu.com (in Chinese): http://www.sohu.com.cn

South China Morning Post (Hong Kong news): http://www.scmp.com

Strategy & Business: http://www.strategy-business.com

Taipei Times: http://www.taipeitimes.com/news

Time Asia: http://cnn.com/ASIANOW/time/

Time.com China:
  http://www.time.com/time/daily/special/newschina/index.html

Transition: http://www.worldbank.org/html/prddr/trans/WEB/trans.htm

Ultrachina.com: http://www.ultrachina.com/english

Virtual China.com: http://www.virtualchina.com

Voices of Chinese: http://www.voicesofchinese.org

Wenhui Bao (in Chinese): http://www.whb.online.sh.cn

World Economic Forum Homepage: http://www.weforum.org/

World Journal/Shijie Ribao (in Chinese):
  http://www.netchina.com/world.htm

World Link Online: http://www.worldlink.co.uk/

Xinhua News Agency (bilingual): http://www.xinhuanet.com

Yazhou Zhoukan Online (in Chinese): http://www.yzzk.com

Zhongwen.com: http://www.zhongwen.com (includes versions of *The Art of War*, certain Confucian works, *Tao Te Ching*, and other classics in both Chinese and English with interactive dictionary)

Glossary of Chinese Terms and Their Pronunciation

biao hui (beow hway): bidding consortium

feng shui (fawng shway): spiritual practice of balancing objects, people, and the environment

guanxi (guan'shi): connections and networks based on trust, common background, and experience

jiaren (jia'ren): family members

Lao Tzu (laow'tz): Chinese philosopher born c. 600 B.C., father of Taoism

lao xiang (laow sheeang): compatriot, old family

mianzi (mien'tz): face

nin (neen): formal second person singular (you)

ni (knee): informal second person singular (you)

renqing (ren'ching): unpaid debts or favors that accrue through *guanxi* relationships; human empathy, human relationship; gift-giving

shengren (soong'ren): strangers

shuren (shoo'ren): nonfamily members with whom one shares a significant connection

Sun Tzu (suwen'tz): general who served the State of Wu (770–476 B.C.), author of the *Bing-fa* or *The Art of War*

tong xiang (tong sheeang): fellow villager

wei-ji (way-jee): crisis; danger and opportunity

wu-bu-wei (oo-boo-way): a philosophical term used by Lao Tzu meaning "in action"

wu-wei (oo-way): a philosophical term used by Lao Tzu meaning "yielding" or "nonaction"

Zhong guo (tzong guoaw): the Middle Kingdom, China

zhong he (tzong huh): balanced harmony

Notes

Chapter 1

1. There are now two forms of written Chinese: traditional and "simplified." By and large, the PRC has been using the simplified form since 1949, while Taiwan, Hong Kong, and other overseas communities continue to use the traditional form. Minorities in China, such as the Mongolians and Tibetans, still use their own languages, but they use the Chinese written language as well.

2. John King Fairbank and Merle Goldman, *China: A New History* (Cambridge, MA: Belknap Press of Harvard University Press, 1998), 183.

3. State Statistics Board of China, *A Statistical Survey of China, 1996, 1997*; IMF, *International Financial Statistics Yearbook 1995*; *People's Daily*, 27 December 1996 and 20 January 1998.

4. "Market Shares of China's Major Car Makers in May," *Xinhua News Agency-CEIS*, 23 July 1999; "Car Output and Sale in China (Year 1999), <http://202.101.18.140/0auto/english/news/news.html> (accessed 28 July 2000).

5. "Motorola in China 2000," <http://www.motorola.com.cn/english/facts2000> (accessed 2 August 2000).

6. Lynn Pan, ed., *The Encyclopedia of the Chinese Overseas* (Cambridge, MA: Harvard University Press, 1999), 24–25.

7. World Economic Forum, *Global Competitiveness Report*, 1998.

8. John Naisbitt, *Megatrends Asia: Eight Asian Megatrends That Are Reshaping Our World* (New York: Simon and Schuster, 1996), 24.

9. Fairbank and Goldman, *China: A New History*, 193–194.

10. George T. Haley, Chin Tong Tan, and Usha C. V. Haley, *New Asian Emperors: The Overseas Chinese, Their Strategies and Competitive Advantage* (Oxford: Butterworth-Heinemann, 1998), 5.

11. Sterling Seagrave, *Lords of the Rim: The Invisible Empire of the Overseas Chinese* (New York: Putnam, 1995), 227.

12. Naisbitt, *Megatrends Asia*, 20. These numbers have been subject to fluctuation as a result of the Asian financial crisis, but the overall trend has remained consistent.

13. *World Journal* (in Chinese), 29 August 1999, Sunday edition.

14. Naisbitt, *Megatrends Asia*, 24.

15. Quoted in Louis Kraar, "The Overseas Chinese: Lessons from the World's Most Dynamic Capitalists," *Fortune*, 31 October 1994, 56.

16. Evelyn Iritani, "In Silicon Valley, China's Brightest Draw Suspicion," 23 October 1999, <http://detnews.com/1999/technology/9910/23/10230016.htm> (accessed 31 August 2000).

17. *Almanac of China's Foreign Economic Relations and Trade* (in Chinese). These figures predate the Asian financial crisis, but the trend continues.

18. It is important to note that part of Hong Kong's investment in the PRC includes domestic capital recycled through Hong Kong. For more information on this subject, see "China's Private Surprise," *Economist*, 19 June 1999, 69.

19. "China-Bound Investment Drops 36 Percent," *China News* (in Chinese), 21 August 1999.

20. Murray Weidenbaum and Samuel Hughes, *The Bamboo Network* (New York: The Free Press, 1996), 27.

21. Thomas Menkhoff, "Chinese Business Networks," in *The Encyclopedia of the Chinese Overseas*, ed. Lynn Pan (Cambridge, MA: Harvard University Press, 1999), 94.

22. John Kohut and Allen T. Cheng, "Return of the Merchant Mandarins," Asia Inc., March 1996, <http://www.asia-inc.com/archive/1996/0396mandarin.html> (accessed 6 February 1998).

23. Naisbitt, *Megatrends Asia*, 230.

24. Quoted in Robert Lenzner and Stephen S. Johnson, "Seeing Things as They Really Are," *Forbes*, 10 March 1997, 125.

25. "Maurice Greenberg Reveals a Little Too Much," *The Financial Times*, 22 May 1998.

26. Naisbitt, *Megatrends Asia*, 21–22.

Chapter 2

1. Tony Shale, "Wang Sticks to the Old Ways," *Euromoney*, October 1994, 100.

2. Margery Wolf, *The House of Lim: A Study of a Chinese Farm Family* (New York: Appleton-Century-Crofts, 1968), 23.
3. Gordon Redding, *The Spirit of Chinese Capitalism* (New York: Walter de Gruyter, 1990), 44.
4. East Asia Analytical Unit, *Overseas Chinese Business Networks in Asia* (Commonwealth of Australia: Department of Foreign Affairs and Trade, 1995), 163.
5. PRC State Statistical Bureau (SSB), *China Statistical Yearbook*, 1998, 1999.
6. See Victor Simpao Limlingan, *The Overseas Chinese in ASEAN: Business Strategies and Management Practices* (Manila: Vita Development Corporation, 1986); Gordon Redding, "Overseas Chinese Networks: Understanding the Enigma," *Long Range Planning* 28, no. 1 (1995): 61–69; Murray Weidenbaum, "The Chinese Family Business Enterprise," *California Management Review* 38, no. 4 (1996): 141–156.
7. Katherine Bruce, "The World's Working Rich: Asia," *Forbes*, 6 July 1998, 196.
8. Shale, "Wang Sticks to the Old Ways," 99; Pete Engardio and Margaret Dawson "A New High-Tech Dynasty? Taiwan's Wang Family Aims to Be a Global Leader in Computing," *Business Week*, 15 August 1994, 90.
9. Leslie Chang, "Slurping Success: Taiwan's Wei Brothers Rule Noodle Market in China," *Asian Wall Street Journal*, 18 November 1997.
10. Andrew Tanzer, "The Amazing Mr. Kuok," *Forbes*, 28 July 1997, 90.
11. Murray Weidenbaum, "The Chinese Family Business Enterprise," *California Management Review* 38, no. 4 (1996): 151.
12. Gordon Redding, "Determinants of the Competitive Power of Small Networking: The Overseas Chinese Case," in *The Global Competitiveness of the Asian Firms*, ed. Helmut Schutte (New York: St. Martin's Press, 1994), 103.
13. Steve Givens, "Best of Both Fields," *Washington University Magazine*, spring 1995, 24–26.
14. Tony Shale, "Roots and Fruits of the Family Trees," *Euromoney*, October 1994, 96.
15. Robert S. Elegant, *The Dragon's Seed* (New York: St. Martin's Press, 1959), 8.
16. "American PR Firm to Set Up Units in Thailand, Indonesia/Edelman Public Relations Worldwide," *Singapore Straits Times*, 4 March 1997.
17. Brian Dumaine, "Asia's Wealth Creators Confront a New Reality," *Fortune*, 8 December 1997, 45.
18. Rahul Jacob, "From Father to Son: One Company's Dilemma," *Time Asia*/Special Souvenir Issue, 15 May 1997.

19. Bruce Einhorn, "Look Who's Taking Asia Digital," *Business Week*, 21 February 2000, 102–112.

20. Dumaine, "Asia's Wealth Creators Confront a New Reality," 42, 44.

21. David K. P. Li, "Family Values in Transition," *Outlook Magazine*, June 1998, <http://www.ac.com/ideas/Outlook/6.98/over_currentf4.html> (accessed 1 June 2000).

22. Joan Magretta, "Fast, Global, and Entrepreneurial: Supply Chain Management Hong Kong Style—An Interview with Victor Fung," *Harvard Business Review* 76, no. 5 (September–October 1998): 113.

23. Joseph Kahn, "Thai Troubles Drive a Dynasty to Sell Its Crown Jewel Bank," *New York Times*, 16 April 1998.

Chapter 3

1. "The Overseas Chinese: Inheriting the Bamboo Network," *Economist*, 23 December 1995–5 January 1996, 79.

2. Jon P. Alston, "Wa, Guanxi, and Inwha: Managerial Principles in Japan, China, and Korea," *Business Horizons* (March–April 1989): 26–31.

3. Fox Butterfield, *China: Alive in the Bitter Sea* (New York: Times Book, 1990), 48.

4. Louis Kraar, "The Overseas Chinese: Lessons from the World's Most Dynamic Capitalists," *Fortune*, 31 October 1994, 91.

5. Jiing-Lih Farh and Orlando Behling, "Doing Business in China: The What, the Why and—Most Importantly—the How of *Guanxi*," working paper, Hong Kong University of Science and Technology, 1998.

6. Kuang-Kuo Hwang, "Face and Favor: The Chinese Power Game," *American Journal of Sociology* 92, no. 4 (1987): 957.

7. Michael Steinberger, "U.S. Investment Banks Catch a Cold in China," *The Times of London*, 29 December 1994.

8. Ambrose Yeo-Chi King, "Kuan-shi and Network Building: A Sociological Interpretation," *Daedalus* 120 (1991): 63–84.

9. Quoted in Irene Y. M. Yeung and Rosalie L. Tung, "Achieving Business Success in Confucian Societies: The Importance of *Guanxi* (Connections)," *Organizational Dynamics* 25, no. 2 (1996): 61.

10. Kris Day and Lori Tansey, "Business Ethics in China," *Ethikos* (March–April 1998): 8–9, 11, 14.

11. Seth Faison, "China Fetes Capitalists, but the Air Is Tense," *New York Times*, 29 September 1999.

12. Tsun-Yan Hsieh, "Prospering through Relationships in Asia," *McKinsey Quarterly*, no. 4 (1996): 4–13.

13. Rosabeth Moss Kanter, "Using Networking for Competitive Advantage," *Strategy and Business* (third quarter 1996), <http://www.strategy-

business.com/casestudy/96306/page1.html> (accessed 16 July 1998), provides an in-depth study of Mochtar Riady as an example of Chinese relationship-based strategy.

14. Ibid.
15. Joan Magretta, "Fast, Global, and Entrepreneurial: Supply Chain Management, Hong Kong Style," *Harvard Business Review* 76, no. 5 (September–October 1998): 113.
16. Erik W. K. Tsang, "Can Guanxi Be a Source of Sustained Competitive Advantage for Doing Business in China?" *Academy of Management Executive* 12, no. 2 (1998).
17. Kanter, "Using Networking for Competive Advantage."
18. Rajan Anandan, Anil Kumar, Gautam Kumra, and Asutosh Padhi, "M & A in Asia," *McKinsey Quarterly*, no. 2 (1998): 71.

Chapter 4

1. In chapter 4, we are making the important clarification that Chinese society is not merely relationship-based, but role-based. By this we mean that people act in accordance with the roles prescribed by Confucian tradition. These roles determine the nature of relationships and expected social behavior in all areas of life, from family to friends and even to business, where the demands of one's functional role in the company (i.e., vice-president, managing director, etc.) must still be considered in light of one's broader social role.
2. Gary P. Ferraro, *The Cultural Dimension of International Business*, 3d ed. (Upper Saddle River, NJ: Prentice-Hall, 1998), 50.
3. Anne S. Tsui and Jiing-Lih Larry Farh, "Where Guanxi Matters: Relational Demography in the Chinese Context," *Work and Occupations* 24, no. 1 (1997): 60.
4. Edwin C. Nevis, "Cultural Assumptions and Productivity: The United States and China," *Sloan Management Review* (Spring 1983): 20.
5. Geert Hofstede and Michael Harris Bond, "The Confucius Connection: From Cultural Roots to Economic Growth," *Organizational Dynamics* 16, no. 4 (1988): 4–21.
6. Melissa Chan, Winnie Ching, Huijn Kong, Jack Sheu, "Chinatrust: Making Tough Decisions in a World of Giants," Student paper, The Wharton School, 27 April 1999.
7. Quoted in Chang Hui-Ching and G. Richard Holt, "A Chinese Perspective on Face as Inter-relational Concern," in *The Challenge of Facework: Cross-Cultural and Interpersonal Issues*, ed. Stella Ting-Toomey (Albany: State University of New York Press, 1994), 122.

8. Quoted in Janet T. Landa, "The Political Economy of the Ethnically Homogeneous Chinese Middlemen Group in Southeast Asia: Ethnicity and Entrepreneurship in a Plural Society," in *The Chinese in Southeast Asia, vol. 1, Ethnicity and Economic Activity,* ed. Linda Y. C. Lim and L. A. Peter Gosling (Singapore: Maruzen Asia, 1983), 93.

9. "Company: AT&T Learns to Save Face," *Economist Intelligence Unit Asia,* <http://biz.yahoo.com/ifc/cn/news/80999-6.html> (accessed 15 August 1999).

10. Quoted in Michael Vatikiotis and Prangtip Daorueng, "Survival Tactics," *Far Eastern Economic Review,* 26 February 1998, 44.

11. Joseph Weber and Andy Reinhardt, "From Rags to 3D Chips: How K. Y. Ho Traded Chinese Woes for High-Tech Wealth," *Business Week,* 21 June 1999, 90.

12. Marcus Brauchli and Dan Biers, "Ethnic-Chinese Family-Owned Businesses in Asia Break with Tradition to Court Foreign Partners," *Wall Street Journal,* 24 April 1995.

13. Jim Rowher, "Where Does China Get Its Money?" *Fortune,* 5 July 1999, 66.

14. Quoted in Rosabeth Moss Kanter, "Using Networking for Competitive Advantage," *Strategy and Business* (third quarter 1996), <http://www.strategy-business.com/casestudy/96306/page3.html> (accessed 16 July 1998).

15. Fons Trompenaars, *Riding the Waves of Culture: Understanding Diversity in Global Business* (London: The Economist Books, 1993), 121.

Chapter 5

1. Lynn Sharp Paine and Robert J. Crawford, "The Haier Group (A)," Case 9-398-101 (Boston: Harvard Business School, 1999).

2. Serene Lim, "Warrior Guru," *Asia Inc.,* March 1999, <http://www.asia-inc.com/aimag/aimagdet.asp?id=1413> (accessed 28 January 2001).

3. Joan Magretta, "Fast, Global, and Entrepreneurial: Supply Chain Management, Hong Kong Style—An Interview with Victor Fung," *Harvard Business Review* 76, no. 5 (September–October 1998): 104–112.

4. Josiane Cauqueline, Paul Lim, and Birgit Mayer-König (eds.), *Asian Values: An Encounter with Diversity,* (Richmond, England: Curzon Press, 1998), 5.

5. David Ho, personal conversation with Kathryn Kai-ling Ho, 19 March 1999.

6. William Doyle as quoted in *Wind and Water Tools for Self-Improvement,* "Feng Shui Endorsements," <http://www.artofplacement.com/endorsements.htm> (accessed 1 May 2000).

7. Evelyn Lip as quoted in *Wind and Water Tools for Self-Improvement*, "Feng Shui Endorsements," <http://www.artofplacement.com/endorsements.htm> (accessed 1 May 2000).

8. Fritjof Capra, *The Turning Point: Science, Society, and the Rising Culture* (New York: Bantam Books, 1982), 43.

9. From communication with N. T. Wang, who interviewed the businessman in 1997.

10. Quoted in Louis Kraar, "The Overseas Chinese," *Fortune*, 31 October 1994, 57.

11. Edward Twitchell Hall and Mildred Reed Hall, *Understanding Cultural Differences* (Yarmouth, ME: Intercultural Press, 1989), 16.

12. Maxine Hong Kingston, *The Woman Warrior* (New York: Vintage, 1975).

13. Brian Mertens and Mariko Hayashibara, "Entrepreneurs Turn Crisis into Cash Cow," *Asian Business* (April 1998): 24.

14. Ben Dolven, "Opening a Portal," *Far Eastern Economic Review*, 3 June 1999. <http://www.feer.com/9906-03/p48entre.html> (accessed 2 February 2000).

15. Quoted in Justin Doebele, "Fast as a Rabbit, Patient as a Turtle," *Forbes*, 17 July 2000, 74–75.

16. Peter J. Williamson, "Asia's New Competitive Game," *Harvard Business Review* 75, no. 5 (September–October 1997).

Chapter 6

1. C. K. Prahalad and Gary Hamel, "The Core Competence of the Corporation," *Harvard Business Review* 68, no. 3 (May–June 1990), 79–91.

2. Ajit S. Nair and Edwin R. Stafford, "Strategic Alliances in China: Negotiating the Barriers," *Long Range Planning* 13, no. 1 (1998): 143.

3. Murray Weidenbaum, "The Chinese Family Business Enterprise," *California Management Review* 38, no. 4 (1996): 144.

4. East Asia Analytical Unit, *Overseas Chinese Business Networks in Asia* (Commonwealth of Australia: Department of Foreign Affairs, 1995), 149.

5. Mark McNeilly, *Sun Tzu and the Art of Business: Six Strategic Principles for Managers* (New York: Oxford University Press, 1996), 9–22.

6. Michael E. Porter, *Competitive Strategy: Techniques for Analyzing Industries and Competitors* (New York: The Free Press, 1980).

7. Rongping Kang and Yinbin Ke, *Firm Diversifications* (in Chinese) (Beijing: Economics and Science Press, 1999), 348.

8. Peter J. Williamson, "Asia's New Competitive Game," *Harvard Business Review* 75, no. 5 (September–October 1997): 56.

9. "Telecoms Huawei Looks to Africa," *China Economic Review* (in Chinese), 17 January 2000.

10. Dexter Roberts, Joyce Barnathan, and Bruce Einhorn, "How Legend Lives Up to Its Name," *Business Week*, 15 February 1999, 76.

11. Ibid.

12. According to 1999 Transparency International Bribe Payer Index, Chinese companies are the most likely in the world to pay bribes. These statistics, however, are open to different interpretations, especially with regard to differences in such social and cultural practices as gift-giving. See "The Transparency International Bribe Payer Survey," 20 January 2000, <http://www.transparency.de/documents/cpi/bps.html> (accessed 3 August 2000).

13. "Haier's Brand-Name Boldness Sets Pace for Recognition Overseas," *South China Morning Post*, 6 April 1998.

14. Richard C. Wei, "The Acer Group: Vision for the Year 2000," Case 9-495-001 (Boston: Harvard Business School, 1994).

15. Rita G. McGrath, Ming-Jer Chen, and Ian C. MacMillan, "Multimarket Maneuvering in Uncertain Spheres of Influence: Resource Diversion Strategies," *Academy of Management Review* 23 (1998): 724–740; Michael E. Porter, *Competitive Advantage* (New York: The Free Press, 1985)

16. Robin Paul Ajello and Ron Gluckman, "The Maverick vs. the Establishment: with his Internet Play, Jimmy Lai Faces the Fight of his Life," *Asiaweek*, 3 December 1999.

17. Lori Dandridge, Ben Hughes, Peter McWilliams, and Bill Sussman, "Chess or Checkers or Basketball" (student paper, Columbia Graduate School, 1995) researched from "Nike vs. Reebok," *Fortune*, 18 September 1995, 90, and "Can Reebok Regain its Balance?" *Business Week*, 20 December 1993, 108.

18. Gao Yuan, *Lure the Tiger Out of the Mountains: The Thirty-Six Stratagems of Ancient China* (New York: Simon and Schuster, 1991).

19. Niraj Dawar and Tony Frost, "Competing with Giants," *Harvard Business Review* 77, no. 2 (March–April 1999): 122.

20. Hong Kong Trade Development Council, *Mainland's Increasingly Sophisticated Consumer Market Offers Favourable Environment for Hong Kong Companies to Explore*, 30 September 1998, <http://www.tdc-trade.com/tdcnews/9809/98093001.htm> (accessed 1 July 2000); The Wirthlin Report, *Domestic Brands Rule the World*, 1997, <http://209.204.197.52/publicns/report/wr9710.htm> (accessed 1 July 2000).

Chapter 7

1. Linda Beamer, "Bridging Business Cultures," *China Business Review* 25, no. 3 (1998): 54.
2. David K. Tse, Kam-Hon Lee, Ilan Vertinsky, and Donald A. Wehrung, "Does Culture Matter? A Cross-Cultural Study of Executives' Choice, Decisiveness, and Risk Adjustment in International Marketing," *Journal of Marketing* 52 (October 1988): 81–95.
3. Edward Twitchell Hall and Mildred Reed Hall, *Understanding Cultural Differences: Germans, French, and Americans* (Yarmouth, ME: Intercultural Press, 1989), 6.
4. May O'Hara-Devereaux and Robert Johansen, *Globalwork: Bridging Distance, Culture, and Time* (San Francisco: Jossey-Bass, 1994), 55.
5. S. Karene Witcher, "Chief Executives in Asia Find Listening Difficult," *Asian Wall Street Journal*, Weekly Edition, 9–15 August 1999.
6. Robert O. Joy, "Cultural and Procedural Differences that Influence Business Strategies and Operations in the People's Republic of China," *SAM Advanced Management Journal* (Summer 1989): 30.
7. Christopher Engholm, *When Business East Meets Business West: The Guide to Practice and Protocol in the Pacific Rim* (New York: Wiley, 1991), 115.
8. "Schwab Opens Chinatown Branch," *PR Newswire*, 31 March 2000.
9. Michael Marriott, "English-Dominant Internet Fast Becoming Multilingual" *San Diego Union-Tribune*, 8 September 1998.
10. Ching-Ching Ni, "Web Portals Opening Doors to Asian Market," *Los Angeles Times*, 6 December 1999.

Chapter 8

1. Quoted in Richard H. Solomon, *Chinese Negotiating Behavior: Pursuing Interests through "Old Friends"* (Washington, DC: Institution of Peace, 1999), 38.
2. Oded Shenkar and Simcha Ronen, "The Cultural Context of Negotiations: The Implications of Chinese Interpersonal Norms," *The Journal of Applied Behavioral Science* 23, no. 2 (1987): 266.
3. Thomas Leung and L. L. Yeung, "Negotiation in the People's Republic of China: Results of a Survey of Small Business in Hong Kong," *Journal of Small Business Management* 33, no. 1 (1995): 73.
4. "China Bumps MV from Car Project; Minivan Hits Snag," *Automotive News*, 24 March 1997.
5. Quoted in Christopher Engholm, *Doing Business in Asia's Booming "China Triangle"* (Englewood Cliffs, NJ: Prentice Hall, 1994), 317.

6. Allison Bisbey Colter, "Morgan Stanley to Transfer Staff from CICC Venture to MWD," *Dow Jones News Service*, 9 April 1999.
7. Engholm, *Doing Business in Asia's Booming "China Triangle,"* 320.
8. Min Chen, *Asian Management Systems: Chinese, Japanese, and Korean Styles of Business* (London: Routledge, 1995), 239.
9. Ajit S. Nair and Edwin R. Stafford, "Strategic Alliances in China: Negotiating the Barriers," *Long Range Planning* 31, no. 1 (1998): 144.
10. Engholm, *Doing Business in Asia's Booming "China Triangle,"* 315.
11. Joel Brockner, Ya-Ru Chen, Elizabeth A. Mannix, Kwok Leung, and Daniel P. Skarlicki, "Culture and Procedural Fairness: When the Effects of What You Do Depend on How You Do It," *Administrative Science Quarterly* 45, no. 1 (2000): 146.
12. Christopher Engholm, *Doing Business in Asia's Booming "China Triangle"* (Englewood Cliffs, NJ: Prentice Hall, 1944), 317.
13. **Goh** Bee Chen, *Negotiating with the Chinese* (Brookfield, VT: Dartmouth, 1996), 60.
14. Nair and Stafford, "Strategic Alliances in China," 142.
15. Lucian W. Pye, "The China Trade: Making the Deal," *Harvard Business Review* 64, no. 4 (July–August 1986): 74–79; Frank Lavin, "Negotiating with the Chinese: Or How Not to Kowtow," *Foreign Affairs* 73, no. 4 (1994): 16–22.
16. Zhao Shuming and Zhong Yang, eds., *Multinational Enterprises: Cross-Cultural Management* (in Chinese) (Nanjing: Nanjing University Press, 1994), 264.
17. Nancy Adler, Richard Brahm, and John L. Graham, "Strategy Implementation: A Comparison of Face-to-Face Negotiations in the People's Republic of China and the United States," *Strategic Management Journal*, 13 (1992): 461.
18. Danny Ertel has proposed a new set of measures for negotiating success based on a consideration of both economic and relationship gains. See "Turning Negotiation into a Corporate Capability," *Harvard Business Review* 77, no. 3 (May–June 1999): 69–78. Howard Raiffa has introduced the concept of "post-settlement settlement" into Western negotiation practices. "Post-Settlement Settlements" in *Negotiation Theory and Practice*, ed. J. W. Breslin and J. Z. Rubin (Cambridge, MA: PON Books, 1991), 323–26.

Chapter 9

1. Quoted in Daniel Burstein and Arne de Keijer, *Big Dragon: China's Future: What It Means for Business, the Economy, and the Global Order* (New York: Simon and Schuster, 1998), 161.

2. Quoted in Thomas Friedman, *The Lexus and the Olive Tree* (New York: Farrar, Straus and Giroux, 1999), 314.

3. Government of Hong Kong, "Hong Kong Chief Executive's—Mr. Tung Chee Hwa—speech to the Royal Institute of International Affairs at Chatham House," Wednesday, 22 October 1997, <http://www.info.gov.hk/ce/speech/1022cesplon.htm> (accessed 27 July 2000).

4. John King Fairbank and Merle Goldman, *China: A New History* (Cambridge, MA: Belknap Press of Harvard University Press, 1998), 181.

5. Louis Kraar, "Five Chinese Myths," *Fortune*, 10 May 1999, 30.

6. Based on my conversation with the managing director of China operations of a leading global consulting company.

7. Qiang Zhiyuan, "Enterprise Transformation in China and the Construction of the Target Enterprise Model," *Nankai Economic Studies* (in Chinese), no. 4 (1998).

8. Ben Dolven, "Wounded Pride," *Far Eastern Economic Review*, 8 July 1999, 73.

9. "China Seeks Foreign Investors for Pharmaceuticals," *China Online*, 24 May 2000, <http://www.chinaonline.com> (accessed 24 May, 2000).

10. Wilfried Vanhonacker, "Entering China: An Unconventional Approach," *Harvard Business Review* 75, no. 2 (March–April 1997): 130–140.

11. "Unilever Seeks to Become First Listed Foreign Company," *Asian Wall Street Journal*, 3–9 July 2000, 6.

12. Brian Palmer, "What the Chinese Want," *Fortune*, 11 October 1999, 233.

13. "Unemployment Has Risen Substantially," *World Journal* (in Chinese), 30 October 1999.

14. Tsun-Yan Hsieh, Johanne Lavoie, and Robert A. P. Samek, "Think Global, Hire Local," *McKinsey Quarterly*, no. 4 (1999): 92–101.

15. A. J. Frazer, "A Scouting Report on Training Options," *China Business Review*, January–February 1999, 44.

16. Paul Jensen, telephone conversation with author, 25 August 1999.

17. M. W. Peng, *Business Strategies in Transition Economies* (Thousand Oaks, CA: Sage Publications, 2000).

18. Kraar, "Five Chinese Myths," 30.

19. Adapted from Zhan G. Li and Diana E. Eadington, "Marketing Agricultural Products to China," *Business Horizons*, 1 March 1999.

20. "Forum: China's Prospects," *Asiaweek*, 15 October 1999.

21. James P. Walsh, Er Ping Wang, and Katherine R. Xin, "Same Bed, Different Dreams: Working Relationships in Sino-American Joint Ventures," *Journal of World Business* 34, no. 1 (1999): 69–93.

Index

About the Author

MING-JER CHEN is a leading international management and strategy specialist, well known throughout Greater China and the rest of the world. He has been the Founding Director of the Global Chinese Business Initiative at The Wharton School, University of Pennsylvania since 1997. As of July 2001, he will hold the Bigelow Research Professorship of Business Administration at the Darden School of the University of Virginia. From 1988 to 1997 he was on the faculty at Columbia Business School. Besides these posts, Dr. Chen has international affiliations with the Chinese University of Hong Kong, the National University of Singapore, and The Imperial College of Science, Technology, & Medicine in the U.K.

Ming-Jer Chen specializes in business strategy, competitive dynamics, and managing East-West enterprise. His corporate teaching and consulting clients include: Morgan Stanley Dean Witter (U.S.A.); BOC Gases (U.K.); the State Economic & Trade Commission, Kelon Electric Holdings, and the People's Construction Bank of China (China); the Institute for Information Industry and the Ruentex Group (Taiwan); and the Executive Talent Association (Hong Kong).

Renowned for his extensive scholarship in premier management journals, Dr. Chen has received several prestigious awards from such organizations as the Academy of Management. He has also received wide coverage in major business newspapers and magazines around the world, including the *China Daily*, the *Commercial Times* (Taiwan), and the *Wall Street Journal*.

Addressing business groups internationally, Ming-Jer Chen has made major contributions to the cause of East-West business and management dialogue, including his keynote speech to the World Economic Forum's *China Business Summit 2000* in Beijing.